Cinema and Sacrifice

I0867704

Cinema has a long history of engaging with the theme of sacrifice. Given its capacity to stimulate the imagination and resonate across a wide spectrum of human experiences, sacrifice has always attracted filmmakers. It is on screen that the new grand narratives are sketched, the new myths rehearsed, and the old ones recycled. Sacrifice can provide stories of loss and mourning, betrayal and redemption, death and renewal, destruction and re-creation, apocalypses and the birth of new worlds.

The contributors to this volume are not just scholars of film but also students of religion and literature, philosophers, ethicists, and political scientists, thus offering a comprehensive and interdisciplinary approach to the relationship between cinema and sacrifice. They explore how cinema engages with sacrifice in its many forms and under different guises, and examine how the filmic constructions, reconstructions, and misconstructions of sacrifice affect society, including its sacrificial practices.

This book was originally published as a special issue of *Angelaki: journal of the theoretical humanities*.

Costica Bradatan is Associate Professor of Humanities at Texas Tech University, USA, and Honorary Research Associate Professor of Philosophy at the University of Queensland, Australia. He has authored or edited several books, including *Dying for Ideas: The Dangerous Lives of the Philosophers* (2015) and *Philosophy as a Literary Art: Making Things Up* (2014).

Camil Ungureanu is Lecturer in Political Theory at the Universitat Pompeu Fabra, Spain. He is co-editor of *Law, State and Religion in the New Europe* (2012) and *Jürgen Habermas' Theory of Law and Democracy* (2011). His work has been published in a number of journals including the *Journal of Political Philosophy* and the *European Journal of Political Theory*.

Cinema and Sacrifice

Edited by
Costica Bradatan and Camil Ungureanu

Routledge
Taylor & Francis Group
LONDON AND NEW YORK

First published 2016
by Routledge
2 Park Square, Milton Park, Abingdon, Oxon, OX14 4RN, UK

and by Routledge
711 Third Avenue, New York, NY 10017, USA

First issued in paperback 2017

Routledge is an imprint of the Taylor & Francis Group, an informa business

British Library Cataloguing in Publication Data
A catalogue record for this book is available from the British Library

ISBN 13: 978-1-138-19688-9 (pbk)
ISBN 13: 978-1-138-93682-9 (hbk)

Typeset in BodoniMT
by RefineCatch Limited, Bungay, Suffolk

Publisher's Note
The publisher accepts responsibility for any inconsistencies that may have arisen during the conversion of this book from journal articles to book chapters, namely the possible inclusion of journal terminology.

Disclaimer
Every effort has been made to contact copyright holders for their permission to reprint material in this book. The publishers would be grateful to hear from any copyright holder who is not here acknowledged and will undertake to rectify any errors or omissions in future editions of this book.

Contents

Citation Information

The chapters in this book were originally published in *Angelaki: journal of the theoretical humanities*, volume 19, issue 4 (December 2014). When citing this material, please use the original page numbering for each article, as follows:

Chapter 1: Introduction
Editorial Introduction: "The joy of destruction is also the joy of creation"
Costica Bradatan
Angelaki: journal of the theoretical humanities, volume 19, issue 4 (December 2014)
pp. 1–5

Chapter 2
Odysseus Unbound: sovereignty and sacrifice in Hunger *and the* Dialectic of Enlightenment
Banu Bargu
Angelaki: journal of the theoretical humanities, volume 19, issue 4 (December 2014)
pp. 7–22

Chapter 3
Heart of the Matter: bodies without organs and biopolitics in organ transplant films
Patricia Pisters
Angelaki: journal of the theoretical humanities, volume 19, issue 4 (December 2014)
pp. 23–36

Chapter 4
Clôtural *Sacrifice: liminal representation of race in film*
Farhang Erfani
Angelaki: journal of the theoretical humanities, volume 19, issue 4 (December 2014)
pp. 37–50

Chapter 5
Sacrifice, Violence and the Limits of Moral Representation in Haneke's Caché
Camil Ungureanu
Angelaki: journal of the theoretical humanities, volume 19, issue 4 (December 2014)
pp. 51–64

Chapter 6
Bodies of Estrangement: Mel Gibson, sacrifice and history
Jorge Bastos da Silva
Angelaki: journal of the theoretical humanities, volume 19, issue 4 (December 2014) pp. 65–78

Chapter 7
Faith, Sacrifice, and the Earth's Glory in Terrence Malick's The Tree of Life
George B. Handley
Angelaki: journal of the theoretical humanities, volume 19, issue 4 (December 2014) pp. 79–94

Chapter 8
"When I swallow his heart and lungs, Jesus is pleased": the transmediation of sacrifice in The Journals of Knud Rasmussen
Russell J.A. Kilbourn
Angelaki: journal of the theoretical humanities, volume 19, issue 4 (December 2014) pp. 95–110

Chapter 9
Anatomy of Melancholia
Robert Sinnerbrink
Angelaki: journal of the theoretical humanities, volume 19, issue 4 (December 2014) pp. 111–126

Chapter 10
"We will die and will be free": a gnostic reading of The Double Life of Véronique
Costica Bradatan
Angelaki: journal of the theoretical humanities, volume 19, issue 4 (December 2014) pp. 127–140

Chapter 11
A Sacrificial Economy of the Image: Lyotard on cinema
Ashley Woodward
Angelaki: journal of the theoretical humanities, volume 19, issue 4 (December 2014) pp. 141–154

Notes on Contributors

Banu Bargu is Associate Professor of Politics at the New School for Social Research, New York City, USA. Her main area of specialization is political theory, especially modern and contemporary political thought, in conjunction with political anthropology and a regional focus on the Middle East. Her research interests include theories of sovereignty, biopolitics, and resistance, as well as aesthetics and materialism. She is the author of *Starve and Immolate: The Politics of Human Weapons* (2014), and she is currently working on a book-length manuscript on Althusser and aleatory materialism.

Jorge Bastos da Silva teaches in the Department of Anglo-American Studies at the University of Porto, Portugal. His main fields of research are English literature and culture, intellectual history, and utopian studies. He is the author and editor of several works, including *The Epistemology of Utopia: Rhetoric, Theory and Imagination* (2013), *A Instituição da Literatura. Horizonte Teórico e Filosófico da Cultura Literária no Limiar da Modernidade* (2010), and *Shakespeare no Romantismo Português. Factos, Problemas, Interpretações* (2005).

Costica Bradatan is Associate Professor of Humanities at Texas Tech University, Lubbock, Texas, USA, and Honorary Research Associate Professor of Philosophy at the University of Queensland, Brisbane, Australia. He has authored or edited several books, including *Dying for Ideas: The Dangerous Lives of the Philosophers* (2015), and *Philosophy as a Literary Art: Making Things Up* (2014).

Farhang Erfani is Associate Professor of Philosophy at the American University, Washington, D.C., USA, and a Research Associate at the Nelson Mandela Metropolitan University, Port Elizabeth, South Africa. He is also a Faculty Member of the Global Center for Advanced Studies. He has published *Aesthetics of Autonomy* (2011) and *Iranian Cinema and Philosophy: Shooting Truth* (2011). His forthcoming monograph is entitled *Against Deconstructive Eurodecentrism.*

George B. Handley teaches Environmental Humanities at Brigham Young University, Provo, Utah, USA. He is the author, most recently, of *New World Poetics: Nature and the Adamic Imagination of Whitman, Neruda, and Walcott* (2007) and of an environmental memoir, *Home Waters: A Year of Recompenses on the Provo River* (2010). He is also the co-editor of *Caribbean Literature and the Environment* (2005) and *Postcolonial Ecologies* (2011). He is currently working on a book-length study, *From Chaos to Cosmos: Literature as Ecotheology.*

Russell J.A. Kilbourn is Associate Professor of English and Film Studies at Wilfrid Laurier University, Waterloo, Canada. He is the author of *Cinema, Memory, Modernity: The*

Representation of Memory from the Art Film to Transnational Cinema (2010), and is co-editor, with Eleanor Ty, of *The Memory Effect: The Remediation of Memory in Literature and Film* (2013).

Patricia Pisters is Professor of Film Studies in the Department of Media Studies at the University of Amsterdam, the Netherlands. She is Programme Director of the research group 'Neuraesthetics and Neurocultures', and co-Director (with Josef Fruchtl) of the research group 'Film and Philosophy' at the Amsterdam School of Cultural Analysis. She is one of the founding editors of *Necsus: European Journal of Media Studies*. Her publications include *The Matrix of Visual Culture: Working with Deleuze in Film Theory* (2003) and *Mind the Screen* (ed., with Jaap Kooijman and Wanda Strauven, 2008). Her latest book is *The Neuro-Image: A Deleuzian Film-Philosophy of Digital Screen Culture* (2012).

Robert Sinnerbrink is an Australian Research Council Future Fellow and Senior Lecturer of Philosophy at Macquarie University, Sydney, Australia. He is the author of *New Philosophies of Film: Thinking Images* (2011) and *Understanding Hegelianism* (2007), co-editor of *Critique Today* (2006), and a member of the editorial board of the journal *Film-Philosophy*. He is currently completing a book titled *Cinematic Ethics: Exploring Ethical Experience through Film*, and co-authoring another book (with Lisa Trahair and Gregory Flaxman) titled *Understanding Cinematic Thinking*.

Camil Ungureanu is Lecturer in Political Theory at the Universitat Pompeu Fabra, Barcelona, Spain. He is co-editor of *Law, State and Religion in the New Europe* (2012) and *Jürgen Habermas' Theory of Law and Democracy* (2011). His work has been published in a number of journals including the *Journal of Political Philosophy* and the *European Journal of Political Theory*.

Ashley Woodward is Lecturer in Philosophy at the University of Dundee, UK. He is a member of the Melbourne School of Continental Philosophy and an editor of *Parrhesia: A Journal of Critical Philosophy*. His book, *Lyotard and the Inhuman Condition*, is forthcoming in 2016.

INTRODUCTION

costica bradatan

"THE JOY OF DESTRUCTION IS ALSO THE JOY OF CREATION"

They say that every year on Christmas Eve, Eugenio d'Ors, one of the finest minds Spain ever had, performed a special ritual: he would identify the best page he had written over the course of the year about to end, and then give it to the flames. Not some random fragment, or something of whose quality he wasn't certain, but the best thing he wrote that year. If you are writer, parting like this from something you've written is painful enough, but destroying the best thing you've come up with must be unbearable. Yet that's precisely the meaning of *sacrifice*: what d'Ors was doing was a sacrificial ritual. For whatever reasons, he took the performance of such an act to be an important part of his life as a writer. Even though the story may not be accurate in every detail, it is exemplary. *Se non è vero, è ben trovato.*

Like other things that make us human, sacrifice is paradoxical in nature: it is destruction for the sake of creation, annihilation that brings something into being. It turns death into its opposite, new life is grafted onto that which perishes. In sacrifice waste is a path to riches and killing to new life forms. For George Bataille destruction is the essence of "sacrificial production." As Girard's sacrificial victim expires in the midst of orgiastic violence, her annihilation gives the community a renewed sense of being. Girard calls the event a "founding murder." How can a murder found anything? It can, provided that certain conditions are met. When Mikhail Bakunin quipped that "the joy of destruction is also the joy of creation," perhaps unwittingly he came as close to the essence of sacrifice as few moderns ever have.

In different forms and under various guises, sacrifice is manifest in virtually all known cultures and religions. In some, it occupies a central position. At the heart of Christianity, to give just one example, there lies the sacrifice of the Son of God; the instrument of torture that was used to kill him became the symbol of the religion itself. Not only is Christ's death the founding event of Christianity, but to be a good Christian, at the limit, is to try to imitate it: *imitatio mortis Christi*. Yet even in religions where there is no discernible "founding murder," sacrifice remains central. For through sacrifice human beings signal a certain positioning in relation to transcendence: they recognize a higher existence and submit to it. It doesn't really matter what we sacrifice; what's important is the sheer *act of sacrificing* something: "It is not their meat nor their blood that reaches God. It is your piety that reaches Him," we read in the Qur'an (22.37).

As killing of living creatures to obtain the gods' benevolence, elimination of one individual to put an end to a state of generalized violence (scapegoating), symbolic offering to the other-world, gifts to fellow-humans or just sharing something with them, fasting, dedication to a cause, destruction of something in order to save something else ("faire la part du feu"), sacrifice can perform a wide range of religious, social, political, cultural or psychological functions. The act of giving something valuable away – one's possessions, one's time and work, or even one's life – for the sake of something greater than oneself is a fundamental human gesture. The manner of its performance, its rituals, codes and protocols, as well as the significance we attach to it, define who we are, and shape the cultures in which we live. Sacrifices can please the gods and bring forgiveness to humans; they can pacify enemies and make friends; they can solve crises, heal collective traumas, make or remake communal bonds.

Conceptually, sacrifice lies at the center of a network of related notions such as gift-giving, reciprocity, crisis, regeneration, renewal, propitiation, substitution and exchange. Rooted in religious experience, as the Latin etymology of the word makes clear (it comes from *sacer* and *facere*, "to make it holy"), sacrifice has undergone continuous metamorphoses and has acquired new and more complex meanings. What's even more significant, sacrifice has permeated the non-religious spheres of life. Economy and politics, personal relationships and ordinary social interactions, international relations and global commerce – all presuppose different practices of sacrifice. Indeed, in a certain sense, as we have become more secularized our interest in sacrifice as a general human phenomenon has expanded. An original body of literature on the topic has grown and flourished over the last century; thinkers as diverse as Emmanuel Levinas, Georges Bataille, Marcel Mauss and Henri Hubert, René Girard, and Giorgio Agamben, to name just a few, have made important contributions to a more comprehensive, sophisticated, and nuanced understanding of sacrifice, sacrificial practices and rituals.

Sacrifice, then, may be genetically tied to religion, but its religious component is far from exhausting its significance and complexity. That's why the relative decline in traditional religiosity (in the West at least) hasn't diminished the importance of sacrifice. People may no longer make offerings to God, but they still engage in a wide range of sacrificial practices: they contribute to charities, help the needy, and make donations; they give up certain foods (meat, for example) and engage in other forms of abstention; they donate their organs; they volunteer in humanitarian projects, sometimes at the risk of their lives; they make gifts and counter-gifts; they sacrifice themselves for their loved ones; they can even sacrifice their lives for a cause, for their country, for their ethnic group, or for things they think to be worth dying for: freedom, dignity, respect. Sometimes they go as far as to set themselves on fire or to blow themselves up, believing that somehow this will help their communities. Indeed, such radical forms of self-sacrifice have come to influence our world in ways both unsettling and difficult to deal with. With suicide-bombing religious sacrifice seems to have undergone a revival as its perpetrators and apologists frame these acts in terms of "martyrdom." Yet this remains a hotly contested issue because even within Muslim circles suicide-bombing is thought to be sinful and against the Qur'an.

The beginning of the twenty-first century makes for a configuration of economic, political, social and cultural factors within which sacrifice is set to play a distinctive role. Political radicalization, new religious fundamentalisms, a sense of powerlessness and defeat in the face of globalized, omnipotent political and economic entities, climate change and the fears of extinction and the sense of doom it induces, apprehension about the diminishing role of humans in a technology-dominated, "post-human" future – these are only some of the issues that foreground sacrifice as a focus of philosophical, artistic and intellectual concern.

• • •

Cinema has a long history of engaging with the theme of sacrifice. Given its capacity to stimulate the imagination and resonate across a wide spectrum of human experiences, sacrifice has always attracted filmmakers. From Dreyer's *The Passion of Joan of Arc* to Pasolini's *Mamma Roma* to Tarkovsky's *Sacrifice* to many of Ozu's films to Kar Wai Wong's *In the Mood for Love* or to Lars von Trier's *Breaking the Waves* and Bruno Dumont's *La Vie de Jésus*, to give just a few examples, sacrifice has nourished, informed and shaped filmmaking. Sacrifice is a fundamental human act, and cinema has always, in some way or another, danced around it.

Yet that's not all. In a world like ours from which the gods have mostly withdrawn, but people haven't stopped feeling the need to believe, in an important sense film has taken over the myth-factory. It's on screen that the post-Christian grand narratives are sketched, the new myths rehearsed, and the old ones recycled. Our contemporaries may no longer be church-goers, but they go to the movies religiously. And the sacrificial theme makes for the perfect raw material for this new production line. For sacrifice can provide stories of loss and mourning, betrayal and redemption, death and renewal, destruction and re-creation, apocalypses and the birth of new worlds – a steady flux of precious, malleable, inexhaustible material.

The ways in which sacrifice is processed cinematically and the manner in which society responds to this process make for a fascinating topic of thought and scholarly reflection. This is precisely the belief from which this project was born. Indeed, its impetus was the felt need for a more comprehensive, ecumenical and interdisciplinary approach to the relationship between cinema and sacrifice. The project revolves around two main tasks. On the one hand, this special issue explores how cinema engages with sacrifice in its many forms and under different guises – here cinema "absorbs" sacrifice. On the other hand, it examines how the filmic constructions, reconstructions and misconstructions of sacrifice, in turn, come to affect society, including its sacrificial practices – and here the circle closes as society reabsorbs cinematically processed sacrifice.

Undertaking such a project is not easy, nor can it be the job of one academic specialty alone. The contributors to this special issue are not just scholars of film but also students of religion and of literature, philosophers, ethicists, and political scientists. It is strongly hoped that such an integrated, interdisciplinary effort will translate into a more nuanced understanding of the film–sacrifice nexus.

• • •

This collection is divided into two large sections. The contributions in the first one ("Sacrifice and the Body Politic") map out forms of sacrifice that operate eminently within the societal sphere, follow a logic pertaining to "this world," and have conspicuous political effects, even though their political character does not always exhaust their significance. In the first contribution, "Odysseus Unbound: Sovereignty and Sacrifice in *Hunger* and the *Dialectic of Enlightenment*," Banu Bargu focuses on Steve McQueen's film *Hunger*, and reads it through the lens of contemporary hunger strikes and their political programs. She examines the film along with Horkheimer and Adorno's *Dialectic of Enlightenment*, exploring how both works problematize the Enlightenment's sacrificial subjectivity and instrumental rationality, at the same time articulating a critique of Western civilization itself. In the next contribution, "Heart of the Matter: Bodies without Organs and Biopolitics in Organ Transplant Films," Patricia Pisters discusses four films in terms of Jean-Luc Nancy's notion of the "intruder": Alejandro González Iñárritu's *21 Grams*, Claire Denis's *L'Intrus*, Stephen Frears' *Dirty Pretty Things*, and Leon Geller and Markus Vetter's *Heart of Jenin*. What emerges from this analysis is a renewed concept of sacrifice, one that brings about a switch from the original sense of religious offering to that of political and ethical resistance, areligious in nature.

In "*Clôtural* Sacrifice: Liminal Representation of Race in Film," Farhang Erfani uses the film *The Cyclist*, by Iranian filmmaker Mohsen Makhmalbaf, as a springboard for a larger theoretical discussion about the limits of representation, a conversation in which Lacan and Heidegger are cast as main participants. In the *The Cyclist* an Afghan immigrant is "sacrificed" for the entertainment of the Iranian onlookers. The author looks at the film through Lacanian lenses, and comes up with a critical reading of its depiction of racism. In "Sacrifice, Violence and Limits of Moral Representation in Haneke's *Caché*," Camil Ungureanu reads Michael Haneke's film in light of "the traditional bond between sacrificial violence, morality and community building." Engaging with Jacques Derrida's views on the "mystical" origin of authority, the author proposes a "postsecular" interpretation of the "ghost director" in the film, as well as of Majid's theatrical self-sacrifice. In the final contribution of this section, "Bodies of Estrangement: Mel Gibson, Sacrifice and History," Jorge Bastos da Silva considers Mel Gibson's oeuvre as filmmaker in terms of narratives of sacrifice. Especially in *Braveheart*, *The Passion*, and *Apocalypto*, the author discerns a vision of history as "fundamentally dependent on acts of ritualization, at the centre of which lies the sacrifice of the individual." This vision, articulated from one film to the next through recurring cinematic techniques and visual-thematic motifs, comes from a certain understanding of death and transcendence. This way, Bastos da Silva's essay marks the transition to the second part of the issue.

The contributions in this section ("Sacrifice, Transcendence, Self-Transcendence"), with one exception, consider sacrifice either from an openly religious standpoint or at least from some transmundane perspective. In the first contribution, "Faith, Sacrifice, and the Earth's Glory in Terrence Malick's *The Tree of Life*," George B. Handley uses Malick's film to re-examine a number of questions pertaining to the Christian theodicy. In this reading, Malick makes accident and sacrifice part of human destiny. Through an ongoing, invisible dialogue with Job, Dostoevsky, and Kierkegaard he re-evaluates the function of sacrifice and relates it to a new appreciation of existence as such, even at its biological and geological levels. In "'When I swallow his heart and lungs, Jesus is pleased': The Transmediation of Sacrifice in *The Journals of Knud Rasmussen*," Russell J.A. Kilbourn focuses on the second, yet central piece of the Isuma "Fast Runner" trilogy in order to examine the metamorphoses of sacrifice in a historical context where competing religious views clash (*The Journals of Knud Rasmussen* follows the impact that the introduction of Christianity had on the traditional Inuit culture in the 1920s). As the author sees it, the film "sets the stage for literal and metaphorical sacrifice," which came from the double threat of conversion and the transvaluation of traditional Shamanistic beliefs.

In the third contribution of this section, "Anatomy of *Melancholia*," Robert Sinnerbrink argues that Lars von Trier's work performs a "complex ethical critique of rationalist optimism in the guise of a neo-romantic allegory of world-destruction." In his view, the film also seeks to "work through" the loss of worlds, be they cinematic, cultural or natural, which defines our historical mood. Finally, placing *Melancholia* within a broader historical lineage (represented by Ingmar Bergman's *Shame* and Andrei Tarkovsky's *The Sacrifice*), Sinnerbrink reads this aestheticization of world-destruction as a preparation for a posthumanist beginning.

In my own contribution, "'We will die and will be free': A Gnostic Reading of *The Double Life of Véronique*," I perform a double task. First, I propose a Gnostic interpretation of Kieślowski's film, in which the figure of the puppeteer, who turns out to be the maker of the film's story and universe, stands for the Demiurge. Kieślowski's techniques of "dematerializing" the world (through deformed lenses, alienating camera angles, and filters) are read in the same Gnostic key. Second, I use the film as a springboard for a broader philosophical conversation on the world as farce, in which such figures as Schopenhauer, Dostoevsky and Cioran participate. Finally, I touch on the significance that our sacrifice to the "cosmic farceur" may have.

The exception I mentioned earlier is the final contribution, "A Sacrificial Economy of the Image: Lyotard on Cinema," by Ashley Woodward. Here sacrifice is not considered politically or socially, not in relation to "this world" nor with "the next" one but in relation to the medium of film itself. Woodward reconstructs Lyotard's philosophy of cinema from several disparate essays, and articulates a notion of sacrifice in terms of the economy of the images from which a film is formally constructed. Film of any variety, this reconstruction goes, includes some sequences and images which are "sacrificial" – they are "other" to the chronological narrative. These images "liberate us from the seductive effects of the narrative," and the "invitation to fantasize," which perform the function of "imposing and reproducing dominant social and cultural norms." There is a distinct degree of self-reflexivity in Woodward's contribution, which makes it a fitting, if unplanned, conclusion to this special issue.

• • •

The editors of this collection are grateful to all those who have contributed to the project: Pelagia Goulimari and Gerard Greenway, *Angelaki*'s editors; James Hypher, its copy-editor; the issue's contributors, as well as the anonymous reviewers involved. Without these people's dedication, hard work, and passion, you wouldn't be reading what you are reading.

bibliography

Bataille, Georges. *Visions of Excess: Selected Writings, 1927–1939*. Trans. Allan Stoekl. Minneapolis: U of Minnesota P, 1989. Print.

Derrida, Jacques. *The Gift of Death*. Trans. David Willis. Chicago: U of Chicago P, 2007. Print.

Girard, René. *The Scapegoat*. Trans. Yvonne Freccero. Baltimore: Johns Hopkins UP, 1989. Print.

Girard, René. *Violence and the Sacred*. Trans. Patrick Gregory. Baltimore: Johns Hopkins UP, 1977. Print.

Hedley, Douglas. *Sacrifice Imagined: Violence, Atonement, and the Sacred*. London: Bloomsbury, 2011. Print.

Lyden, John C. *Film as Religion: Myths, Morals and Rituals*. New York: New York UP, 2003. Print.

Mauss, Marcel. *The Gift: The Form and Reason for Exchange in Archaic Societies*. Trans. W.D. Halls. New York: Norton, 2000. Print.

Mitchell, Jolyon, and S. Brent Plate, eds. *The Religion and Film Reader*. London and New York: Routledge, 2007. Print.

Pahl, Jon. *Empire of Sacrifice: The Religious Origins of American Violence*. New York: New York UP, 2010. Print.

Pizzato, Mark. *Theatres of Human Sacrifice: From Ancient Ritual to Screen Violence*. Albany: State U of New York P, 2004. Print.

Plate, S. Brent, ed. *Representing Religion in World Cinema*. New York: Palgrave Macmillan, 2003. Print.

Sontag, Susan. *Regarding the Pain of Others*. London: Penguin, 2004. Print.

PART ONE

sacrifice and the body politic

banu bargu

ODYSSEUS UNBOUND

sovereignty and sacrifice in hunger *and the* dialectic of enlightenment

In a speech delivered in Belfast on 5 March 1981, Margaret Thatcher famously remarked: "There is no such thing as political murder, political bombing or political violence. There is only criminal murder, criminal bombing and criminal violence."[1] The visceral and deeply moving portrait of Bobby Sands – the first of the ten men who starved themselves to death in their struggle for "political status" in the infamous Maze Prison – in Steve McQueen's critically acclaimed movie *Hunger* provides an excellent exposition of the untruth of Thatcher's statement.[2]

In *Hunger*, we are dragged into the prison of a liberal-democratic state, a prison where the only law is the sovereign will, performing and reproducing itself through the security forces' labor of intimidation and vengeful violence. This sovereign will is donned with the legitimacy of the law, but the law now appears like a bad copy of itself, a broken façade that scarcely hides the duel between an existing sovereign in whose hands it is used to criminalize, discredit, and thereby neutralize its opponents, on the one side, and a movement whose violent struggle for national liberation is no less than its own law, on the other. And yet, even with the help of special legislation directed at terrorism – one of the pioneers of the kind that has come to define securitized states in the post-September 11 world – the mighty sovereign is able to punish but unable to discipline. The violent clash of the wills takes on a decidedly corporeal form in the claustrophobic atmosphere of the high-security prison, movingly depicted by *Hunger*, where the contrast between the repetitive violence of the forces "upholding" the law and the self-destructive resistance of those "breaking" it is soon revealed to be the reversal of what is political and what is criminal. Unable to bend the prisoners to its own will, the state folds back upon and criminalizes itself, in the face of the moral and political indictment put forth by the violent self-destruction of the prisoners themselves. If *Hunger* thereby chronicles how sovereignty and democracy enter into a frontal collision in the conditions of the high-security prison, its immanent critique of British politics raises the question of whether it is not democracy that thereby self-destructs with the hunger strike and eventual death of its political prisoners.

While the movie centers on what McQueen calls "*the* most important event in British history in recent times,"[3] it actually speaks to the present: it stages a principled intervention into our political landscape where the question of hunger strikes hovers as urgently as ever, hailing most notably (but not only) from Guantánamo Bay Prison. As of 1 May 2013 (at the time of writing), 100 of the 166 prisoners held under "indefinite detention" have been starving themselves.[4] Unlike the Maze Prison, however, no death by self-starvation occurs in Guantánamo.[5] This is because prisoners are continually resuscitated by nonconsensual medical intervention, most notoriously by the insertion of nasal feeding tubes while they are tied to restraint chairs.[6] Even though Obama has publicly disowned Guantánamo, in contradistinction to the late Thatcher's position on the Maze Prison, he has not kept his long-standing promise to close the prison and has turned a blind eye to the violation of international human rights laws as well as the global ethical standards of medical practice that condemn forced feeding as "cruel, humiliating, and degrading treatment."[7]

Guantánamo may be the most conspicuous example of the "liberal" exceptions taken from fundamental human rights, but it is hardly the only one. "Special" prisons and detainment centers have proliferated around the globe, a proliferation which lends evidence to the thesis that exceptional regimes – perpetuated through executive decrees, counter-insurgency tactics, or the outright suspension of liberties as part of counterterrorism measures – are fast becoming recurrent and normalized, if not constitutive, features of liberal-democratic states.[8] In parallel, hunger striking has become a recurrently utilized form of resistance as part of an emergent necropolitical repertoire of struggle.[9] Regrettably, the experience of Irish political prisoners continues to hold important resonance for the present, exposing the dark side of liberal-democratic states that can no longer be written off as exceptions.[10] *Hunger*, therefore, is not only about Bobby Sands; it is about the hunger strikers of our time whose names we do not even know.

sovereignty and sacrifice

If the immediate political resonance of *Hunger* does not exhaust its power, it is because the movie, as a genuine work of art, calls for deeper philosophical reflection. Its stunning beauty, due as much to McQueen's keen aesthetic as it is to the excellent performance of Michael Fassbender in his role as Bobby Sands, augments the force of what I take to be the movie's most central question: how far are we willing to go in order to dominate, how far in order to be free? *Hunger* thus speaks to a nexus defined not only by the lavish excesses of securitized state sovereignty but also by the quest for freedom and the role of sacrifice in the struggle for its attainment. Embedding us in a life-and-death struggle, it forces us to reconsider the meaning and implications, the potentialities and limitations of our agency, especially when that agency takes a sacrificial form.

Indeed, *Hunger* is a movie about sacrifice as much as it is about sovereignty, but it would be wrong to conclude that it is unequivocal in its approach to either. The movie does not equate the critique of the British state with an unquestioned espousal of the Provisional IRA, nor does it abstain from depicting the human tragedy involved in the everyday enactments of the claim to sovereignty from either side. With great attention to the complexity of the conflict, the movie chooses to depict it through individuals on opposing sides: both the prison guards and the prisoners emerge as non-identical to the roles that their structural positions in the asymmetry of power relations require them to play. On the one hand, the prison guards who are the laborers of the state's security apparatus are themselves without security; they live in fear of their lives. Meanwhile, they have to dehumanize the prisoners in order to brutalize them on a recurrent basis, but they too lose something of their humanity in the process.[11] On the other hand, the prisoners in the Dirty Protest, living in the midst of bodily excrements and smearing their shit on the cell walls, reduce themselves to "animality" in order to reclaim their human dignity.[12] Meanwhile, they, too, must bear the cost of their claim to sovereignty, which comes most painfully through the protracted labor of dying they carry out on the hunger strike. However, it is worth noting that while pointing to the shared humanity of the prisoner and the prison guard, McQueen nevertheless avoids "repeating liberal humanism's common mistake of flattening the differences in power relations."[13] *Hunger* thereby sustains an uneasiness until the very end, which amplifies its powerful effect.

Like its equivocity to sovereignty, the movie is far from an unhesitating endorsement of sacrifice in the struggle for freedom. While the sympathies of the movie toward the prisoners' cause is clear, *Hunger* is far from being a work of political propaganda aiming for a crude glorification of self-destruction.[14] Despite its realistic conveyance of the conditions of the high-security prison, the movie avoids presenting the decision of the prisoners to go on hunger strike as an inevitable outcome, and more transparent and obvious than it actually is. *Hunger* makes room for agency; in fact, an uninterrupted twenty-two-minute sequence in the middle of the movie stages a heated conversation between Bobby Sands and a West Belfast priest (played skillfully by Liam Cunningham), in which Sands gives an account of the moral and political reasons for embarking on this journey of self-destruction, defends his decision against the priest's effort to convince him to negotiate with the British government instead (which, not incidentally, is also the position of the outside leadership of the Provisional IRA), and presents a rebuttal of criticisms. One does not have to agree with Sands' reasoning to understand that his decision is a well-contemplated and difficult one, made with the knowledge of its consequences and the awareness that there is little chance of its success. If the priest's refusal to support the fast unto death does not cast sufficient doubt on the movie's championship of sacrifice, its final part, which follows Sands in the painful corporeal deterioration of his last days, most certainly does. As the director puts it: "In the end we are alone with one man, living out his last days in the most extreme manner possible – but only one decision away from choosing to surrender and live. The simplest physical action becomes an odyssey."[15] Indeed, the award-winning movie, co-authored by McQueen and Enda Walsh, goes a long way in courageously and thoughtfully portraying the wealth of troubling moral, personal, and political dilemmas and difficulties that surround the choice of pursuing self-destructive acts in political struggle, without necessarily lionizing or vilifying the endeavor, and they should be commended for this achievement.[16]

As the hunger strike takes Sands to the limits of biological existence, it also provides an implicit commentary on the liberal foundations of the Western political imaginary, which, centered on the presupposition of the primacy of self-preservation, sustains a deep contradiction with self-sacrifice. This tension is most forcefully recognized by Max Horkheimer and Theodor Adorno, who present it as a fundamental tenet of civilization as such, in their renowned *Dialectic of Enlightenment:*

> [t]he history of civilization is the history of the introversion of sacrifice. In other words: the history of renunciation. Everyone who practices renunciation gives away more of his life than is given back to him: and more than the life that he vindicates.[17]

Stated differently, the predicament of civilization is precisely that the way to sublate the contradiction between self-preservation and self-sacrifice is the condemnation of everyone to a system of perpetual repression in which the renunciations made to stay alive outweigh the benefits. Self-destructive protest challenges this imaginary based on renunciation because it shifts the dictum that life is the highest value toward the question of what kind of life is worth living.

From this perspective, *Hunger* shares a significant commonality with Horkheimer and Adorno's interpretation of Homer's *Odyssey*. Both advance a strong critique of the enlightened Western civilization and its consequences. They do so by redefining civilization on the basis of the constitution of subjectivity in a dual process of subjectification and subjection, which they situate in the entwinement of sovereignty and sacrifice. Both works, I would like to argue, problematize the sacrificial subjectivity of enlightenment and its instrumental rationality while they also interrogate the conceptions of time that go into their making.

For Horkheimer and Adorno, Odysseus' adventures, and especially his encounter with the Sirens, can be read as a formative moment for the constitution of the identity of the modern subject because they point to the entanglement of myth and reason: myth is already enlightenment and enlightenment reverts to myth. Homer's *Odyssey* is an epic whose structure forebodes the very dialectic of enlightenment; it sketches out how freedom from the domination of nature creates new forms of domination that are destructive to the self and others. With *Hunger*, the odyssey of Bobby Sands can be read as a modern epic, which skillfully situates our contemporary moment within the dialectic of enlightenment. If the high-security prison can be read as the political culmination of the self-destructive tendency of enlightenment, wherein democratic sovereignty's promise of liberation from arbitrary and violent domination has become a new form of domination, self-destructive resistance emerges not only as a response to this domination but also as the interruption of the dialectic itself. The figure of Sands is the dialectical reversal of the figure of Odysseus, supplanting the sacrificial subjectivity of enlightenment with one that is re-constituted by *insurgent* sacrifice.

Reading Horkheimer and Adorno's excursus on Odysseus in the *Dialectic of Enlightenment* together with McQueen's *Hunger*, my intention is to draw attention to the ways in which modern subjectivity – a philosophical problem common to both works and central to furthering the critical project of reason – is being politically challenged and reconfigured in the present. In this light, I want to pose *Hunger* as a response to the enlightenment narrative proposed by Horkheimer and Adorno, one that not only validates their observations but also points to some of their limitations. Such a reading takes art seriously as an independent grounding for the self-critique of reason and attends to how the aesthetic can bring into sharp focus the political contradictions of the present and their implications for liberation.

critiquing enlightenment

In their formidable and controversial work, Horkheimer and Adorno begin from a simple yet crushing observation regarding the relationship of reason and power; namely, that while the process of humanity's enlightenment by the use of reason contains the ambition to dissolve domination (or, at the very least, to question and unsettle the supremacy of those who wield power and reveal the precarity of their power), it acts as the handmaiden of power instead, which reduces the masses to passivity and blind obedience. This observation, aiming to make sense of the experience of fascism and subject its technological-instrumental rationality to critique, is based on the view that fascism is not an aberration of enlightenment, an exception from its otherwise liberating course, but rather internal to its development. Expressed more sharply, fascism is nothing less than the culmination of enlightenment's course and an index of its self-destruction.

Horkheimer and Adorno define enlightenment as the process by which men are liberated from fear and transformed into sovereign subjects (sovereign over nature, both external to them and their own). In order to avoid being subjected to the forces of nature, humanity learns how to dominate nature but denies and subjugates its own nature in the process.[18] Enlightenment proceeds with the acquisition of knowledge and the dissolution of myth, but that knowledge, while it allows freedom from fear, does not necessarily bring justice.[19] Instead, the mastery of nature and other "men" in the service of self-preservation now becomes the ultimate end imposed by domination and a new source of subjection.[20] The reversal of sovereignty to subjugation is the reversal of enlightenment to myth. Rationality becomes deeply engulfed in myth even as it tries to escape from and destroy it.[21] This dual character of enlightenment defines a dialectic between liberation and domination in the maelstrom of which the subject is forged into being. As reason attempts to dominate nature, within and without, through struggle and labor, it helps construct a unified self. It is not just that subjectification proceeds hand in hand with subjection, however. It also prostrates its bearer, irrevocably transforming the self toward something less that it could be – mutilating, sacrificing, damaged and damaging, leaving behind it a trail of unrealized hopes and disappointments.

The reason for the overarching pessimism of the text has generally been attributed to the implicit negative teleology that informs the reconstruction of enlightenment as culminating in "totalitarian capitalism." Horkheimer and Adorno's radical critique of rationality, it has been argued, especially by Jürgen Habermas, not only overlooks the achievements of modernity in scientific knowledge, universalism, democracy, and aesthetics but also puts forth a reductive understanding of modernity itself. Habermas maintains: "The critical ability to take a 'yes' or 'no' stand, to be able to distinguish between what is valid and invalid, is *undercut* by the unfortunate fusion of power and validity claims."[22] Horkheimer and Adorno's conflation of power and validity claims, or reduction of reason to instrumental rationality, also undermines the text's ability to ground its own criticism in reason. The "totalizing critique" put forth by Horkheimer and Adorno in "their blackest, most nihilistic book," Habermas asserts, "turns against reason as the foundation of its own analysis."[23] Habermas considers this aporia problematic because it ignores the "rational content of cultural modernity," which Horkheimer and Adorno's critique takes for granted even as they indict reason for its complicity with domination.[24] If the distinction between power and reason is obfuscated, asks Habermas, how can reason retain a critical potential that can be used for an analysis of itself – is it not always-already part of power? In a similar way, Seyla Benhabib argues, if domination is built into the structure of Western reason, "then the theory of the dialectic of the Enlightenment, which is carried out with the tools of this very same reason, perpetuates the structure of domination it condemns."[25]

While Habermas is right to insist on the necessity of critique to account for its own conditions of possibility, he also recognizes that the aporetic qualities of the text do not necessarily render Horkheimer and Adorno's critique invalid. For it is precisely the ability of the text to operate in such a "performative contradiction,"[26] one that Habermas himself notes, which enables it to provide a critique of an unreasonable truth by recourse to reason – thereby locating the contradiction in the conditions that give rise to their critique – and to call for a necessary self-reflection of enlightenment.[27] The problem hinges, at least in part, on whether or not Horkheimer and Adorno consider the process of self-destruction that they find in enlightenment's trajectory to be inevitable. There are many moments in this text that warrant such an interpretation and Habermas is certainly not alone in taking that to be the text's ultimate position.[28] However, there is also much to suggest in the text that it is Horkheimer and Adorno's goal to salvage enlightenment from itself, for example, when the authors write: "If enlightenment does not accommodate reflection on this recidivist element, then it seals its own fate."[29] In this light, Richard J. Bernstein argues that despite the pessimism regarding enlightenment, Adorno's thought contains a utopian promise, "the vision of a nonantagonistic, nonhierarchial, nonviolent, and nonrepressive society."[30] Such a hope perhaps also sheds light on the risk that Horkheimer and Adorno have taken in occupying that aporetic position Habermas underscores, as a gesture that attempts to bring enlightenment's self-destructive process to a halt by critical reflection whose grounding is precarious, if not altogether dubious.

As Benhabib points out, the way Horkheimer and Adorno navigated this paradox was an appeal to the logic of non-identity, which could be found in the aesthetic.[31] Indeed, the aesthetic constituted a refuge for the critique of rationality in which one could (hope to) escape the complicity of reason in its own demise.[32] According to Horkheimer and Adorno, art is the only form in which the past can be rescued without being reduced to an instrument of progress: "The compulsion to rescue what is gone as what is living instead of using it as the material of progress was appeased only in art, to which history itself appertains as a presentation of past life."[33] This recuperative dimension of Adornian aesthetics provides the possibility of a memory of the past against the progressive historical narrative of enlightenment. It also provides the possibility of enlightenment's self-critique.[34]

A different way to approach the text's pessimism, then, one enabled by art, is to disentangle its implicit negative teleology from a story of the "fall." When Horkheimer and Adorno read Odysseus as the "prototype of the bourgeois individual,"[35] they clearly suggest that the modern subject is no less immune to the struggle between reason and myth than its prehistoric counterpart might have been. Homer's text, which the authors call the "basic text of European civilization," offers "eloquent testimony of the mutual implication of enlightenment and myth," an implication that lies at the origin of Western civilization and continues to characterize it.[36] If they thereby oppose the conventional, progressive, and triumphalist enlightenment narrative that posits the ultimate overcoming of myth by reason, they do not necessarily suggest demise as the inevitable *telos* of this process. In fact, the authors unsettle the very conception of a "golden age" that lies at the *origin* of civilization when they take away the classical world as a safe haven. Instead, they posit the classical world as a premonition of the catastrophes to come.[37] At the same time, they put into question the necessity of history's unfolding toward catastrophe. It is their polemical intent, according to Susan Buck-Morss, that animates the juxtaposition of ancient Greece to the "most barbaric, most irrational phenomena of the present," a juxtaposition which sought to "demythologize the present and the past's hold over it."[38] Horkheimer and Adorno construct a genealogy of the subject that stretches the limits of a historiography that claims fidelity to facts, but they do so in order to expose what they see as a fundamental truth; namely, that the history of the formation of modern subjectivity, which is dependent on the dialectic of enlightenment in which it is forged, is a story of unfulfilled promises rather than that of the "fall." In this dialectic, there is room for contingency. But contingency depends on the struggles for freedom that, not having been successful, wait as ever-present potentialities even though they are relegated to history. The problem for the critical theorist, then, "is not the conservation of the past, but the redemption of the hopes of the past."[39]

If this interpretation is correct, then Horkheimer and Adorno's text not only leaves the door open for change but also gestures to indicate a way to achieve it. Their work teaches the necessity of recuperating the emancipatory promise of enlightenment, but it also performs this teaching by engaging in a reading that crisscrosses different temporalities, interweaving the present and the past. For Horkheimer and Adorno, Homer's *Odyssey* sheds light on *their* present while the present casts a new light on the past.[40] In Christopher Rocco's words,

> [t]heir strategy thus works in two directions at once: it aims to free us from a reified present in which political and economic structures of domination appear natural and it works against any nostalgic return to a falsely idealized past.[41]

The tragedies of the authors' present allows them to excavate the past for opportunities missed and potentialities lying dormant, which in turn help unsettle the conclusion that what has become was predestined and cannot be changed. Repeating their gesture, as it were, we can theorize the predicaments of subjectivity today through a similar practice of a *transtemporal* reading, but this time through the mediation of their text. Horkheimer and Adorno's method may allow us to understand that the self-destructive reconfiguration of modern subjectivity in the forceps of domination is not the end but an attempt to realize the unfulfilled promise of freedom. In this reading, the aesthetic continues to provide a fruitful, engaging site for grounding critical reflection. However, as I hope to show, the refuge of art is bound to remain inadequate and utopian if it cannot address political forms of resistance to domination.

sacrificial subject and sovereign time

It is well known that Horkheimer and Adorno situate sacrifice at the heart of the Odyssean journey to constitute the self. The struggle with myth is fundamentally asymmetric and dangerous; the self is always less powerful than the frightening mythical powers that threaten to destroy it. Sacrifice becomes a form of exchange with the mythical powers and gods because it grants the possibility of self-preservation.[42]

Crucial to the process of subjectification through sacrifice is the element of deceit embedded within the exchange relation characterized by asymmetry. Deception, Horkheimer and Adorno point out, is a rational survival strategy: it allows the subject to exercise agency from a position of powerlessness before the gods. Odysseus' success depends on his ability to "outwit" the gods through the very medium of exchange that honors them. His cunning depends, in turn, on the calculability of sacrifice. Appeasing the gods with gifts is not only to acknowledge their power but also to demand something in return, such as protection, which turns the gift into a calculated act. If the gods accept the sacrifice, they confirm their divine status before which the individual has bowed in recognition; however, by that very acceptance, they have also been cajoled into serving the individual's ends, especially the end of self-preservation. Horkheimer and Adorno argue: "All human sacrifices, when systematically executed, deceive the god to whom they are made: they subject him to the primacy of human ends, and dissolve his power."[43]

The element of calculation within the act of sacrifice exposes sacrifice in its essential character: a relation of exchange, a contract. An exchange of equivalents is never completely equal; however, when this exchange is embedded within a structural asymmetry, the power differential among the parties of the exchange cannot but vitiate any semblance of equality. And yet, in that very inequality, deceit carves a space of reversal and implodes the sacrificial contract from within. Calculation within the sacrificial relation provides a way to overturn the asymmetry because it injects a logic that tries to salvage what is commensurate to or more than what is being forgone in the exchange. "By calculating his own sacrifice, [Odysseus] effectively negates the power to whom the sacrifice is made. In this way he redeems the life he had forfeited."[44]

Horkheimer and Adorno make it clear that while Odysseus renders the element of deception in sacrifice more visible, he neither invents nor exhausts it. In drawing a historical line stretching from the immortality attributed to the deified victim in ancient rituals of human sacrifice, whose blood is to flow back into the community as some form of primordial energy, to the sacrifice of individuals to modern collectivities, especially in warfare, Horkheimer and Adorno posit deception as integral to sacrifice. However, while in the first case the gods are being outwitted, in the latter case it is the individuals who are being outwitted by the state, which has become the new god. And yet modern sacrifice need not be fatal; it takes on subtler forms. The struggle to free oneself from bondage to nature becomes a struggle that leads to one's own bondage in the form of self-denial, sublimation, and repression. Horkheimer and Adorno contend that the domination of the self in the effort to master nature and others becomes destructive of the subject; it destroys what it is supposed to preserve. The path laid out by domination is a sacrificial contract that has outlasted its necessity; upholding the contract, originally intended to protect life, becomes its own rationale. The irrationality of domination reaches its extreme point with "totalitarian capitalism" – in order to uphold it, one must go down the path that leads to the "extermination of mankind."[45] In the regulated, rationalized form of sacrifice that is constantly demanded by the system – a mastered and "masterful" renunciation – deceit is now directed to the self. It is those thus dominated who are being cheated by the new god, and "the subjected repeat upon themselves the injustice that was done to them, enacting it again in order to endure it."[46]

Horkheimer and Adorno locate a turning point in the development of the cunning of reason in Odysseus' encounter with the Sirens, whose temporality is revealing and constitutive. This encounter takes place in "mythic time," the temporality characterized by repetition for the mythical powers – the Sirens must lure every traveler – and the suspension of ordinary time for the mortals. Repetition is the curse that the Sirens cannot break, but it also lies at the source of their lure.[47] Deceit is in the Sirens' offer when they act as the voice of history: they deliver the knowledge of the past but at the expense of the future, for "the promise of the happy return is the deception with which the past ensnares the one who longs for it."[48] Their temporality is that of sovereignty; they control time. By contrast, Odysseus has little in the way of his own temporality; that is why his adventures are spatially, rather than temporally, separated and serialized through the image of voyaging or wandering. Where "historical time is detached from space" and suspended, Odysseus is subject to the Sirens' temporality as much as he is subject to their lure: "their allurement is that of losing oneself in the past."[49]

The song of the Sirens, dangerous as it is beautiful, is Odysseus' test of subjectification, of achieving the internal development of the self-preserving, centered, and instrumentally rational subject of enlightenment. Mythical time requires that the subject has no independent relation with history but loses itself in the suspension of temporality in which the mythical powers can endlessly repeat and reproduce themselves. However, Odysseus' emancipation from myth relies on the transformation of nature into history. Thus, while he can entertain the knowledge he has acquired from the past to ensure his survival, he cannot tolerate the appeal of a return to what has passed.[50] Odysseus must dissociate the past from the present and the present from the future, grounding the unity of his nascent self in the "now." His success requires a narrative of history as progressive rationalization and instrumental knowledge – otherwise the memory of natural history is strong enough to engulf the subject. The fear of subjection to nature lingers in the definition of civilization.[51] It is the remainder that cannot be subsumed into civilization, nor can it be destroyed.

Sacrifice appears in dual form in the solutions for escaping the lure of the Sirens' song. Either their song must not be heard at all or a way must be found to resist its temptation. Odysseus finds the first solution fit for the laborers on his ship. Because their ears are waxed, the oarsmen are left to labor in silence and submission to Odysseus' will, without any conflict between the Sirens' lure, their own desires, and the rationality of self-preservation. The deceit in their sacrifice is simple: in order to avoid being engulfed by nature, they agree to submit themselves to the domination of sovereignty. For the oarsmen, sovereignty takes on a dominant, repetitive temporality, which brings survival at the cost of not only their freedom but also the knowledge and experience of the Sirens' song. The second solution is for Odysseus who has himself bound to the mast of the ship while he listens to the Sirens. Even though he tries to cast off his bonds once he hears the song, he struggles in vain since the oarsmen cannot hear him either. Here, the conflict between desire and reason is resolved by a different sacrifice, one that is more controlled and calculated. In yielding to the power of the Sirens, or displaying only a rationalized resistance, Odysseus "has found an escape clause in the contract, which enables him to fulfill it while eluding it. The primeval contract does not provide for the possibility of the seafarer listening bound or unbound to the bewitching voices."[52] Cunning means taking charge of one's own subjugation not only for safe passage but also for the advantageous use of knowledge and the enjoyment of the Sirens' song. If the oarsmen's sacrifice is their submission to Odysseus' will and to repetitive labor, Odysseus' sacrifice is subduing his instincts to the discipline of instrumental reason, or giving up the nature in himself in order to dominate nature and the oarsmen. Odysseus thus internalizes and re-rationalizes sacrifice; it becomes a controlled "renunciation" that appears to neutralize his subjection. This is also the appropriation and internalization of a sovereign temporality of repetition, ensuring the fixity of time for the emergent subject. Cunning thus allows Odysseus to navigate the asymmetric relation of exchange and transform the inevitability represented by the power of myth to his own advantage: "his rationality necessarily assumes a restrictive form – *that of an exception*."[53] As Odysseus takes exception from myth, he embarks on the path that renders the *exceptional* form of rationality the *rule* of enlightenment.

This encounter is symptomatic for showing how deceit used toward the goal of self-preservation vis-à-vis nature ends up eating away at the subject's own nature, deceiving the deceiver in the process. The domination achieved through this very denial or the internalization of sacrifice renders Odysseus the figure of the *sacrificial* subject. This subjectivity is constituted through a dialectic between nature and history, a dialectic in which sovereignty over nature is achieved through the negation of human nature as part of nature, and sovereignty over time is achieved through a controlled and self-imposed subjection of desire. Odysseus' submission to renunciation defies the truth of the subject's hard-earned sovereignty, implicating him in the logic of "equivalent" exchange, which entails the preservation of life by forgoing a *fulfilling* life. After all, "the annulment of death," argue Horkheimer and Adorno, "constitutes the very core of all antimythological thinking."[54] Consequently, the song of the Sirens can be heard for what it really is: the *mythical interpellation of the sacrificial subject into a sovereign subject.* In this light, we can understand Horkheimer and Adorno as presenting a compelling critique of sovereignty, in which domination over nature and others is always-already domination over oneself. The dialectic of enlightenment is a dialectic of sovereignty and sacrifice in which:

> Man's domination over himself, which grounds his selfhood, is almost always the destruction of the subject in whose service it is undertaken; for the substance which is dominated, suppressed, and dissolved by virtue of self-preservation is none other than this very life as functions of which the achievements of self-preservation find their sole definition and determination: it is, in fact, what is to be preserved.[55]

hunger's siren song

Odysseus listens to the Sirens' song while he is bound to the mast, but his cunning attempt to overcome its lure results in the neutralization of the aesthetic that is thereby transformed into a mere source of pleasure rather than a way of experiencing the world. However, against the self-destructiveness of enlightenment and the reversal of reason to myth, true art is the source of a redemptive critique.[56] According to Robert Hullot-Kentor:

> In art, domination is able to become liberation, the truth of the whole, because the same process of the domination of nature that society carries out occurs within the art work; the same sacrificial act of reason is carried out by art through its construction ... However, whereas the sacrifices required by self-preservative reason in the actual domination of nature are silenced by the semblance of necessity woven by the principle of identity, art mourns the sacrifices it carries out.[57]

McQueen's *Hunger* is precisely such a work, which offers sensory experience as a critical perspective from which to evaluate the dialectic of enlightenment and the non-identical as a refusal to forget what is sacrificed. It offers knowledge of the past not as a practical tool of self-preservation in the present but as the reminder of a moment of unfulfilled promise, as the constituent element of a memory against history as well as a form of mourning of loss. The movie can therefore be interpreted as an engaged response to Horkheimer and Adorno's critique of modernity, which it shares and advances. Like the *Dialectic of Enlightenment, Hunger* attends to the dialectical constitution of modern subjectivity and problematizes instrumental rationality. Similarly, it transtemporally gestures to unsettle the present by salvaging a precious moment of the past from oblivion, without, however, overlooking its contradictions or idealizing it. However, just as the *Dialectic of Enlightenment* enables us to arrive at a new appreciation of *Hunger*, the movie also enables us to point to some limitations of Horkheimer and Adorno's analysis.

The figure of Bobby Sands as depicted in *Hunger* presents a strong contrast to the figure of Odysseus as interpreted by Horkheimer and Adorno. Odysseus hears the Sirens' song, but he cannot let himself listen freely. He is interpellated as a sovereign subject, but the cost of his sovereignty is his ongoing renunciation. On the other hand, Sands, too, hears the Sirens' song, but not only does he listen to it, he also lets himself be taken by it, by transforming his renunciation into self-destruction. If Odysseus is the allegory for the constitution of the modern sacrificial subject defined by instrumental reason, Sands can be read as its fruition, inversion, and ultimate destruction. Sands' interpellation by the Sirens' song in order to redeem the unfulfilled promise of freedom from domination radicalizes sacrifice and turns it against the self. However, the destruction of the logic of domination based on a regime of renunciation for the sake of survival is only possible through the destruction of Odysseus. Sands is the self-destruction of Odysseus, whose advantageous contract with sovereignty implodes to reclaim a free subjectivity.

The distance between the two figures can be found in Sands' account of a childhood moment when he ventured deep into the woods with a group of friends while preparing for a cross-country race. In the woods, they encountered a little foal in pain with a broken leg. The other children deliberated what to do without doing anything. Sands tells how he drowned the foal, exactly at the moment when they were seen by one of the priests, who reprimanded them for the death of the foal. Sands takes the blame in everyone's name. The lesson is clear: in order to alleviate the suffering of others, he will act without fearing its consequences. If Sands' encounter with the foal is a test of subjectification, a challenge he must overcome to become the self that he is, it already indicates the possibility of a different pathway than the cunning of Odysseus. Sands' actions are not about outwitting the powers that threaten him but silently confronting the challenge, taking moral responsibility, and suffering the repercussions of his actions. Subjectification is not centered on self-preservation but on putting an end to suffering and the preservation of friends.

The contrast between Sands and Odysseus becomes most vivid in the prison encounter. Here, the struggle for subjectivity is no longer about the conquest of an external nature. Unlike the *Odyssey* where nature remains the unconquered "other" of civilization, in *Hunger* we are deep in the bowels of civilization, in a "civilized" prison where domination has become *second nature*. The mythical powers that Odysseus struggled against have mutated into the "enlightened domination" of the sovereignty of the state. Nature's mythical powers are no longer a threat to the survival of the self but nature is a source of freedom from civilization. On the one hand, an idealized nature naively protrudes into the movie with the suffering foal, the fly that visits the prisoner's cell, the rat that accompanies the prison guard smoking in the yard, and the birds that fly away to signify Sands' eventual yielding to death. McQueen's projection of freedom on nature, juxtaposed against civilization as the index of humanity's alienation from itself, appears curiously romanticized and nostalgic from the perspective afforded by Horkheimer and Adorno. On the other hand, *Hunger* recuperates its critical perspective when it turns to depict how human nature already objectified and colonized by civilization can be turned back against civilization in the form of resistance to domination: in the naked bodies that refuse clothing themselves in prison uniforms, the excrements that are smeared on the cell walls, the urine that is poured from the cell doors, the transformation of the body's cavities into vessels of political messages, and the sustained refusal of food. Just as the most basic corporeal functions of human nature become objects of oppression, they can be reversed into the means of resistance against oppression. Radicalized self-domination in the form of the repression of the desire to eat is forged into a weapon against the domination of the state. Nature is once again pitted against civilization, but now as the source of its internal or self-critique and the possibility of its transformation.

If *Hunger* thereby charts the dialectic of subjectivity suggested by the *Dialectic of Enlightenment*, it attends to what Horkheimer and Adorno tend to overlook: resistance. *Hunger* situates the present as part of this dialectic but draws upon resistance to show how the dialectic can be interrupted: the modern self built on the renunciation of nature can radicalize renunciation into self-sacrifice. It does so not only by its transtemporal gesture to critique the present but also by interweaving different temporalities within the movie, temporalities that resonate with those of Odysseus. The temporality of sovereignty is chronicled in the movie's first part through the juxtaposition of the experience of a new prisoner and the prison guard who enter into the same prison. This is time organized, regulated, and dominated by the power of the state. Ordinary time is suspended. The only evidence of the passing of time for the prisoners is the rhythm of recurrent beatings, forced haircuts and baths, cavity searches.[58] The prison guard's recurrent relief from the beatings he gives to the prisoners by soaking his bruised knuckles in water shows how the guards' labor is subject to the same rhythmic organization of time. Both the prisoners and the guards are rooted in the "now," without any real connection to the past or the future. Like the "mythic time" in the *Odyssey*, sovereign time is abstract and detached, and characterized by compulsory repetition. Only, the power of the Sirens has now been supplanted by Odyssean sovereignty – Odysseus' ability to achieve domination over myth by reason has been objectified in the modern state, which reproduces itself through the repeated labor of violence.

The only way to survive this temporality is through renunciation. The prison guards must have their ears waxed and keep on rowing while the prisoners must remain tied to the mast. Like Odysseus, they must formally subject themselves to the state, recognize its laws, make compromises, do their time in submission. Their resistance must be calculated and advantageous. But there is a problem: the prisoners refuse the Odyssean strategy; they reject wearing the prison uniforms, they do not clean themselves, they rebel against the sacrificial contract with power, dictated by instrumental rationality. Already in sovereign time, or the eternal repetition of mythical violence, prisoners become non-identical with their roles, beginning to point beyond the rationalized and deceptive resistance of Odysseus toward the *refusal* of domination. The assassination of the prison guard outside of the prison marks the beginning of the end of sovereign time, by acting as the symbolic destruction of the possibility of rowing in silence for the oarsmen. It also acts as a segue way to the second part of the movie, hailed by critics as its heart – the long conversation between Sands and the priest, in which the two debate Sands' proposed course of action as resistance comes to its own by articulating its self-consciousness. This is the moment in which the historic rupture from the dominant temporality is articulated through the decision on the hunger strike unto death and its justification in political and moral terms before the tribunal of the priest. Pointing to the failure of the first hunger strike, which was called off when the government agreed to prisoner demands but never kept its promises, Sands argues that prisoners end up being cheated when they negotiate with the state. Stated differently, the controlled renunciation of the prisoners, in which they think they are utilizing the situation to their advantage, ends up in deception: it destroys the possibility of achieving their goals while it threatens to diminish, if not erase altogether, the prior work of resistance. Echoing Horkheimer and Adorno's critique of the sacrificial subject symbolized in the figure of Odysseus, Sands refuses the reconciliatory line, which implies conceding to the sovereignty of the state as a strategy of renunciation in which self-preservation is bound to end up undermining the very life to be preserved. Instead of a negotiating tool for gaining leverage or concessions, the proposed hunger strike unto death is the expression of a staunch rejection to be determined and dominated by the state. This is an absolute and *insurgent* form of sacrifice, fundamentally at odds with controlled and calculated renunciation. Regardless of its chances of success, this strategy is seen as the only way to achieve freedom. Against the priest's objection that such self-destructive action amounts to suicide, a disregard for life, Sands responds that it is necessary to lay down one's life for a *dignified* life, one lived in line with the deepest moral and political convictions. Sands argues: "My life means everything to me. Freedom means everything ... Putting my life on the line is not just the only thing I can do, Dom. It's the right thing."

Sands' position thus radicalizes the critique of the sacrificial subject by proposing a break with instrumental rationality. Self-preservation no longer dominates the terms of an exchange with the powerful, in which cunning would be necessary to transform the asymmetry of the exchange from within. Since there is no "equivalent" that can be exchanged for self-imposed death, such action refuses compromise and deceit and obliterates the possibility of renunciation being translated into further domination. The subjectivity entailed by the radicalization of renunciation to the limit is an insurgent subjectivity fundamentally at odds with that of Odysseus. In *Hunger*'s temporality of the decision for resistance we therefore encounter the articulation of the desire to break free from one's bonds, not in order to ensure survival but in order to upend domination and destroy the sacrificial subjectivity brought into being in the dialectic of enlightenment. The consequences of such a decision, however, are far from clear: it can lead to the collapse of enlightenment or open an opportunity for its recuperation.

This brings us to the final part of the movie, which narrates the corporeal journey that takes Sands to his death and where a novel temporality is introduced. This temporality, radically alien to the coming into being of sovereign time that dominates Horkheimer and Adorno's interpretation of Odysseus' encounter with the Sirens, is *scatological* time, the temporality of corporeal deterioration.[59] *Hunger* painfully portrays the famished body of Sands as he is slowly reduced to bed. But the material traces of self-starvation – the blood in the toilet, the vomit, the stains on the bed sheets from the ulcers of his skin, the muffling of voices, the blurring of vision – document the invisible: glimpses of a new subjectivity in defiance of the destruction of the body, in the form of an inextinguishable spirit of freedom that resists both the domination of the state and the fear of death itself. This is the temporality of refusal that, on the one hand, gestures toward an indefinite futurity, a time of ultimate redemption to come, while, on the other hand, it connects back to the past. We see a young Sands staring at his dying self and the dying Sands merging with his young self, freely running in the wilderness. The temporality of *insurgent sacrifice* breaks the cast of a partitioned time between the past, present, and future, which made possible the nascent subjectivity of enlightenment in the figure of Odysseus. In *Hunger*, these three temporalities intertwine and re-merge in a new whole, which comes to define the new self claimed through a struggle against one's former subjectivity, as well as the domination that rendered it damaged and lacking. Odysseus' price for self-preservation was continual self-denial and the introversion of sacrifice into renunciation. Sands resorts to self-destruction in order to reclaim his freedom. As the sacrificial subject of enlightenment is subverted, we encounter the flickering vision of a new subjectivity, reconfigured by the radicalization of internalized sacrifice. Insurgent self-sacrifice interrupts sovereign time, bringing the dialectic of enlightenment to a halt. In this new temporality, Odysseus is no longer bound to the mast. Sands is *Odysseus unbound.*

dialectic interrupted

Reading *Hunger* with the *Dialectic of Enlightenment* allows us to arrive at a new appreciation of both works as commentaries on subjectivity in modernity as constituted by sovereignty and sacrifice. Read transtemporally alongside the "primal history of subjectivity" put forth in the *Dialectic of Enlightenment*, the figure of Bobby Sands in *Hunger* provides a history of the present: he emerges as the inversion of Odysseus and reveals how the subversive potentialities embedded within our subjection can be activated in a staunch resistance against domination. At the same time, he shows how the dark side of our rational self-domination involves a violence that is directed against the self, made visible by the self-imposed and willed corporeal decay of the subject, deconstructing itself as it rejects the sacrificial subjectivity of enlightenment. In contrast to the insurgent sacrifice epitomized by the figure of Sands, Odysseus of the *Dialectic of Enlightenment* appears as a cautionary tale of the trajectory of reason that surrenders itself to domination so absolutely in its struggle against nature and myth that its redemption comes at the cost of self-destruction.

If *Hunger* thereby pressures the *Dialectic of Enlightenment* toward its logical conclusions in bringing it to bear on our present, it also throws some of its limitations into sharp relief. While Horkheimer and Adorno are right to diagnose the self-destructive tendency in enlightenment, perpetuated by the reversal of the struggle to break free from nature into a cage of domination and repression, reproduced by asymmetries of power and calculated renunciation, their call for enlightenment to engage in critical self-reflection in order to counteract its destructive dynamic appears to be a curiously feeble solution. There are moments when self-reflection is not sufficient, both because it can remain isolated from action and because that self-reflection is also subject to the same dialectic, which tends toward its own demise. The aesthetic provides a refuge from which to criticize this self-destructive tendency, but change requires the political struggle of those subjects who are shaped by and who in turn shape that self-destructive tendency. If Horkheimer and Adorno's text is pervaded by a deep pessimism, this is also because radical resistance is absent from it. Such resistance does not completely overturn the devastating account of enlightenment proposed by the authors, but it militates against its inevitability and renews our faith in the possibility of change as well as our commitment to bring it about.

The *embodied and fatal* critique of Sands – and of those individuals in prisons and detention centers around the world whose names are much less known – resounds from those "civilized" sites in which the line between the political and the criminal is blurred to remind us that the struggle for freedom and the desire to bring domination to an end are ever present, however bleak and violent are the forms they take. This critique interrupts the dialectic of enlightenment, even if it does not eliminate it, not only by providing an opportunity of self-reflection concerning the predicaments of modern subjectivity but also actively opening new trajectories for enlightenment. As such, *Hunger* is a rejoinder to Horkheimer and Adorno, perhaps not amending their pessimism but at least showing that the self-destructive resistance of subjects who politicize life to its limits are also part of the legacy of enlightenment and its promise of liberation. It gives a nod to the later Adorno who argues that the "subject's nonidentity without sacrifice would be utopian"[60] by seeking to destroy the sacrificial subject through radicalization of sacrifice. The radical temporality of insurgent sacrifice points, however briefly, to a dignified life beyond domination but one it cannot sustain.

Rather, it sings to us, lures us, and brings us to a halt, long enough that we might not just listen to the Sirens' song but begin singing our own.

notes

1 Thatcher.

2 *Hunger*, directed by Steve McQueen.

3 McQueen, "Video Interview."

4 Savage.

5 On the adoption of force-feeding not as an ad hoc but planned tactic of the Guantánamo base clinic under the guise of a discourse on the protection of life, see Anderson 1729–36.

6 See, for example, al Hasan Moqbel.

7 World Medical Association.

8 Agamben.

9 Bargu.

10 For an in-depth account, see Feldman esp. 147–217.

11 McNamee.

12 Ibid.

13 El-Khairy 191.

14 However, the movie was chided for its political sympathies. See, for example, O'Toole; Tookey.

15 McQueen, "Director's Statement" 2.

16 However, *Hunger* generated mixed responses: while celebrated for its ability to provide a truthful portrait of the dirty protest and the hunger strike, the movie was also criticized for glossing over the broader historical context of the Troubles. Cf. O'Hagan; Brown 73.

17 Horkheimer and Adorno 55.

18 For a critique of Horkheimer and Adorno's reading of enlightenment in Homer exclusively as the attempt to master nature, which leads them to overlook the spiritual dimension, see Ruderman 138–61.

19 Horkheimer and Adorno 17.

20 Ibid. 22.

21 Ibid. 12.

22 Habermas 18. On Habermas's rift with Horkheimer and Adorno, see Hohendahl.

23 Habermas 13, 22. For a counterargument to Habermas claiming that the fragmentary structure of the *Dialectic of Enlightenment* resists the charge of "totalizing critique," see Rocco 81–97.

24 Habermas 23.

25 Benhabib 1442.

26 Habermas 22.

27 Honneth captures this aspect of Horkheimer and Adorno's critique, which he calls "world-disclosing" and defends as a form warranted by a particularly "pathological" type of social disorder. See Honneth 116–27.

28 In this line, for example, Brunkhorst identifies an ambivalence in the text, which oscillates between utopian critique of domination and the rationality that is in line with it, and a fundamentalist critique, based on a metaphysical philosophy of history that presents the trajectory of enlightenment as one of decay. See Brunkhorst 133–40.

29 Horkheimer and Adorno xiii.

30 Bernstein 197.

31 Benhabib 1443.

32 Hullot-Kentor 23–44.

33 Horkheimer and Adorno 32.

34 For an insightful account on the role of art for Adorno, see Wellmer, "On the Dialectic of Modernism" 337–62.

35 Horkheimer and Adorno 43.

36 Ibid. 45–46.

37 On Horkheimer and Adorno's interpretation of Homer in relation to its cultural significance for the German philhellenic tradition, see Fleming 107–28.

38 Buck-Morss 61.

39 Horkheimer and Adorno xv.

40 On the allegorical dimension of their reading, see Owens. For the link between Horkheimer and Adorno's allegorical reading and that of Walter Benjamin in his *The Origin of German Tragic Drama*, see van Reijen.

41 Rocco 77.

42 Horkheimer and Adorno 10.

43 Ibid. 50.

44 Ibid.

45 Ibid. 55.

46 Ibid. 51.

47 Much has been written on the sexual identity of the Sirens, its implications for the constitution of gender relations and the patriarchal order, which I will have to sidestep in this discussion. See, for example, Comay; Salecl; Hewitt; Love.

48 Horkheimer and Adorno 33.

49 Ibid. 32.

50 Ibid.

51 Ibid. 31.

52 Ibid. 59.

53 Ibid. 58; my emphasis.

54 Ibid. 76.

55 Ibid. 54–55.

56 For an interpretation that locates the emergence of self-reflexive aesthetic contemplation in Odysseus' encounter with the Sirens, see Wellmer, "Death of the Sirens" 5–19.

57 Hullot-Kentor 43.

58 According to Melvin, the sonic motifs of the movie, especially the rhythmic pulse (i.e., the banging of dustbins that opens the movie, the batons of the prison guards, the water in the sink, and the soft breathing of the hunger striker near his end), drive the narrative forward. See Melvin 26, 28, 29.

59 Feldman 165.

60 Adorno 281.

bibliography

Adorno, Theodor. *Negative Dialectics*. Trans. E.B. Ashton. London and New York: Routledge, 1973. Print.

Agamben, Giorgio. *State of Exception*. Trans. Kevin Attell. Chicago and London: U of Chicago P, 2005. Print.

al Hasan Moqbel, Samir Naji. "Gitmo is Killing Me." *New York Times* 14 Apr. 2013. Web. 19 Oct. 2014. <http://www.nytimes.com/2013/04/15/opinion/hunger-striking-at-guantanamo-bay.html>.

Anderson, Patrick. "There will be No Bobby Sands in Guantánamo Bay." *PMLA* 124.5 (2009): 1729–36. Print.

Bargu, Banu. *Starve and Immolate: The Politics of Human Weapons*. New York: Columbia UP, 2014. Print.

Benhabib, Seyla. "Critical Theory and Postmodernism: On the Interplay of Ethics, Aesthetics, and Utopia in Critical Theory." *Cardozo Law Review* 11 (1989–1990): 1435–48. Print.

Benjamin, Walter. *The Origin of German Tragic Drama*. Trans. John Osborne. Intro. George Steiner. London: Verso, 1998. Print.

Bernstein, Richard J. "The Rage against Reason." *Philosophy and Literature* 10.2 (1986): 186–210. Print.

Brown, Matthew. "Cities under Watch: Urban Northern Ireland in Film." *Éire-Ireland* 45.1/2 (2010): 56–88. Print.

Brunkhorst, Hauke. "The Enlightenment of Rationality: Remarks on Horkheimer and Adorno's *Dialectic of Enlightenment*." *Constellations* 7.1 (2000): 133–40. Print.

Buck-Morss, Susan. *Negative Dialectics: Theodor Adorno, Walter Benjamin and the Frankfurt Institute*. New York: Free, 1977. Print.

Comay, Rebecca. "Adorno's Siren Song." *New German Critique* 81 (2000): 21–48. Print.

El-Khairy, Omar Assem. "Snowflakes on a Scarred Knuckle: The Biopolitics of the 'War on Terror' through Steve McQueen's *Hunger* and Kathyrn Bigelow's *The Hurt Locker*." *Millennium – Journal of International Studies* 39.1 (2010): 187–91. Print.

Feldman, Allen. *Formations of Violence: The Narrative of the Body and Political Terror in Northern Ireland*. Chicago: U of Chicago P, 1991. Print.

Fleming, Katie. "Odysseus and Enlightenment: Horkheimer and Adorno's *Dialektik der Aufklärung*." *International Journal of the Classical Tradition* 19.2 (2012): 107–28. Print.

Habermas, Jürgen. "The Entwinement of Myth and Enlightenment: Re-reading *Dialectic of Enlightenment*." Trans. Thomas Y. Levin. *New German Critique* 26 (1982): 13–30. Print.

Hewitt, Andrew. "A Feminine Dialectic of Enlightenment? Horkheimer and Adorno Revisited." *New German Critique* 56 (1992): 143–70. Print.

Hohendahl, Peter U. "The Dialectic of Enlightenment Revisited: Habermas' Critique of the Frankfurt School." *New German Critique* 35 (1985): 3–26. Print.

Honneth, Axel. "The Possibility of a Disclosing Critique of Society: The *Dialectic of Enlightenment* in Light of Current Debates in Social Criticism." *Constellations* 7.1 (2000): 116–27. Print.

Horkheimer, Max, and Theodor Adorno. *Dialectic of Enlightenment*. Trans. John Cumming. New York: Continuum, 1972. Print.

Hullot-Kentor, Robert. *"Back to Adorno." Things beyond Resemblance: On Theodor W. Adorno*. New York: Columbia UP, 2006. 23–44. Print.

Hunger. Dir. Steve McQueen. Blast! Films/Pathé Distribution. 2008. 96 minutes. Color 2.35:1. English. DVD.

Love, Nancy S. "Why Do the Sirens Sing? Figuring the Feminine in *Dialectic of Enlightenment*." *Theory & Event* 3.1 (1999). Web. 3 Nov. 2013. <http://muse.jhu.edu/login?auth=0&type=summary&url=/journals/theory_and_event/v003/3.1love.html>.

McNamee, Eugene. "Eye Witness – Memorializing Humanity in Steve McQueen's Hunger." *International Journal of the Law in Context* 5.3 (2009): 281–94. Print.

McQueen, Steve. "Director's Statement." *Hunger: A Film by Steve McQueen*. Pamphlet. Web. 16 Oct. 2013. <http://www.offestival.com/images/upload/presse/greve_de_la_faim.pdf>.

McQueen, Steve. Video Interview. *Hunger*. Special Features. DVD.

Melvin, Adam. "Sonic Motifs, Structure and Identity in Steve McQueen's Hunger." *The Soundtrack* 4.1 (2011): 23–32. Print.

O'Hagan, Sean. "McQueen and Country." *The Guardian* 11 Oct. 2008. Web. 28 Oct. 2013. <http://www.guardian.co.uk/film/2008/oct/12/2>.

O'Toole, Fintan. "Hunger Fails to Wrest the Narrative from the Hunger Strikers." *Irish Times* 22 Nov. 2008. Web. 28 Oct. 2013. <http://cain.ulst.ac.uk/victims/docs/newspapers/irish_times/otoole_it_221108.pdf>.

Owens, Clide. "The Allegorical Impulse: Toward a Theory of Postmodernism." *October* 12 (1980): 67–80. Print.

Rocco, Christopher. "Between Modernity and Postmodernity: Reading Dialectic of Enlightenment against the Grain." *Political Theory* 22.1 (1994): 71–97. Print.

Ruderman, Richard S. "Odysseus and the Possibility of Enlightenment." *American Journal of Political Science* 43.1 (1999): 138–61. Print.

Salecl, Renata. "The Sirens and Feminine Jouissance." *Differences: A Journal of Feminist Cultural Studies* 9.1 (1997): 14–28. Print.

Savage, Charlie. "Amid Hunger Strike, Obama Renews Push to Close Cuba Prison." *New York Times* 1 May 2013. Web. 19 Oct. 2014. <http://www.nytimes.com/2013/05/01/us/guantanamo-adds-medical-staff-amid-hunger-strike.html?pagewanted=all&_r=0>.

Thatcher, Margaret. "Speech in Belfast." Public Statement. 5 Mar. 1981. Web. 5 Nov. 2013. <http://www.margaretthatcher.org/document/104589>.

Tookey, Chris. "Hunger: More Pro-terrorist Propaganda." *Daily Mail* 28 Oct. 2008. Web. 28 Oct. 2013. <http://www.dailymail.co.uk/tvshowbiz/reviews/article-1081911/Hunger-More-pro-terrorist-propaganda.html>.

van Reijen, Willem. "The Dialectic of Enlightenment Read as Allegory." *Theory, Culture & Society* 5 (1988): 409–29. Print.

Wellmer, Albrecht. "On the Dialectic of Modernism and Postmodernism." Trans. David Roberts. *Praxis International* 4.4 (1985): 337–62. Print.

Wellmer, Albrecht. "The Death of the Sirens and the Origin of the Work of Art." *New German Critique* 81 (2000): 5–19. Print.

World Medical Association. *Declaration of Tokyo: Guidelines for Physicians Concerning Torture and other Cruel, Inhuman or Degrading Treatment or Punishment in Relation to Detention and Imprisonment*. Adopted by the 29th World Medical Assembly, Tokyo, Oct. 1975. Rev. 2005 and 2006. Web. 19 Oct. 2014. <http://www.wma.net/en/30publications/10policies/c18/>

patricia pisters

HEART OF THE MATTER

bodies without organs and biopolitics in organ transplant films

In "L'Intrus" Jean-Luc Nancy describes the alienating experience of his heart transplant. Most vividly his words make sensible how from "pain to pain, strangeness to strangeness" his proper "I" withdraws and becomes an intruder. The suffering of an opened, invaded, vulnerable body is infinite and the image of the tortured body of a crucified Christ almost automatically comes to mind.[1] And yet this religious connotation of sacrifice and martyrdom is precisely what Nancy puts into question. The expropriation of organs, the torments of the body bring us not closer to God but are rather an indication of the death of God:

> *Corpus meum* and *interior intimo meo*, the two together state very exactly, and in a complete configuration of the death of god, that the truth of the subject is its exteriority and excessivity: its infinite exposition. The *intrus* exposes me, excessively. It extrudes, it exports, it expropriates: I am the illness and the medical intervention, I am the cancerous cell and the grafted organ [...][2]

Nancy explains this further by adding that we are at the beginning of a mutation where man is going infinitely beyond man (again, implying the death of God) and becoming what he is and always has been, namely the most terrifying and troubling technician who refashions nature, and re-creates creation.[3] Organ transplantation, which is an old phenomenon but only recently successful since the first non-rejected kidney transplant in 1954, is one more step in this essential and troubling characteristic of mankind.[4] In both its legal and illegal practices in the world market of globalized capitalism today, organ transplantation is a form of biopower and biopolitics in the Foucauldian sense: where life and its mechanisms are "brought into the realm of explicit calculations and power–knowledge [is] an agent of transformations of human life."[5]

However, the death of God that Nancy encountered in his intruding and extruding experience of cardiac transplantation also implies biophilosophical questions relating to the potentiality of the body and a new kind of ethics that this may imply. Nancy starts "L'Intrus" with a quote from Antonin Artaud: "There is nothing in fact more ignobly useless and superfluous than the organ called the heart, which is the vilest means that one could have invented for pumping life into me."[6] For Deleuze and Guattari, Artaud's declaration of war on the organs, expressed on 28 November 1947 in the radio play "To Have Done with the

Judgement of God," is the beginning of thinking the organism outside its habitual and automatic composition, the beginning of thinking beyond a religious framework. Artaud shows us "how to create a Body without Organs."[7] The Body without Organs as a concept has to be situated on a different level of experience than the biopolitical concerns related to organ transplantation. Rather than knowledge and power, it addresses an ethics of intensities, vibrations, gradients, joyful and sad affects, all marked by a "striving to persist." But what is this striving to persist, what strives to persist in the experience of organ transplantation? What is the "strange *conatus* of infinite excrescence," as Nancy calls his heart transplant?[8] In what sense does this experience involve the death of God and undo the judgement of God? And how does this relate to the concept of sacrifice?

In this essay I will look at four recent films that have organ transplantations "at their heart": *21 Grams* (Alejandro González Iñárritu, 2003), *L'Intrus* (Claire Denis, 2001), *Dirty Pretty Things* (Stephen Frears, 2002) and *Heart of Jenin* (Leon Geller and Markus Vetter, 2008).[9] Each film in its own way shows how Nancy's concept of the intruder balances in a different dynamics between biopolitical and biophilosophical concerns. Each film participates in the biopolitical discourse that surrounds the question of the body that concerns us here. As such the camera registers the surface of reality, representations that could be considered as the visible skin of reality. The films, however, also offer more than representations. Hidden within the visible body of the image, on a more profound and invisible level, they also produce "Bodies without Organs" that change the concept of sacrifice from religious offering into political or ethical resistance and allow a-religious strivings to persist. Therefore, more than an instrument for capturing the world in representations, the camera thus also functions as a surgical instrument itself, putting reality on the operating table. Walter Benjamin's famous observation about the film camera as scalpel serves here as an underlying principle to approach the power of the filmic images discussed:

> [The surgeon] greatly diminishes the distance between himself and the patient by penetrating into the patient's body, and increases it but little by the caution with which his hand moves among the organs [...] The painter maintains in his work a natural distance from reality, the cameraman penetrates deeply into its web [...] Thus, for contemporary man the representation of reality by the film is incomparably more significant than that of the painter, since it offers, precisely because of the thoroughgoing permeation of reality with mechanical equipment, an aspect of that reality which is free of all equipment.[10]

Laying bare what lies beneath the surface, these films are not just about organ transplantation, but by touching and moving organs they point to biopolitical and biophilosophical questions that are at the heart of the matter of contemporary reality.

hearts and kidneys

In all four films that form the "corpus" of my examinations, the heart is literally the most vital and problematic organ. In *21 Grams* and *L'Intrus* the main characters undergo a heart transplant. In *21 Grams* Paul (Sean Penn) is a terminally ill maths professor who receives the heart from a man killed (together with his two young daughters) in a hit-and-run car accident. Iñárritu's film presents to us the crossing paths of Paul, his donor's widow and now childless mother Cristina (Naomi Watts), and the hit-and-run driver Jack (Benicio del Toro).[11] Claire Denis's film *L'Intrus* is directly inspired by Nancy's essay on his heart transplant.[12] Although there is nothing of Nancy's essay that finds direct cinematographic translation, practically every scene of the film is permeated with intrusion. Its enigmatic and dark principal character, Louis Trebor (Michel Subor), undergoes an illegal heart transplant and travels from the North (the snowy white mountains of the Jura on the French–Swiss border) to the South (one of the French Polynesian islands of Tahiti in the Pacific Ocean).

In both *21 Grams* and *L'Intrus* the proper heart of the characters, by failing, appears as the first intruder. The second intruder is the grafted heart, a heart that, as Nancy notes, is identified by the host body as foreign, which necessitates the lowering of the immune system "so that his body will better tolerate the foreign element. Medical practice thus renders the graftee a stranger to himself: stranger, that is, to his immune system's identity – which is something like his physiological signature."[13] Both *21 Grams* and *L'Intrus* ask ontological questions about what it means to be human, how we relate to others and deal with intrusions of the other, the stranger, to the point where we are strangers to ourselves. *21 Grams* shows the mysterious connections between individual fates. In *L'Intrus* every body is fundamentally disconnected.

Dirty Pretty Things and *Heart of Jenin* present more directly political stories of the heart. In *Dirty Pretty Things* Stephen Frears uncovers some of the invisible dimensions of contemporary London (or any globalized metropolis for that matter), featuring asylum seekers who work as cab drivers, night porters, cleaners, and prostitutes.[14] A Nigerian doctor, Okwe (Chiwetel Ejiofor) works as a cab driver during the day and as a night porter in an expensive hotel after dark. One night while checking on a clogged toilet in one of the hotel rooms, he finds the cause of the blockage: a human heart. Then he discovers that the hotel manager Juan (Sergi López) runs an illegal operation trading kidneys of immigrants for forged passports. I will return to the significance of the kidney below. Here I want to remain with the heart that in this film is not transplanted but the starting point of an investigation into illegal practices, asking pertinent questions about the globalized traffic of biomaterial. *Heart of Jenin* is in a different way immediately political. This film is a documentary about Ahmed Khatib, a Palestinian boy shot by Israeli soldiers in 2005. His father, Ismael Khatib, decides to give his son's organs to six children in Israel. The documentary follows the father when two years later he visits some of the children who received his son's body parts. One of Ahmed's kidneys went to a Bedouin boy, another to an Orthodox Jewish girl. Although the father initially had doubts about donating Ahmed's heart, it now beats in the chest of a Druze girl.[15]

Of all the organs the heart seems to be most loaded with both vital and cultural significance. While many organs come in pairs (lungs, kidneys), the heart is a single organ and living donation of a heart is impossible. Someone has to die for another person to receive a heart, to live. The heart is a muscle that pumps blood into the vessels with rhythmic contractions. It is often considered as the soul of a person, containing someone's innermost thoughts and feelings. In the Bible (Genesis 6.5) God sees that the evil thoughts of mankind are seated in their hearts. But goodness is also situated in the heart. The sacred hearts of Jesus and Mary stand as exemplary for this broader connotation of the heart. Even though we do not see the heart, we can sense it easily, feel it working by putting a hand on our chest, or a finger on our pulse to sense it beating faster or slower in different circumstances. Metaphorically, also, we "know" the heart: it can jump with joy, recoil with empathy, freeze with fear, it can break.[16]

L'Intrus and *21 Grams* both refer to the heart in this sense of hosting good and evil souls. Denis's film opens with a preamble, an ominous image of an unnamed character in a dark grotto, played by Katerina Golubeva, who will return in the film as the haunting figure of an angel of doom. While she lights a cigarette we hear her voice whispering "Your worst enemies are hiding inside, in the darkness, in your heart." Throughout the film the main character Louis Trebor is portrayed as cold and "heartless," unable to connect to his son, to his lover, or to anyone else, living alone with his two huskies in a cabin in the woods. Even the huskies are left behind when he leaves the Jura to have his transplant operation. This man getting a new heart does not fill our own heart with sympathy. In *21 Grams* Paul follows Caterina, the widow of his donor. Rather than a stalker, he acts more like a protective angel with "a good heart." His confession to

Caterina that he is the recipient of her husband's heart first meets her immense anger, and then helps her in the unspeakable grief over her terrible loss. The title of the film refers to the idea that a person's soul, contained in the heart, has some kind of spiritual materiality that has actual physical weight. As Paul's voiceover reflects: "They say we all lose 21 grams at the exact moment of our death. Everyone. And how much fits into 21 grams?" The weight of a heart beat perhaps?

Kidneys are differently connoted organs. Situated in the lower back they come in pairs, one kidney each side of the vertebral column. They serve many purposes, most crucially the filtering of blood, removing waste that is diverted to the bladder. The kidneys also regulate blood pressure, balance bodily homeostasis and produce certain hormones. In short, they are just as vital as the heart, but they are more hidden, operating more unnoticed, and because we have two kidneys, living donation is possible. Kidneys, sometimes referred to as reins, also feature quite prominently in the Bible where they are mentioned more than thirty times.[17] In the Bible, animal kidneys are frequently referred to as sacrificial offerings made in seeking divine intervention to cure diseases.[18] More metaphorically, human kidneys, just like the heart, are seen as the mirror of the soul. Several times, the kidneys are mentioned as "the organs examined by God to pass judgement on a person [...]": "Examine me, O Lord, and prove me; try my reins and my heart (Psalms 26:2)"[19] In newer translations of the Bible, however, kidneys and reins have gradually been replaced by "mind" or "soul." As Garabed Eknoyan explains, this may have to do with the success rate of kidney transplants that makes the kidney more "soulless."[20]

In *Dirty Pretty Things* the kidneys are quite literally sacrificed. Unlike in the Bible they are not animal organs but human ones, offered not to cure a physical disease but to cure a social-political "disease," trading it for a legal identity. In his review of *Dirty Pretty Things*, Ted Hovet refers to further symbolism of the central role of kidneys in the film: the kidney is invisible, just like the secret and invisible lives of the immigrant service workers. As such they are nevertheless fully part of the "economic life of the city, providing manufacturing, transportation, and cleaning – especially, like the kidney, those functions that dispose of the waste that other's don't want to experience."[21] At the end of the film Okwe, the illegal immigrant from Nigeria, a Turkish asylum seeker Senay (Audrey Tautou) and Juliette (Sophie Okonedo), a black prostitute without legal papers, work together to plot against the hotel manager and, instead of Senay's body parts, take *his* kidney to an organ traffic dealer in the parking lot of the hotel. At his surprise to see people he has never met before, Okwe answers the dealer: "We are the people you don't see. We drive your cabs. We clean your rooms. We suck your cocks." *Dirty Pretty Things* exposes the "underworld of British service culture."[22] Kidneys in both their materiality and metaphoric sense are part of this exposition. And as such kidneys are part of the shadow apparatus of globalized capitalism, which makes it nonetheless a biopolitical issue where life is at the (dark) centre of political order and trade.

biopolitics and border transgressions

Dirty Pretty Things exposes this hidden aspect of biopolitics. The film shows how an invisible anonymous part of society can form a new collective, a multitude, presenting a resistance to the apparatus of power of global capitalism.[23] At the end of the film Okwe and Senay are able to leave the anonymous border location of the hotel, which could be seen as a metaphor for the British nation-state, regulating and "accommodating strangers into the home/nation."[24] With their forged passports they manage to get to that other anonymous border space, the airport. Senay leaves for her sister in New York; Okwe calls his daughter whom he had to leave behind in Nigeria after he was falsely accused of murdering his wife on the operating table. *Dirty Pretty Things* forms a counter-discourse and is part of a biopolitical power–knowledge apparatus that could be defined in a broader sense than Foucault proposes. As Agamben argues, we can

> call an apparatus literally anything that has in some way the capacity to capture, orient, determine, intercept, model, control, or secure gestures, behaviors, opinions, or discourses of living beings. Not only, therefore, prisons, madhouses, the panopticon, schools, confession, factories, disciplines, juridical measures, and so forth (whose connections with power is in a certain sense evident), but also the pen, writing, literature, philosophy, agriculture, cigarettes, navigation, computers, cellular telephones and – why not – language itself, which is perhaps the most ancient of apparatuses – one in which thousands and thousands of years ago a primate inadvertently let himself be captured, probably without realizing the consequences that he was about to face.[25]

The camera or film is another apparatus is this sense. *Dirty Pretty Things* is a fiction film that nevertheless addresses actual practices and that can provide empowering discursive resistance by showing, on the level of representation and storytelling, what is hidden in society's biopolitics of illegal organ traffic.

Heart of Jenin is a documentary and addresses biopolitical issues in an even more complicated network of power because it is at the heart of one of the most pertinent political conflict zones of the modern world: Jenin, the occupied territories of the West Bank. The film starts with an Israeli news item on the death of the twelve-year-old Palestinian Ahmed Khatib, innocently killed by Israeli soldiers who mistook him for a terrorist while he was playing with a toy gun. While Ahmed's body, covered in the Palestinian flag, is carried around as a martyr and the cries for vengeance are growing louder in the streets of Jenin, in the Israeli hospital where Ahmed died a male nurse had already set in motion a different response to the tragedy. At the bedside of his diseased son, he had asked Ahmed's father to donate his son's organs to sick children in other hospitals who might in this way get a chance to life. When after reflection the father takes a heartbreaking decision and agrees, the Israeli news reports again about this remarkable deed. Some of the families of the receiving children are interviewed, just before the operations on their children. Two years later the documentary makers follow the father and a relative in Israel when he visits some of the children who received one of his son's organs. In this way *Heart of Jenin* portrays the story of a father who instead of burying his son like a martyr and calling for vengeance, chose "gifts of life" instead. In a political situation as explosive as the Palestinian–Israeli conflict this profoundly humane decision is immediately political. As is the media coverage and the documentary itself that starts to operate in the discursive field. The film travelled and stirred quite some debates.

While it is widely acknowledged that the story in itself is very moving and the decision of the father to donate his son's organs is a remarkable choice, both this choice and especially the film's depiction of it are received with mixed feelings and disappointment from both Palestinian and Israeli sides.[26] Palestinians complain that the news report of the death of a Palestinian boy suggests that the Israelis would care about the loss of Palestinian innocent casualties. From the Israeli side, consciousness of the discursive effects of media representations have led to criticism of one-sided depiction of bad Israelis and victimized Palestinians because of the narrow focus on Ismael Khatib's decision and journey. On the PBS website of the film, Rabbi Haskel Lookstein counterbalances the story of Ahmed with that of an Israeli woman, killed in a terrorist bomb attack, who donated one of her vital organs to an Arab person. Steven Stotsky, in a review for CAMERA (Committee for Accuracy in Middle East Reporting in America), argues that the decision of Ismael Khatib to donate his son's organs could not have taken place without the intercession of Israeli doctors and medical staff, whom he calls "the unseen heroes, who continue to administer critical care to individuals on both sides of the conflict despite the risks."[27] As a result, Stotsky argues, the film reinforces antagonism instead of offering new insights into the conflict. Stotsky adds other background information to contextualize Ismael Khatib's noble gesture, reproaching the filmmakers especially in having portrayed the Orthodox family as grudging and prejudiced Israelis.

Granted, when the Orthodox father Yakov Levinson is interviewed in the first instance, while his daughter is unexpectedly on the operating table, he expresses the wish for the kidney of his little daughter preferably to be a Jewish organ. And one can question here the filmmakers for capturing people at a very anxious and vulnerable moment of their life. When two years later the family receives Khatib and his relative the situation certainly is very painful, partly because of this initial interview. Moreover, the political situation weighs heavy on the shoulders of both the hosts and the visitors. And yet the film does not give the one-sided image of the Jewish family as is argued in Stotsky's review and in other online commentaries. In fact, the Orthodox family is genuinely grateful: "We owe you so much," Yakov Levinson says while the little girl with Ahmed's kidney gives Ismael a present. Moreover, the fact that the family agreed to be filmed in these circumstances (not all recipients of Ahmed's organs gave their permission) is quite courageous because it exposes them. It makes them liable to the accusation of betrayal and it shows a willingness to enter into some kind of dialogue, even if, as Orthodox Jews, they have a strict lifestyle and the father does not know how to express himself very well. The film acknowledges this perspective. When Ismael and his relative drive back home, the uncle comments about Yakov Levinson: "This man really regrets what he said earlier. Did you see the little girl? I think she has a secret energy behind her. Her name is Menuha, which means tranquillity, comfort." In these words there is a ray of hope that in the vastness of the political blockages and deadlocks something can still connect, quite literally, a shared source of life. But the political situation is so incredibly complex and so deeply painful that any representation becomes part of a much larger discursive network. *Heart of Jenin* literally goes to the heart of these matters, presenting a biopolitical story that is profoundly related to all kinds of power relations that need contextualization and vigilance, but that operate also at the level of the heart and soul. And hence, just like *Dirty Pretty Things*' exposure of the invisible side of contemporary London, it starts cutting through the skin of discursive representations.

intense cruelty of bodies without organs

At this point we have to start asking how organ transplantation, this trans-individual exchanging of vital body parts, with all its political connotations entangled in discursive apparatuses and biopolitical networks of power, relates to biophilosophical questions. Eric Alliez has argued that "biophilosophy realizes itself as biopolitics."[28] Can we now also ask how biopolitics might imply biophilosophy? Does the discursive representation of organ transplantation relate to the concept of the "Body without Organs"? Does the literal and corporeal "opening of being" that Nancy describes as so powerful in "L'Intrus" relate to the pre-individual and trans-individual ethics of immanent vitalism that is implied in the biophilosophy of Deleuze and Guattari and that is most vividly expressed in Artaud's Body without Organs? Before turning back to the films, let's have a closer look at the concept itself.

First, it is useful to clarify that transplant organs should not be confused with the concept of "organs without bodies" that Slavoj Žižek proposes in his (reverse and perverse because related to sexual difference and desire) reading of the Body without Organs. Žižek gives the examples of Edward Norton's hand that starts fighting itself in *Fight Club*, or the recorded voice that sings without being embodied in *Mulholland Drive*. These "organs without bodies" are, according to Žižek, Lacanian partial objects:

> The hand acting on its own is the drive ignoring the dialectic of the subject's desire: drive is fundamentally the insistence of an undead

> "organ without a body," standing, like Lacan's *lamella*, for that which the subject had to lose in order to subjectivize itself in the symbolic space of the sexual difference.[29]

It is quite clear, however, that a grafted organ and the experience of organ transplantation has nothing to do with partial objects that are lost in order to be subjectivized or with the symbolic space of sexual difference and desire negatively defined as "lack" (of the symbolic organ, of castration). Quite the contrary, as Nancy suggests, the gift of life in organ donation

> institutes among us, without any limit other than the incompatibility of blood type (and, in particular, without the limits of sex or ethnicity: my heart may be the heart of a black woman), the possibility of a network wherein life/death is shared out, where life connects with death, here the incommunicable communicates.[30]

What is communicating in the material exchange of body parts (donating and receiving an organ) communicates on a pre-individual, transversal level, beneath the habitual organization of the body and representation. Beyond the laws of transcendental subjectivity that, as Deleuze and Guattari argue, "always has a priest behind it": the hierarchical organization of power and knowledge against normative white, male faciality (which has the "face of Christ" as its reference).[31] In organ transplantation the "Christian" (or other national or religious normative) organization of subjectivity is literally undermined. Even an Orthodox Jewish family is happy with a Palestinian heart. And so a biopolitical practice of "organs without bodies" operates on an intensive pre-individual level. It obtains the deterritorializing powers of the Body without Organs that is not organized following the laws of the judgement of God.

"The Body without Organs hurts," Alliez asserts.[32] The references to Artaud indicate that for Deleuze and Guattari a particular way in which it hurts is in the confrontation with madness. Artaud, who was diagnosed as schizophrenic, in his theatre performances resists the organic use of language and bodily code by uttering "only gasps and cries that are sheer unarticulated blocks of sound."[33] Deleuze and Guattari argue that the schizo has his own system of coordinates at his disposal, which does not coincide with the social code. "It might be said that the schizophrenic passes from one code to the other, that he deliberately scrambles all the codes."[34] Organs are regenerated, re-inscribed in a "litany of disjunctions" on the own body.[35] This disorganization of the body can be realized in less pathological forms in artistic experimentation. But it can be argued as well that it has a techno-physiological form in the donation and reception of organ transplantation. The way Nancy describes his grafted body undergoing an additional excruciating treatment for cancer that invaded his body as a side-effect of the lowering of his immune system is in a sense a "schizoid" experience, an experience that changes the habitual organization of his body completely:

> My heart is twenty years younger than I am, and the rest of my body (at least) a dozen years older. So having at the same time become younger and older, I no longer have an age proper, just as, properly speaking, I am no longer my own age. Just as I no longer have an occupation, although I am not retired, so too I am nothing of what I am supposed to be (husband, father, grandfather, friend) unless I remain subsumed within the very general condition of the *intrust*, of diverse *intrus* that at any moment can appear in my place in my relations with, or in the representations of, others.[36]

This is, quite literally, a body with scrambled codes, a Body without Organs. It is a body full of intensities that underneath the organized body starts to make new and different connections, experience new (sometimes excruciating) affects. "We don't know what a body can do," is Spinoza's famous question that Deleuze has emphasized as the most central one that is the basis of the Body without Organs. In the transcription of his courses on Spinoza, Deleuze explains further: "Knowing what you are capable of. This is not at all a moral question, but above all a physical question, as a question to the body and to the soul [...] The only question is the power of being affected."[37] Artaud, in his schizoid experiments of the Body without Organs, created a "theatre of cruelty." In her article on Deleuze and Artaud, Laura Cull mentions that Artaud's system of cruelty was directed at allowing cruelty as affective power to penetrate everything, especially the relationship to his audience: "Making yourself a theatre of cruelty, then, is not about 'wielding a butcher's knife on stage at every possible opportunity' in order to represent cruelty, Artaud explained; rather it means creating a 'real transformation' in your audience by acting 'deeply and directly' on their sensibilities."[38]

We have seen that *Dirty Pretty Things* and *Heart of Jenin* are films with huge biopolitical signification, but they remain mostly at the level of narrative representation. The Body without Organs in these films can be sensed only indirectly, underneath the acting, the storylines, the visibility of the representation. They are empowering discursive tools (or perhaps even weapons) but they do not cut directly into the "organs" of the audience. *21 Grams* and *L'Intrus* are films that respect less the rules of classic narration and representation. And therefore these films perhaps cut deeper, in that they deal more saliently with the biophilosophical implications of organ transplantation. Aesthetically they perform cruelty (as a disorganizing force) on the audience. *21 Grams* has been criticized for its scrambled and fragmented narration.[39] At the beginning of the film we see flash-forwards of the main characters that chronologically only come to know each other later:

> We see Cristina asleep on a bed while Paul sits beside her, smoking, gazing down; we see Paul slumped in a wrecked chair outside a desolate motel, in gray light; we see an abandoned swimming pool, choked with debris, under a brooding sky full of floating snow. These introductory epiphanies yield to choppy glimpse of the plot's frantic climax (Jack driving a car at high speed, rushing an injured, bleeding Paul and a screaming Cristina to the hospital).[40]

This is a disorienting prelude indeed, but it is also a very expressive way of putting the power of affect before any narrative development or organization. Before we can make sense of the story, before we can identify with the characters, the sensations and affects have already grasped us, at a deep and cutting pre-individualized level. This primacy of the affect and the fact that we start from a point in the future, that the narrative or narration speaks from a perspective of the future, are what I call elsewhere the schizo-aspects of contemporary cinema in the digital age.[41] The frantic camera work and the editing style are the scalpels of the surgeon filmmaker. With its jumping, slicing, looping structure *21 Grams* is a Film without Organs. Moreover, this sense of unavoidable fate that the film's encircling structure brings about makes *21 Grams*, as Robert Hahn argues, in spite of its melodramatic materials, reminiscent of Greek tragedies.[42] But, as Hahn rightly notices, it is not the individual fate of the characters that interests Iñárritu but rather the impersonal or pre-individual experience of time as such. It is in time that we become, in time that our fate gets entangled with that of others, the strangers that intrude on our life and become entangled with ours. Relative to the normal organization of the body and human psychology *21 Grams*

> undercuts the premise that we are most ourselves when we are confident in self-definition and successful in self-presentation; we are equally real, it suggests, when we are out of control, confused, obsessed, deluded, ill, pathetic: we are all of those people – the people we were then, and the people we will be.[43]

All characters in *21 Grams* have become strangers to themselves. Paul's heart transplant is not just his own struggle with that question of a becoming and transforming self. Within the intense structure of this film, the heart transplant puts us in touch with those fundamental intruding questions at the core of our identities.

Denis's *L'Intrus* is even more alienating in its aesthetics. As a European art film it is less expected to follow a Hollywood organization of its material, and hence it is met with different evaluation criteria, even if it is still seen as an "evasive and difficult" film.[44] In Denis's adaptation (or rather "adoption" as Nancy had called the film version of his text) the concept of the intruder is not only related to the physical dimension of the transplanted body. Rather, the idea of intrusion is sensible in every scene. Compared to *21 Grams'* emphasis on time, Denis's film is more concerned with space. Moving from the Northern hemisphere (the Jura) to the Southern hemisphere (Tahiti), with transits in Geneva (Switzerland) and Pusan (South Korea), the intrusion is first presented as a spatial phenomenon. The film starts at a border control with police dogs, sensing illegal traffic. Dogs, as guardians of the territory, as first to alert an intrusion, are in practically every scene of the first part of the film. And many scenes in the snowy mountain forests of the Jura are haunted by dark shadows of strangers who want to enter the country and whose glimpses we see regularly in the woods, the camera sometimes taking their place as a spying gaze from the shadows – for instance when "they" observe how Trebor's own heart becomes an intruder, failing him whilst swimming.

The illegal immigrants who in *Dirty Pretty Things* get a face, a story and agency remain abstract but nevertheless real and present forces in *L'Intrus*. In this film they are haunting and haunted Bodies without Organs. Some scenes have oniric or even delirious qualities and we don't know whether Louis Trebor actually kills one of those shadowy intruders who is later found under the ice; whether the bloody heart found in the snow is the heart of a girl who intruded Trebor's cabin is really her heart, or whether it is a metaphoric image for his (illegally obtained) transplanted organ. Denis leaves these options open, while the political implications are nevertheless always sensible. In the Pacific, Trebor himself is the intruder. He clearly stands out among the islanders and is regarded with suspicion as a European foreigner. His attempts to find his Polynesian son, whom he left many years ago, fail, even if the islanders try to find a replacement son for him. Instead his body starts to reject his new heart, so the intrusion comes again from the inside, from the grafted heart. Trebor ends up at sea, with a pretended son whom he is too weak to reject, destiny unknown. The film returns to the Jura and ends (without Trebor) with the image of his neighbour (Beatrice Dalle) who is a dog keeper, who leads a pack of dogs through the snow. On the move, a new circle (of hunting?) starting.

The physical intrusion of his own body that Nancy describes in the experience of his heart transplant is not only translated in the film's highly intrusive elliptic spatial structure but also in the completely de-psychologized painting of the characters that gives a sense of alienation. We will never get to know Trebor's motives, his thoughts or feelings; he is certainly not a sympathetic character. As Martine Beugnet emphasizes in her reading of *L'Intrus*:

> Drawn into the film's circular flow (the journey takes us around the world and back), the characters operate less like psychological constructs than like chemical bodies reacting to a series of contrasted environments, or like cells traveling through the body of the film, set on their course by its internal kinesthesia.[45]

The rhythm of a perpetual mobile (the beatings of a heart), this continuing movement is more important than narrative continuity, which is demanding and "cruel" for the audiences. Where *21 Grams'* scrambling of filmic codes is confusing, Denis's *L'Intrus* is enigmatically alienating. Beugnet refers to an interview with Denis where she characterizes her films as having a limp, one arm shorter, or a big nose, some kind of unfitting "excrescence" that wants to be felt, experienced. In another interview Denis explains that she likes philosophy because it is circular, like a meridian that encircles the world, and you can jump on another meridian and see things differently. "I need things to be open, nothing is definitive. I am just incapable of being 'sliced' (*tranchée*)," she explains.[46] With this form of "nomadic narration" *L'Intrus* is a Film without Organs, a Body without Organs, in the sense that

Beugnet concludes: "The film thus offers itself as a body of sensations through which, as spectators, we might sense and practice our ability to let our defences down – to be drawn into and infused by the unfamiliar."[47] With the abstract but explicit connection between the stranger as territorial, physical and cinematographic intruder, *L'Intrus* presents perhaps the most balanced view between biopolitical and biophilosophical questions that organ transplantation and Bodies without Organs can bring about. But also the most unsettling ones. Unlike the other films, there is no hope as in *Heart of Jenin*, or agency and political visibility as in *Dirty Pretty Things*, or even catharsis and redemption as in *21 Grams*. Just a continuation on another "meridian" and the desire to continue in an open whole.

sacrifice resurrected

All the above lead us to the final question: what happens with the concept of sacrifice when we consider organ transplantation in light of the Body without Organs? In many accounts of organ transplantation the Christian concept of charity is mentioned as an important motivation for organ donation.[48] And, as stated at the beginning of this essay, the suffering body of the organ-receiving body does remind us of the suffering body of Christ. In *Jesus of Montreal*, organ transplantation is explicitly linked to this religious sense of sacrifice. On the website of *Heart of Jenin* religious leaders of the big monotheist religions (a priest, a rabbi, an imam and a Baptist reverend) all comment that the gift of life is the greatest act of charity one can offer (even the pope has signed a donor certificate). And so *Heart of Jenin* participates in the religious discourses surrounding organ donation, even if this level is not addressed explicitly in the documentary itself. Organ transplantation is inscribed in biopolitical issues that are guided by religious institutions, albeit in a complex network of other apparatuses that go beyond institutional power, such as the individual decision to donate organs in particular (legal and illegal) circumstances.

At the same time Nancy has argued that the medical technology involved in transplantation practices signifies "the death of God" and implies an explicit transgression of this religious framework, in any event the institutional frameworks that are related to the type of normative or habitual organization of the body.[49] In the different films the concept of sacrifice is related in different ways to (the death of) God. In *Dirty Pretty Things* the main character Okwe, who is a doctor, mentions loud and clear that he has no religion, except to survive. Also in *21 Grams* and *L'Intrus* the characters are moving in a world without God. But the issue of religion is more complicated in the latter two films. First of all, as Laura McMahon has noted, for Nancy the dead of God "remains pregnant with the possibility if not necessity of a resurrection that restores both man and God to a common immanence."[50] In *21 Grams* and *L'Intrus* multiple references to Christianity refer to this idea of resurrection. In *21 Grams* Jack, the ex-con, turns fanatically to religion to seek salvation and seems at first a Christ figure. However, it is finally Paul who becomes a resurrected Christ figure, a protective angel. He who receives the heart transplant sacrifices himself in the end (shooting himself in the chest) to help Jack and Cristina to somehow find redemption and repair themselves (Cristina turns out to be pregnant from Paul, Jack returns home to his family, leaving Christian dogmas behind).

In *L'Intrus* the (difficult) father–son lineage is inscribed with Christian connotations. Louis Trebor's neglected French son (Grégoire Colin) is seen in his father's deserted cabin, putting on a crown of leaves that was left behind by a young girl who first intruded the place. The crown certainly looks like Jesus' crown of thorns, and both the girl and Trebor's son later have their hearts ripped out. As suggested above, Trebor could have taken either of those hearts: an illegal one, or the (metaphoric) heart of his son whom he never loved. Moreover, the film features multiple resurrections, the main one being, of course, Trebor himself who gets a second chance through his heart transplant. When he travels to Tahiti, Denis also inserts a young Michel Subor arriving forty years earlier on the same shore in another film, *Le Reflux* (Paul Géauff, 1965), which is a cinematographic resurrection.[51] So while the sacrifice in Christian terms is deconstructed and questioned by "the death of God" that organ transplantation implies, there is a second life, a resurrection of God, precisely in the different forms of sacrifice and reception of "the other" as a stranger. Perhaps what organ transplantation makes quite literally tangible is the immanent life force that we share on a pre-individual level through which we can sense the immanence of God (and not God as a transcending judging principle). Perhaps, indeed as Philip Adamek suggests, "Christianity [itself] is like a heart transplant."[52] Sacrifice and redemption are still part of our secular medicalized and technologically mediated culture. But biophilosophy and the concept of the Body without Organs shows us that this resurrection after the death of God also implies "to have done with the Judgement of God," entering a theatre of cruelty that asks us to perceive our relations to others in a new way. If Christianity is a heart transplant then God may well be a Body without Organs, responding, as Steven Shaviro has argued, both to the same necessity: "that of conceiving a non-totalizing and open 'whole' in which all potentiality may be expressed [...] without any sort of finality or closure."[53] The image, according to Nancy in *The Ground of the Image*, is always "sacred," distinct from reality but with its own force.[54] If Artaud has put man and God on the anatomy table to re-organize his body, the film-maker can help with his scalpel to imagine this resurrected concept of sacrifice with new intensities and new power of transformation at the heart and soul of the matter beyond the institutional framework and dogmas of religious discourse.

notes

1 In Denys Arcand's film *Jesus of Montreal* (1989) this was made explicit. Here, the actor who plays Jesus in a modern update of the passion play dies and his organs are taken from his body. Filmed from a high angle, Jesus' body on the operating table seems to be on a cross.

2 Nancy, "L'Intrus" 12–13.

3 Ibid. 7. For the inclusion of technics and technology in Western philosophy, see also Bernard Stiegler's three volumes of *Technics and Time*.

4 For the emergence and scope of organ transplantation and global trade in biomaterial, see Geesink and Steegers, *Nier te Koop, Baarmoeder te Huur* [*Kidney for Sale, Womb for Hire*].

5 Foucault, *History of Sexuality* 143. Here, the word biopower appears for the first time. The first explicit mention of biopolitics is in Foucault's "Il faut défendre la société." See also Hardt and Negri, *Empire*. For an insightful account of various conceptions of biopolitics, see Dean.

6 Nancy, "L'Intrus" 1.

7 Deleuze and Guattari, "The Body without Organs" in *Anti-Oedipus* 9–16; and "How Do You Make Yourself a Body without Organs?" in *A Thousand Plateaus* 149–66.

8 Nancy, "L'Intrus" 13.

9 Other organ transplantation films that go beyond the Frankenstein myth are, among others: *Coma* (Michael Crichton, 1978), *EMR* (James Erskine and Danny McCullough, 2004), *Valley of the Wolves: Iraq* (Serdar Akar and Sadullah Sentürk, 2006), *Seven Pounds* (Gabriele Muccino, 2008), *My Sister's Keeper* (Nick Cassavetes, 2009), and *Never Let Me Go* (Mark Romanek, 2010). There are quite a few Korean films that have organ trafficking in their action-plot. For instance, *Heartbeat* (Yoon Jae-keun, 2010), *The Man from Nowhere* (Lee Jeong-beom, 2010) and *The Traffickers* (Kim Hong-Sun, 2012). For an extended discussion of *Coma*, see Pisters, *Matrix of Visual Culture* 61–64. Another film that should be mentioned here is Anand Gandhi's film *Ship of Theseus* (2012) which brings together three different stories of organ transplantation in a beautiful and intelligent way. For an analysis of this film, see Pisters, "Transplanting Life."

10 Benjamin, "The Work of Art in the Age of Mechanical Reproduction" in *Illuminations* 227.

11 For a review, see Hahn.

12 For a special issue on the Nancy–Denis encounter, see *Film-Philosophy* 21.1. See

<http://www.film-philosophy.com/2008v12n1/morrey.pdf> for an introduction by the editor of this issue which features an article by Nancy on Denis's film *Trouble Every Day* and four other articles on the Denis–Nancy collaboration.

13 Nancy, "L'Intrus" 9.

14 See also Hovet.

15 See the PBS Wide Angle series website for background information and the full documentary: <http://www.pbs.org/wnet/wideangle/episodes/heart-of-jenin/introduction/4991/>.

16 For elaborate studies of the different significances of the heart, see Jager; Young.

17 Eknoyan.

18 Ibid. 3467.

19 Ibid. 3468.

20 Ibid. 3470.

21 Hovet 3.

22 Gibson 700.

23 Hardt and Negri, *Multitude*. See also Bordeleau.

24 Gibson 694.

25 Agamben 14.

26 See, for instance, the hundreds of responses to the introduction of the film on the PBS website: <http://www.pbs.org/wnet/wideangle/episodes/heart-of-jenin/introduction/4991/>. Basically, every responder has new facts and additional perspectives to add. Or the blog post on Jewlicious: "Was Heart of Jenin Heartfelt or Heartless?" available at <http://www.jewlicious.com/2009/07/was-heart-of-jenin-heartless-or-heartfelt/>.

27 Stotsky. While Stotsky is very right that all this could never have happened without the excellent Israeli medical staff, one could continue the contextualization and ask why there are few Arab medical staff and facilities on the West Bank. But his point is well taken and valuable. A similar point is actually made at the end of Arcand's film *Jesus of Montreal*. Here the Catholic hospital is overcrowded and simply sends the severely wounded Jesus back on the streets. The Jewish hospital, on the other hand, acts adequately and while being too late to save him they do rescue his organs for transplantation.

28 Alliez 1.

29 Žižek 174.

30 Nancy, "L'Intrus" 8.

31 Deleuze and Guattari, *A Thousand Plateaus* 154. Here, Deleuze and Guattari talk about the curse on desire when desire is uprooted from its field of immanence and brought in connection to a (normative) transcendental principle. In the following plateau Deleuze and Guattari explicitly address European racism and degrees of deviance in relation to the White-Man face as the Christ face in painting where "the face of Christ [is used] to produce every kind of facial unit and every degree of deviance" (178).

32 Alliez 1.

33 Deleuze and Guattari, *Anti-Oedipus* 9.

34 Ibid. 15.

35 Ibid. 12.

36 Nancy, "L'Intrus" 11.

37 Deleuze 9.

38 Cull 48.

39 See, for example, the reviews by Rene Rodriguez, Rob Gonsalves and others at <http://www.rottentomatoes.com/m/21_grams/>.

40 Hahn 56.

41 Pisters, *The Neuro-Image* 98–124.

42 Hahn 53.

43 Ibid. 56.

44 Morrey i.

45 Beugnet 43.

46 *Claire Denis – L'Intrus Entretien: Olivier Bombarda*, available <http://www.youtube.com/watch?v=yPGmjCq-OFo>.

47 Beugnet 46.

48 Weeda, "Nieren afstaan uit naastenliefde" [Donating Kidneys out of Charity] 8–9.

49 Nancy, "L'Intrus" 12–13, qtd at the beginning of this essay. In his book on Nancy, Derrida also emphasizes the link between the opening of the body by technology and the need to go beyond the Christian body in Nancy's work. See Derrida.

50 McMahon 70.

51 For an extended analysis of images of resurrection in Denis's films, see Morrey, "Open Wounds."

52 Adamek 196.

53 Shaviro 129–30.

54 Nancy, *Ground of the Image*. As he explains in the first essay of the book, "The Image – the Distinct," Nancy defines "sacred" here in a non-religious way as something that is distinct, separate.

bibliography

Adamek, Philip M. "The Intimacy of Jean-Luc Nancy's *L'Intrus*." *CR: The New Centennial Review* 2.3 (2002): 189–201. Print.

Agamben, Giorgio. *What is an Apparatus? And Other Essays*. Trans. David Kishik and Stefan Pedatella. Stanford: Stanford UP, 2009. Print.

Alliez, Eric. "The BwO Condition or, The Politics of Sensation." *Multitude: Revue Politique, Artistique, Philosophique* 9 (2004). Web. 12 Oct. 2014.

Benjamin, Walter. *Illuminations*. Ed. and intro. Hannah Arendt. Trans. Harry Zorn. London: Pimlico, 1999. Print.

Beugnet, Martine. "The Practice of Strangeness: *L'Intrus* – Claire Denis (2004) and Jean-Luc Nancy (2000)." *Film-Philosophy* 12.1 (2008): 31–47. Web. 12 Oct. 2014.

Bordeleau, Erik. *Foucault anonymat*. Quebec: Le Quartanier, 2012. Print.

Cull, Laura. "Ethics in Deleuze's Encounter with Artaud." *Deleuze and Ethics*. Ed. Nathan Jun and Daniel W. Smith. Edinburgh: Edinburgh UP, 2011. 44–62. Print.

Dean, Jodi. "Drive as the Structure of Biopolitics: Economy, Sovereignty, and Capture." *Krisis: Journal for Contemporary Philosophy* 2 (2010): 2–15. Web. 12 Oct. 2014.

Deleuze, Gilles. *Les Cours de Gilles Deleuze: Spinoza 24-01-1978*. Trans. Timothy S. Murphy. <www.webdeleuze.com>. Web. 12 Oct. 2014.

Deleuze, Gilles, and Félix Guattari. *Anti-Oedipus: Capitalism and Schizophrenia*. Trans. Robert Hurley, Mark Seem, and Helen R. Lane. London: Athlone, 1984. Print.

Deleuze, Gilles, and Félix Guattari. *A Thousand Plateaus: Capitalism and Schizophrenia*. Trans. Brian Massumi. London: Athlone, 1988. Print.

Derrida, Jacques. *Le Toucher: Jean-Luc Nancy*. Paris: Gallimard, 2000. Print.

Eknoyan, Garabed. "The Kidney in the Bible: What Happened?" *Journal of the American Society of Nephrology* 16.12 (2005): 3464–71. Web. 12 Oct. 2014.

Foucault, Michel. *The History of Sexuality: The Will to Knowledge*. Trans. Robert Hurley. London: Penguin, 1990. Print.

Foucault, Michel. *Il faut défendre la société. Cours au Collège de France 1976*. Paris: Gallimard/Seuil, 1997. Print.

Geesink, Ingrid, and Chantal Steegers. *Nier te Koop, Baarmoeder te Huur: Wereldwijde Handel in Lichaamsmateriaal*. Amsterdam: Uitgeverij Bert Bakker, 2011. Print.

Gibson, Sarah. "The Hotel Business is about Strangers: Border Politics and Hospitable Spaces in Stephen Frears' *Dirty Pretty Things*." *Third Text* 20.6 (2006): 693–701. Web. 12 Oct. 2014.

Hahn, Robert. "21 Grams." *Film Quarterly* 58.3 (2005): 53–58. Web. 12 Oct. 2014.

Hardt, Michael, and Antonio Negri. *Multitude: War and Democracy in the Age of Empire*. New York: Penguin, 2004. Print.

Hardt, Michael, and Antonio Negri. *Empire*. Cambridge, MA and London: Harvard UP, 2000. Print.

Hovet, Ted. "The Invisible London of *Dirty Pretty Things*; or Dickens, Frears, and Film Today." *Literary London: Interdisciplinary Studies in the Representation of London* 4.2 (2006): 1–4. Web. 12 Oct. 2014.

Jager, Erik. *The Book of the Heart*. Chicago: U of Chicago P, 2000. Print.

McMahon, Laura. "Deconstructing Community and Christianity: 'A-religion' in Nancy's reading of *Beau Travail*." *Film-Philosophy* 12.1 (2008): 63–78. Web. 12 Oct. 2014.

Morrey, Douglas. "Introduction: Claire Denis and Jean-Luc Nancy." *Film-Philosophy* 12.1 (2008): i–vi. Web. 12 Oct. 2014.

Morrey, Douglas. "Open Wounds: Body and Image in Jean-Luc Nancy and Claire Denis." *Film-Philosophy* 12.1 (2008): 10–31. Web. 12 Oct. 2014.

Nancy, Jean-Luc. "L'Intrus." Trans. Susan Hanson. *CR: The New Centennial Review* 2.3 (2002): 1–14. Web. 12 Oct. 2014.

Nancy, Jean-Luc. *The Ground of the Image*. Trans. Jeff Ford. New York: Fordham UP, 2005. Print.

Pisters, Patricia. *The Matrix of Visual Culture*. Stanford: Stanford UP, 2003. Print.

Pisters, Patricia. *The Neuro-Image: A Deleuzian Film-Philosophy of Digital Screen Culture*. Stanford: Stanford UP, 2012. Print.

Pisters, Patricia. "Transplanting Life: Bios and Zoe in Images with Imagination." *The Subject of Rosi Braidotti: Concepts and Politics*. Ed. Bolette Blaagaard and Iris van der Tuin. London: Bloomsbury, 2014. 65–71. Print.

Steven Shaviro. *Without Criteria: Kant, Whitehead, Deleuze, and Aesthetics*. Cambridge, MA: MIT P, 2009. Print.

Stiegler, Bernard. *Technics and Time, 1: The Fault of Epimetheus*. Trans. Richard Beardsworth and George Collins. Stanford: Stanford UP, 1998. Print.

Stiegler, Bernard. *Technics and Time, 2: Disorientation*. Trans. Stephen Barker. Stanford: Stanford UP, 2009. Print.

Stiegler, Bernard. *Technics and Time, 3: Cinematic Time and the Question of Malaise*. Trans. Stephen Barker. Stanford: Stanford UP, 2011. Print.

Stotsky, Steven. "Film Review: *Heart of Jenin*." CAMERA: Committee for Accuracy in Middle East Reporting in America. Web. 12 Oct. 2014. <http://www.camera.org/index.asp?x_context=3&x_outlet=18&x_article=1698>.

Weeda, Frederiek. "Nieren afstaan uit naastenliefde." *NRC Next* 21 Nov. 2011: 8–9. Print.

Young, Louisa. *The Book of the Heart*. New York: Doubleday, 2002. Print.

Žižek, Slavoj. *Organs without Bodies: On Deleuze and Consequences*. New York and London: Routledge, 2004. Print.

farhang erfani

CLÔTURAL SACRIFICE
liminal representation of race in film

My broad goal in this essay is to take stock of the constitutive role of sacrifice in representation, which I take to surpass my chosen scope, namely film and specifically cinematic racial representation. By closely analyzing the Iranian film *The Cyclist* (1987), by Mohsen Makhmalbaf, I argue that common concerns about the "limits" of representations are philosophically restrictive and that a liminal approach sheds a new light on often neglected nuances of representation and its troubles. I will better explain liminality in due course, but as a working definition it stands for the structural inability to represent the margins.

The first two sections are devoted to theoretical complexities of representation. I rely briefly on Heidegger to move away from what I call the "vertical" notion of representation and sacrifice's implicit role in its constitution. I then turn to Lacan to shed light on what I call "horizontal" representation and sacrifice. Although Heidegger opens up the space for the horizontal model, Lacan's perspective, as we will see, is more critical and less celebratory of the phenomenological horizon. The final two sections are devoted to *The Cyclist*, respectively as a basic outline and a critical reading of its depiction of racism.

In short, the final analysis confirms the value of Lacan's prominence in (some) film and race studies scholarly circles, but it also demonstrates its restrictions. As much as Lacan explains the process of marginalization, there is a "narcissistic" tendency in the Lacanian approach that inadvertently keeps the marginalized in the periphery. At the same time, by relying on other aspects of the Lacanian framework, I argue for means of solidarity with the "misrepresented" other. As solidarity neither "speaks for the other" nor treats her as radically different, it attends to liminality in a productive manner.

I representation and sacrifice

To start, let me couch my thesis in the very problem of representation. As much as representation is the studied object, it is also this study's philosophical underwriter. My proposed path is akin to matryoshka nesting dolls; each conceptual trope contains a smaller, related, but also slightly different philosophical topic. This problematic assumption is tellingly better seen in reverse order: here, a singular film (*The Cyclist*) presumably "represents" the more generic topic of cinematic racial representation, which again presumably speaks to difficulty of representation in film or in aesthetics at large. Despite each link's limited reach, they are taken together as a chain to anchor the wider philosophical debate regarding sacrifice and representation.

Regardless of one's assessment of my interpretation, the assessment already relies at once on a canonical model of representation on the equally canonical concern about the limits of representation. One might perhaps argue that it does not adequately illustrate the larger concepts, such as racial representation *tout court*, or representation in general. Even if, as I hope, the reader is convinced by my argument, the problem nonetheless remains. Either approach considers representation to be always limited and the debate thereafter is whether this particular representation falls within acceptable limits.

Limits of representation undoubtedly matter and ordinary experience alone confirms its importance. We know that even a faithfully mimetic copy is not quite "it." A portrait, for example, lacks the depth or thickness of the person; the two-dimensional re-presentation is comparatively thin. For analytic purposes, I call this limitation, or this loss of depth, "vertical sacrifice." Verticality, let us tentatively say, is loosely akin to the Platonic divided line wherein each lower level is considered a deficient reflection of its higher reality. I fully appreciate that the "chain of being" has been out of service for some time now and my argument does not require its traditional essentialism. In fact, I now turn to Heidegger to remove any metaphysical residue from the argument.

1.1 heidegger on representation

Heidegger, as we know, distanced himself from traditional understandings of representation that are contaminated by the history of metaphysics. In a nutshell, an entity – be it a physical object such as a hammer, an aesthetic one such as a painting, or even an "idea" such as one's identity – was traditionally taken in the representational paradigm of the one and the many. His famous example of the hammer, for instance, proves the limitation of this model. A hammer "is" not one instantiation of an essential "hammerness." Its being is instead given to us in a network of (primarily) concealed meaning – i.e., Being – that operates beneath our radar. In that backdrop, a hammer is related to nails, boards, and the project of Dasein at work in its worldliness, etc. In sum, what a hammer "represents" is not its own singular essence. Genuine representation – as *aletheia* – unconceals that entity *as* belonging to a world of Dasein that always already also points to the ontological presence of others (as other entities and more importantly as "other" Daseins).

Art, for Heidegger, has a similar capability of unconcealing the pre-thematic world of Dasein (*Being and Time* 63), with two additional advantages. For one, it is less cooperative, and accordingly more helpful, in overcoming the metaphysical model. Consider his famous interpretation of Van Gogh's pair of shoes. As Van Gogh's painting "indicates" nothing but a banal pair of shoes, to say that his work represents the universal form of shoes or "shoeness" is adequate, but a "very general and empty" (*Being and Time* 199) pronouncement. Unlike this "usual view" ("Origin" 17) of aesthetics, Heidegger finds that – much like the hammer – the shoes reveal the worldliness of Dasein and herein lies the second important point. In the famous case of the hammer, it took a crisis of unavailability (*Being and Time* 68–69) for Dasein to take a step back to appreciate not just the hammer's worldliness but its own ontological belongingness, or its being-in-the-world. In art, Heidegger finds a similar opening for ontological unconcealment without crisis or breakdown.

Before applying these two insights to film and sacrifice, let us note that Heidegger's critique of metaphysical representation makes the vertical model – a pair of shoes as embodiment of the higher essence of shoeness – untenable. More importantly, he advocates for something close to the horizontal model I have in mind. "[T]he appropriate ontological horizon" (*Being and*

Time 267) means that meaning is not given in a one-to-one or many-to-one relationship but rather against the phenomenological horizon or backdrop in which meaning is relational. This horizon, we know, is temporal and therefore not a "flat" horizontal space. While I equally take the horizon or the horizontal as dynamic and unstable, I emphasize – with Lacan – that this space is also politically charged. I address this issue specifically in Part 3, but the remarks below will serve as conceptual bread-crumbs to reach that framework.

1.2 film and unconcealment

Aletheia matters to film and race but it is not a perfect transition or translation. In brief, the metaphysical view Heidegger rejects is obviously problematic for film. To take race as a "metaphysical" representation requires "biological essentialism" that is seldom employed today.

What we have instead is non-metaphysical nominalism in today's racism: instead of attaching a minority character, for instance, to a universal ethnic essence, that "subaltern" character may be presented as just being *that individual* character, with allegedly no further claim. Such nominalism falls short of "universal representation" but it is diluted metaphysics in so far as it does not unconceal anything. It is unrevealing.

Nearing Heideggerian grounds is the kind of film – typically anti-racist works – that unconceals the "racist structures" of the "world" and brings to light the ideological background that sustains racism. This is a departure from Heidegger. Dasein's hammer "is" a hammer because Being gives it to Dasein *as* a hammer. In anti-racist films, however, the focus on race is intended to reveal Being *as* crisis or in crisis.

This brings me to the first critical point of my argument. While much of the scholarship on race and film is non-essentialist, the model of representation at work remains strangely vertical. Consider a deserving scholarly critique that mirrors, informs, or is perhaps even informed by a commonplace or widespread concern we find in the "general public." We know that "minority" characters are poorly represented in cinema, especially in Hollywood. Minorities often play secondary roles, they are often "the first to die," and they are often portrayed through stereotypes (Bogle) mapped over white audience's fantasies (hooks).

This criticism is both empirically and conceptually important but it does rest on verticality. For a variety of reasons, any character on screen is bound to be limited or inadequate. That being a given, the critique of racial (mis) representation rests upon equity of limits. Minority characters should not be "thinner" than the protagonists; they should not be more "sacrificed" for the sake of representation. This call for equity of sacrificial representation or equality of "thinness" is more than legitimate, but it remains too focused on limits.

Representation is a luring limelight. It simultaneously locks our attention on a depicted object and blinds us to its surrounding darkness. Liberal solutions to remedy "unfair" darkness are laudable but under-appreciate a sacrificial logic, i.e., the horizontal model, as we will see. To demand the stage be uniformly illuminated or to let the other represent herself by reverse shot ("minority" filmmaking) is philosophically naive. It is not a coincidence that minority characters are often "misrepresented" and the liberal call for equity confuses limits and philosophical liminality, which is the structural incapacity to represent margins and the marginalized.

2 constitutive sacrifice

Sacrifice is indeed not limited to traditional rituals. Because it is neither glorious nor festively indicated, the politically constitutive role of sacrifice in identity formation is often forgotten. Racism, my focus here, is but one instance of the sacrificial logic, which Lacan grasps even better than Freud and Girard.

To post-Heideggerians, such as Lacan, Being itself has holes. Fortuitously and to Lacan's joy, his RSI in French phonetics is *hérésie* (*Le Séminaire XXIII* 15). His philosophical heresy is due to the absence of a single ground in his thought. The *R*eal[1] ghost, the *S*ymbolic father, and the *I*maginary son-ego are not hypostatically unified in Being. Lacan has no cohesive self to speak of since the speaking "self" is already split between these three realms. Subjectivity is not intimate imaginary selfhood but adherence to – being subject to – the Symbolic. Whereas Heidegger and Lacan require our coming to terms with finite belongingness – historicity and the Real, respectively – authentic Dasein festively dwells in Being and Lacanian subjugation gives rise to the subject's symptom. Lacanian "tripartite" lived experience is symptomatically barred from harmony. Even docile neurosis – a symptomatic investment to subjection – is unsatisfying and unable to dwell at home. To be a shepherd of one's roots or symptoms leaves something to be desired because of the Real tears in the social fabric and therefore in one's identity. For both thinkers, an identity represents deeper structures articulated in language but Lacan's heretic process of socialization, however, is politically more valuable.

How can anyone be Iranian, to paraphrase Montesquieu? The Lacanian paraphrase of Beauvoir replies: one is not born Iranian, but one is made to become one. Assimilation begins before the father enjoys a celebratory cigar or the surrounding of the mother with blue or pink balloons to signify gendered birth. The Symbolic is positively discriminatory – hermeneutically prejudicial – as a linguistic roadmap. Each experience is gradually integrated in differentiating sedimentation of signifiers. The infant and subsequently the child inherit what the parents were also told. A child's distressing experience will be translated and directed from above, say, "boys don't cry." The father thus represents the Symbolic – the Other. Our desires are hence desires of the Other. Since we are always asymmetrically related to the Other, every human existence desires recognition and assimilation. To Lacan, our lacking existence always seeks love ("Subversion" 689). We desire the Other's recognition and we sacrifice our Imaginary selves and our desires to conform to the Other.

The fracturing Real in the Symbolic (and the Imaginary) makes absolute adaptation, assimilation and conformity structurally impossible. To adapt to "boyhood" and so to please his father, the crying boy represses his emotions. His sacrifice is somewhat praiseworthy, if not glorious – but also never enough. The "vertical" sacrifice of negating from below one's singularity to adhere to the injunction from above is constitutive of identity and sheds light on our aforementioned obsession with the limits – not the liminality – of representation. Representation is structurally and therefore always limited because of the gap (Real) between the signified and the signifier. The "vertical" simile proves lacking, however, for communal identities. In 1935, driven by modernist envy, the Shah began referring to the country no longer as Persia but as Iran – as the land of Aryans, a nod to rising European racism of the 1930s. Persians being only half of Iran's population, Persia was no less discriminatory but it was more honest in its admission of suppressing diversity. Iran and Persia as signifiers are inadequate demonyms.

Consider existing and suppressed identities of a Kurd, Baluch, gay, woman, Christian, Zoroastrian, or Jew in Iran. Unassimilated by the Symbolic, they are Real identities. A rich Persian in Tehran equally makes vertical sacrifices, but his sacrifices are not equal to the others. Given the aleatory linguistic "chain of signification," identities are not identical. At the same time, political differences are hardly aleatory. The political field is anything but leveled. In the linguistic field the signifier "man," for instance, is horizontally differentiated from the signifier "woman." Lacan knew that signifiers do not float too loosely; they get "pinned down" (*point de capiton*). To this day, "man" remains pinned down to represent "mankind," or "human being." By reflecting reified ruling-class ideas, *point de capiton* is also reminiscent of *camera obscura*, except it is not derivative but constitutive of privilege, which is not to say that language alone causes privilege. The constitutive role of the Real is not restricted to the gap between the signified and the signifiers and we can understand its place as long as we do not seek pseudo-Hegelian essentialist engines of history. Political asymmetry indeed exists despite the Real, but the *polis* gathers because of the Real, or because it is finite.

Greeks went to temples, Heidegger correctly says, to reaffirm and to conform to their Greek identity. In the most benign sense, Being is ideologically conservative (Ricœur 176); as "shelter" against lack, it conserves our existence. Without Being, we are indeed nothing instead of some particularly shaped being. Without Symbolic signifiers we have no meaning, yet the Symbolic is politically exclusionary precisely because it promises more than it can deliver. The split-self sooner or later confronts the lacks in the system. For Lacan, fantasy becomes a coping supplement to veil Real holes in the social fabric. Because the norm is inadequate, fantasy is correspondingly "normal" to some extent. The more extensive the lack or crisis, however, the more fantasy extends itself. For instance, one becomes a carpenter by adapting to its Symbolic normative script. The generic signifier – "carpenter" – is itself a fantasy for the multitude of Imaginary Egos struggling with performance anxiety.

Although nobody is entirely represented by a signifier, we typically internalize the blame. We neurotically imagine we must do better; perhaps we must sacrifice more time and effort to "be" the perfect carpenter. When neither a missing hammer nor our own maladaptive hammering can account for a crisis, a pathological fantasy comes to the rescue. We cannot enjoy (*jouir*) our rights and subject-positions – e.g., being a carpenter working in tranquility – because others, say, immigrants, stand in the way. We dare not think that the Other – the Symbolic – failed us; we imagine others are in the way of our being home with the Other. Finding our crises of identity too devastating, Heidegger tellingly longed for a non-metaphysical god to save us. Instead of seeing the cracks in the shelter of Being, his mysticism and quietism turn lacks into setbacks (Caputo; Janicaud). Peaceful home dwelling is postponed but kept alive through the fantasy of various "home invaders."

In sum: as we lack essential unity, we depend upon meaning and linguistic signification. We can only gain meaning in and by our historical and relative perspectives. As there are no "private languages," we sacrificially conform to our communal shared understanding that shelters us from errancy. Being or the Symbolic indeed brings a semblance of order to the chaos of contingency. Semblance is the operative word, however, as the constitutive lack is never eliminated. The ones most invested in the core of a community's identity are the ones who gain the best returns on their investments as well. The well off can first fancy, as in the American Dream, their position as a result of only their hard work and sacrifices. Societal shortcomings are thus veiled; the poor clearly did not work hard enough. The more meager the return becomes, the greater the fantasy. The already privileged "rationalize" the system. They dutifully submitted and did not trespass against the Law of the Father and will not forgive perceived trespassers.

Must that be the case? Linguistic differentiation is ontologically unavoidable (Lacan, *Seminar XI* 72); political marginalization is difficult to avoid. It requires society to "authentically" come to terms with its lacks and finitude. Yet, even ignoring considerable political problems of rootedness, Heidegger still considers authenticity difficult. Cognizant of said obstacles, Lacan prescribed "traversing fantasy." His prominent example is, revealingly, James Joyce. Lacanian traversal of fantasy frees one of the Symbolic blackmail – but only one. It is a lonely walk in the desert because it requires divestment from the Symbolic. For racism, the traversal is particularly impotent, as that too is embedded in the structures one left behind.

2.1 sacrifice represented

Let us temporarily set aside sacrifice in representation and instead consider its representation. In still Heideggerian terms, sacrifice has the overt capacity of unconcealment but the nuances will let the horizontal model of sacrifice emerge.

Let's start with a typical and historical sacrificial ritual, which is tied to an economy of asymmetrical exchange. A heavy price is often paid – sacrificing material goods and animals, self-sacrifice, and in extreme cases sacrificing other persons – to obtain something from the "holy" other: God(s) or "Nature." Such rituals are Heideggerian in at least two ways. For one, they are "symbolic" or "referential" (*Being and Time* 78). By its symbolic nature, sacrifice overtly points to something other than itself and thus has a better chance of unconcealing ontological belongingness. Unlike a hammer that can mistakenly be taken as self-contained, a sign, even a traffic signal, only has meaning in context. Its worldliness is more evident from the start. Second, sacrificial rituals interrupt everydayness. When practiced communally, they are like "holy-days" that Heidegger greatly emphasized (*Elucidations* 67–100; Young 84–101); even when practiced alone, sacrificial rituals imply and rely upon commonly held values and practices. They are, in other words, affirmative of one's horizon, but do they unconceal it?

We find a similar appreciation of sacrifice's symbolic value as the reinforcement of the "social fabric" in other thinkers, such as René Girard and Sigmund Freud. For Girard, the

> common denominator that determines the efficacy of all [...] (sacrifices) [...] is internal violence – all the dissensions, rivalries, jealousies, and quarrels within the community that the sacrifices are designed to suppress. The purpose of the sacrifice is to restore harmony to the community, to reinforce the social fabric. (8)

For Freud, sacrifice is the "repetition and a commemoration of [the] memorable and criminal deed, which was the beginning of so many things – of social organization, of moral restrictions and of religion" (165). The difference with Heidegger is that, to Girard, sacrifice is a "misunderstanding" because it *conceals* past violence (7); to Freud, the totem meal festivity *conceals* unconscious motivations.

The key point here is that Girard and Freud agree with Heidegger that a symbolic act brings the community together by highlighting their common horizontal "attunement," but they rightly insist that this attunement is subject to (ideological) distortions. Ideology need not be metaphysical to remove us from Being; it can very much be a part of Being – its ruling class and its ruling ideas, as Marx said.

3 *the cyclist*

There is no room here to contextualize Makhmalbaf's work within Iranian cinema.[2] Before I provide a synopsis, let me contextualize the film within the framework of my argument. I will leave the analysis for the next section. The key here is to see that because Makhmalbaf cannot rely on easy visual cues, his depiction of racism must attend to the "background" or the sustaining structures.

The Cyclist indeed unveils the underside of (Iranian) racism, which scapegoats Afghan immigrants – such as Nasim, the film's protagonist – for societal ills. The film opens in a dark setting where Nasim's friend, a stunt man, prepares to ride his motorcycle in a dangerous cylinder to spectators' delight. Transitioning to an equally dark scene with a tall window shedding light on Nasim's anxious face, a doctor's authoritative voice informs him that his wife, Noghreh, is gravely ill. The good doctor loses interest and tears up the medical file once he discovers Nasim cannot afford hospitalization and we thus learn nothing of the illness. Other hospitals and doctors prove as unwelcoming. Throughout these brief and uncomfortable dialogues, the camera remains on Nasim's face and the asymmetry between the commanding voice of the doctors and Nasim's feeble words indicate his marginality. The camera, however, continually makes unspecific but unsubtle shifts, which I will address later.

The hospital's cashier is even less compassionate. While rejecting Nasim's Afghan currency, he preemptively declares that Noghreh's looming death is not his problem, but he softens his tone as Nasim's motorcyclist friend volunteers to cover the fees for one night. Nasim had once helped this man – even saved his life – who was involved in illicit traffic between Iran and Afghanistan. Makhmalbaf, however, gives the viewer little to no details beyond that.

On the hospital admission form, he awkwardly signs his name as "Nasim the Cyclist," with no last name. The nightly rate for the hospital bed alone is six times Nasim's daily underpaid wage as a well-digger. He has nothing as collateral, nothing to offer except his body – which is a dime a dozen – for work. Every morning he stands in a crowd of desperate Afghans, hoping to be selected by construction companies for a day. Few are needed daily but they all try to climb into the back of the trucks only to be beaten down by overwhelmed and angry construction managers.

The motorcyclist takes Nasim and his son Jomeh to see Ayas, an Azerbaijani smuggler, who asks whether Nasim can drive a truck to help their trafficking. Though dangerous, it would cover Noghreh's hospitalization. Nasim is reluctant; he is an honest worker, he says. Ayas quips: no one is born an evil smuggler; one chooses to become one. His pseudo-existentialism mirrors the anti-immigration ideological rhetoric that fancies immigrants choosing to break the law in crossing borders. Nasim's signature without a last name indicated his dispossession even in Afghanistan. Desperation, of course, forced Nasim to come to Iran illegally, only to be treated as subhuman. In other words, he never learned to drive, unabling him to "choose" smuggling opium. Ayas is seemingly the perfect Iranian, insisting they are his guests for the night. His generosity conceals his cunning and greed as he knows Nasim is too desperate. He believes that in the morning Nasim will have no choice but to come along. Ayas' plans fail, however. Not only will Nasim not join them, Ayas and his crew are arrested as Nasim, his friend, and Jomeh run away from the police raid.

Ayas was but one option in the illicit free market and Nasim takes his business elsewhere, to a more receptive mobster who is intrigued by a three-day (and night) cycling race Nasim had won. With the approval of the head-mob, the mobster offers a deal. They will cover Noghreh's hospitalization if Nasim rides a bicycle continuously for seven days and nights. Nasim hesitates before this inhumane plan, although he is learning that his humanity has no value in itself. He is further down the chain of being than the motorcyclist who risks his life for only a few minutes, on a mechanical machine that at least pushes forth on its own.

The deal benefits the mob in selling tickets to this makeshift circus freak show. People bet mainly on *when* will Nasim fall, as few expect him to last a week. The show is quite successful, exponentially gaining spectators to watch Nasim ride in a circle. A barber, a fortune-teller, a blind accordion player and others set up shop around the spectacle, creating a sub-economy of rent-paying mobile businesses for the mob to exploit. Significantly adding to the stakes, a rival gang also decides to ride Nasim's misery by betting against him. Both gangs operate in the open, in full view of government officials – who also partake in the betting. Totalitarian states are failures in many ways, ironically including their inability to exert total control.

The mobster turned promoter encourages Afghans to attend the show. The rival gang, in response, hires them for construction jobs to isolate Nasim. They initially double the wage but as the show continues, even quadrupled pay does not persuade Nasim's countrymen. The promoter brings a medical team and an easily bribed umpire to authenticate the bets. While Nasim's inability to afford medicine is the basis of the story, he is not afforded one medical team but two – one from each gang. One doctor dopes Nasim; the other crushes valium in his water. Besides valium, Nasim survives other sabotage attempts by the rival gang, such as their throwing nails under his bicycle wheels.

The initial spectacle takes place near the Soviet embassy, which in the late 1980s was still entangled in Afghanistan. On behalf of the Soviet consul, an Iranian lieutenant governor conveys the embassy's discomfort regarding "all these Afghans" near Soviet sovereign territory! The consul even calls Nasim, who receives the call on a phone held by the umpire running next to his bicycle. The consul knows the truth, or so he says; Nasim is a spy and must immediately stop. Dumbfounded, Nasim does not obey but the promoter moves the circus to another location.

Nasim falls once mid-week but fortunately in the middle of the night when most observers, including the umpire, are asleep. Dragged away, Nasim still pedals in his sleep. The motorcyclist jumps on the bicycle, covering his face with a veil. Given the night temperatures, no one is suspicious of the scarf. The "blind" accordion player turns out not to be blind after all, but since he bet on Nasim winning, he happily turns a blind eye on the switch. The motorcyclist returns for the last time to his own dangerous job in the morning; sleep-deprived, he crashes his bike and dies at the bottom of the cylinder. He had survived difficulties and illicit trafficking. This other border-crossing – his assisting Nasim – is fatal and also disqualifies him from an actual identity. The film's credits (and the official script) refer to him only as the motorcyclist. As I will argue, racism sacrifices the other to create an identity for the self. Racial identity in general, and especially in this film, is not about skin pigmentation. By associating himself with the other, this Iranian friend abdicates his identity.

A few hours of rest at the cost of his friend's life rejuvenate Nasim all the way to the seventh day. In the end, and against all odds, Nasim "wins." Jomeh along with the crowd, now fully behind him, cheering his achievement, beg Nasim to stop. Nasim no longer hears them and continues to ride in the circle, among the spectators. I shall later return to the film's salient points and the camera angles. Without a richer understanding of representation, the film's analysis can hardly surpass ontic indications of discrimination; *The Cyclist* would be reduced to the projection of misery of the cyclist on screen.

4 *clôtural* arguments: sacrificing nasim

Unlike Joycean language, anti-racist films are interpersonal. Instead of abandoning structures, they combat structural marginalization – but too often in terms of equal representation. The latter is ineffective and easily co-opted because signifiers are not equal and are beneficially pinned down to favor Symbolic privilege. Even before Obama's election, Colin Powell and Condoleezza Rice as Secretaries of State supposedly represented conservatives' post-racism.

Racial representation is liminal, since representation is meaningful only when it speaks *from* – even when it speaks against – the roots. As such, in addition to ineffectiveness or fantasy feelings of righteousness, anti-racist films run the risk of inadvertently reinforcing the structure of marginalization. I turn to three aspects of sacrifice in *The Cyclist*: internal, external, and *clôtural*.

4.1 internal sacrifice

"Internal" refers to thematic sacrifices within the plot. The "obvious" sacrifices – e.g., Nasim's personal sacrifices – are Heideggerian representations. Although not ceremonial, they unconceal values. The film also unconceals sacrificial racism and I focus on three such representations: Nasim's proximity to animality, the promoter's play on signifiers, and Nasim as the Real.

4.1.1 nasim's animality

Beyond the inhumane wager itself, Makhmalbaf depicts Nasim's displaced humanity. Before Nasim was relocated away from the Soviet embassy, he had replaced racing horses for gamblers in the same space to be treated like them. The sabotaging medical team worked in a van, a mobile laboratory with medically unnecessary caged lab rats. One hopes the doctor knows enough of his craft to undermine Nasim without testing potions on rats (that all die before the end of the film). Makhmalbaf thus highlights our contingent place under the Symbolic sun that grants identity but can equally exile one from humanity. Nasim in the end is emptied of his personhood. He can no longer stop pedaling or hear people around him. He is merely a human body-machine without the ghost.

4.1.2 sliding signifiers

Makhmalbaf promotes the mobster-promoter to the irresistible Symbolic agent of marginalization. His collecting rent from street vendors aside, the promoter is in a position of privilege. The gypsy fortune-teller he seduces is not gullible but her self-awareness is hardly valuable against his position. As another Symbolically unhinged character, she bitterly warns her daughter not to trust men. In her way, she "speaks truth to power," but, without a seat at the Symbolic table, her speech is impotent. She "reads" the promoter's palm to tell him he is untrustworthy. It takes no supernatural skills, however, to know that; she has been dealt too many bad hands to hide behind fantasies. Still bickering, she nonetheless flees with the promoter. Despite his marriage proposal and commitment to take care of her, she knows that he too will use and abuse her. After all, he just stole all the bets to flee the scene.

The promoter actively profits from his ability to game the system.[3] He rides the Symbolic wedge; he profits from the Real by reweaving together loose signifiers. Nasim was hardly part of the social contract – you cannot sign a contract without a last name – but the promoter demotes him back to the state of nature. Nasim – whose name means "breeze" – is again emptied of humanity. "Nasim once stopped a train in India with his gaze; he lifted two cows on one finger in Pakistan." These fabricated tales and his loudly repeated marketing slogan – "Breeze [Nasim] is a Storm" – fence off Nasim from other human beings. Nasim slides from an initial recognition in life, however limited, to becoming an interchangeable noun.[4]

The mobster needs no elaborate scheme; he openly calls this a circus. On a large, handwritten promotional sign transliterated in Latin alphabet, we read "cyrk." This and other "English" signs in the film are Makhmalbaf's complex transnational codes. The promoter tasks Jomeh with carrying the "cyrk" sign around, even to Afghan quarters, to boost attendance. The uneducated migrants could not read the misspelled sign, but the bastardized Latin is a signifier of legitimacy and importance. The promoter knows which signifiers show merit. This inhumane circus is not a perversion of Heideggerian festivity but its underside. Makhmalbaf accordingly represents the postcolonial roots of the space. Representation of Western power-structures speaks to yet another lack in the Iranian Symbolic.

4.1.3 the real nasim

In a nation, we do not all enjoy the same place under the sun, but Nasim is turned into the ultimate outsider whose exclusion serves to reinforce and to legitimize the existing boundaries of the Symbolic. The promoter is primarily the Symbolic agent because he replicates and reinforces its racist structures. He invites group visitors – prisoners, the elderly consigned to state-run homes, and even lepers. The promoter revealingly reminds each group they are better off than Nasim. They still have a place in society, however marginalized. They could become Nasim, or his anonymous motorcyclist friend who also paid with his life for crossing the Symbolic border. No lack is worse than Nasim's non-place.

Because Nasim's skin is hardly distinguishable from the Iranians on screen – "Nasim" is played by an Iranian actor, further troubling the "color lines" – the actors make cameo appearances within the film. Makhmalbaf cleverly places Nasim and his son in the crowd. Among the young prisoners is a young boy played by Jomeh; one of the visiting lepers is played by the actor playing Nasim. Even the leper's face – despite his scars – looks healthier. "Nasim" slows down on his bicycle in front of his "mirror image," making the equivalence unmistakable. Only the Symbolic can pin down difference out of equivalence.

4.2 external sacrifice

By "external," I refer to the viewers' aesthetic experience – the non-pejorative voyeuristic pleasure we seek from films – a central topic of Lacanian film theory. The denied – even sacrificed – jouissance is unimportant in this case, however, as Makhmalbaf bars viewers from identification with Nasim. Makhmalbaf thus unconceals Nasim as extra-ordinary. Ordinary is the business of the Symbolic from which Nasim is excluded. Internally, the plot provides few details of the protagonist's life. Like his lack of a family name, he remains anonymous to us. Externally, the film's framing represents Nasim's (non-)place and non-belongingness.

Beyond the plot, we have an unconventional vision of Nasim because the camera *purposefully* defies emotional identification. As mentioned above, especially in the early parts of the film, there are numerous unspecific and unsubtle camera shifts. These shifts are indeed quite noticeable, but they appear meaningless – there is no change of camera angles, nothing new to see. They are, however, disruptive. Just when we begin to explore Nasim's face – as he listens in pain to the heartless doctors in the opening scenes, for instance – emotionally draining before our eyes, the camera nudges our proximity and breaks the empathic arc.

When Makhmalbaf proceeds conventionally, he also troubles the viewer's curiosity. Unlike the unconventional shifts, generally in medium shots with Nasim slightly off center, Makhmalbaf's close-ups are frustrating. Nasim's alleged suicide attempt, for example, allows the filmmaker to underscore viewers' cinematic naivety. The close-up depicts at length Nasim's anxious head placed against the oversized truck tire. We seem to have the rare chance of seeing his thoughts. The camera tricks us to hope that Nasim will be placed along the cinematic tropes – a hero, perhaps – but instead we witness an uneventful and awkward failed scheme. Neither a hero nor a villain, Nasim seems unworthy of meaningful agency – barely worthy of pity.

Another early scene portrays Nasim digging in the depth and darkness of a well. The accompanying soundtrack is choral and religious; the camera neutrally observes at a conventional distance and Dasein is revealed in the "tranquility" of work, bathed in rays of light from the top. Nasim masters his tools, but Jomeh, at the top of the well, does not, struggling to lift bags of stones filled by his father. Jomeh, failing at an alarming rate, is predictably pulled down by a heavy bag and the camera follows his screaming fall, allegedly to his death on his father's lap. Nasim is immediately seen waking from what was only a nightmare.

The above are but a few examples; Makhmalbaf's techniques are alienating. Evidently, however, he *failed.* Film critics in unison praised the film's "message," but found it technically uninteresting, or worse: "the occasional quick cuts look more the works of error than planning" (Schneider). I find the viewers' reception disturbing. Undoubtedly Makhmalbaf intentionally plays on our feelings, at times bordering on emotional blackmail. Given his impeccable credentials, accusing him of poor cinematography is naive, if not Orientalist. Perhaps he chose not to give more "body" or life to Nasim's dreams and fantasies – instead of only depicting his nightmares – to represent viewers' sedimented expectation from their privileged seats. Regardless of his intentions, Makhmalbaf kept Nasim as other. Beyond his intentions, the gap between viewers and Nasim, or the gap between Makhmalbaf's activist camera and his reductive representation of Nasim's character speaks to the limits of representation that plague racist and anti-racist films. Both operate within the enclosed – *clôtural* – Symbolic ideological space.

4.3 clôtural *sacrifice*

Despite the clear differences between racism and anti-racism, the latter's tendency to depict the ignorant others (the racists) in turn conceals forms of complicities. Racism and anti-racism are not interchangeable. Traces of the "savior" complex in this film – the *sacrifice* of the Afghan as the object of guilt and pity – are troubling. The *clôtural* reading admits to the "thickness" of representation but also recognizes its complicated relationship with politically motivated representations.

As another post-Heideggerian, Derrida called the "problem of closure" the "*relations* between belonging and the breakthrough" (110) within a text. As Simon Critchley says:

> The deconstruction of logocentrism proceeds by showing how the limit, or closure, of a logocentric text is irreducibly flawed. The closure with which a text's dominant interpretation surrounds itself is shown to

> possess certain faults, or breaks, which are the marks of an alterity which the text is unable to reduce. (74)

The "relations" are indeed problematic, embodying the tension between the weight of the world and ethical resistance against the given. *The Cyclist* seemingly fits the criterion, showing the flaws of the logocentric text – the hegemonic anti-Afghan racism. Even the film's inconclusive ending resists closure. "Closure," adds Critchley, "is the double refusal both of remaining within the limits of the tradition and of the possibility of transgressing that limit" (20). In other words, raging against the racist machine has its limits. And this applies to Makhmalbaf as well as to Lacan.

In a different (legal) context, Derrick Bell argued that racism is "permanent," leading some to unfairly accuse him of defeatism and quietism (Bell; Taylor). Choosing between conservatively submitting to traditions *à la* Heidegger and championing individualism is a false dichotomy, itself contributing to "permanence" of inequalities. I place the "permanence" of racism within the logic of anti-racism, as long as the latter is caught in sacrificing the victim. Heidegger is correct that roots run deep and Derrida is equally right to say that working within a logocentric logic meets limitations from the start. To be clear, I do not fault Makhmalbaf. I do not prescribe surrendering to oppressive structures either. Makhmalbaf, however, replicates the sacrificial gesture he denounces.

The Afghan is presented as an outsider – as Afghan only – and represents the other we keep at bay to cover our own lack – a problem that Makhmalbaf openly deplores elsewhere (Makhmalbaf). His choice of *Iranian* actors is doubly striking. On the one hand, the presence of Iranians as Afghans is subversive, negating the fantasy of color differentiation. On the other hand, since the visual distinction is nonexistent, why not employ Afghans for the same role? "Employment" is at stakes in the narrative, yet Nasim's wife is played by Makhmalbaf's own daughter. Makhmalbaf keeps Iranians as the center. Moreover, the reason why his emotional appeal to pity fell flat is because the film remains within the ideological structure of racism that dehumanizes Afghans. The racism unconcealed is veiled by emotional charity. Unlike racist films enjoying the dehumanization, the anti-racist film nevertheless employs objectifying techniques – making Nasim an object of pity. Persian guilt is as impotent as white guilt.

In overt anti-racist films, the victim at times plays a sacrificial role, representing a *cause célèbre*. While I have relied heavily on Lacan, I find Lacanian scholarship on film, race, and gaze caught in Symbolic navel-gazing. Relying on visual cues, Lacanians seek the Real – as stain – in films. The Real cannot be represented, by definition. It is present via absence, as stain on the white fabric of the Symbolic. As sympathetic as I am to such approaches (Erfani 87–114), the obsession with the Real is costly. Lacanians overemphasize unraveling, without sufficient attention to constitution, to representation. Symbolic representation is entertained in order to catch it red-handed, to show its contingence and lacks. While denouncing Symbolic oppression is commendable, Lacanian film theory is geared toward viewers and *their* perceived lack. Žižek famously considered Charlie Chaplin – the arch-figure of the marginalized – as the stain. Contrasting Chaplin's black clothing to a white sheet, covering a white monument, Žižek calls him "a disturbing stain one tries to get rid of as quickly as possible" (*Enjoy* 4).

Applied to race, the racialized other is accordingly taken as the Real, or as the gaze of the Other (Seshadri-Crooks 59). The Lacanian gaze is the viewer's perspective. The viewer is assumed to be a symbolic subject and the "gaze locates the subject as a screen" (67). The subject is a screen in so far as she too is lacking, but her Symbolic subjection and tranquility masks – screens – her own contingency. Her mastering view is interrupted by a stain – be it Chaplin or a racial other – reminding her of her finitude. In other words, the focus is not actually on the marginalized – the ones lacking privileges – but on the lacks of the already integrated. Like Makhmalbaf, Lacanian film theory turns the experience of witnessing misery into a convoluted appeal to the golden rule – it asks the viewer to admit to equal fragility where there is no equality. Viewers' self-screening off the lack is returned to them; the marginalized is representationally sacrificed for their sake. Anti-racism in this Lacanian vein borders on narcissism. It is not a coincidence that Nasim's character is fairly empty, nor that the Lacanian approach centers on centered subjects.

In a recently published interview with Hamid Dabashi, Makhmalbaf divides his own work into three periods. The first period was rather faithful to the revolution, "portraying the leftists as evil and religious people as good"; the second period shifted in content, where the "poor are all good people and the evil are the rich." He considered both periods as flawed because of their "absolutism," as he calls it.

> In the third period, what has changed are the characters. They've become more complex – one doesn't see good people and bad people; everyone is simultaneously good and bad; everyone is grey. This is the most important change in this period. Also, in these films, there is no centre of truth. (73–74)

One would assume – and Makhmalbaf's language indicates his own valorization – the third period is more philosophically profound. *The Cyclist*, however, belongs to the second "social justice" period. In his later films, such as *Kandahar* (2001), Makhmalbaf represents Afghans but provides them with a meaningful presence on the screen. The fame of *The Cyclist* is not coincidental. Emotional guilt as unconcealment is not merely commercially appealing; it is ideologically and cathartically soothing. Problems are unaddressed and our tried emotions distance us from psychopathic racists, covering the structural complicities. But we should not hastily and instinctively laud nuance. For in the details, race disappears. Liminality persists.

Nuanced films have varieties of interpretations, the multifocal polyphony makes race less central, less represented. When race is represented, it does not speak directly from the margins. And for representation to be meaningful, however critically, it must speak from the center where shared meaning resides. The benevolent anti-racist discourse, vividly in integrative forces of liberalism, runs this risk of *clôtural* sacrifice. The subaltern cannot speak because she cannot be represented without co-option. When she speaks on her own terms, she defies the Symbolic forces at the risk of being incomprehensible. Anti-racism, particularly in its liberal form, is far less radical than it appears. It does not address the actual marginalization but lends a hand in marginal gestures. In America, dashing fantasies connects diversity as one; thus one is African-American, Iranian-American. Whatever precedes the dash is sublimated in the end by "American." While this is better than purely rejecting Africans or Iranians, it does not address the privilege of the Americans without dashes. It reinforces the center, demanding integration.

Clôtural gestures are failures because they work from the center and decentering should not become implicit complicity with the Symbolic, which is likely when the process of socialization and its sacrificial logic are ignored. Not only is Heidegger right to insist on Being, he is also right to insist on its "heaviness." The "teleological suspension of the Symbolic" is difficult but the ethical imperative of crossing the Symbolic picket line is nonetheless possible. Instead of narcissistically identifying the real, we can productively use Lacan and his prescription of identifying *with* the Real, *with* the marginalized, to resist Symbolic exclusion (Žižek, *Looking Awry* 140). Despite the injunction of the Law of the Father, we can refuse to collaborate. Using Nasim's misery for liberal indignation is collaboration. In 2012, Isfahan, one of the largest cities in Iran, proved itself pseudo-Heideggerian by barring Afghans from public parks during the New Year festivities, meant to celebrate only Iranians, keeping holidays as *national* celebrations. The Iranian youth resisted this loathsome act. In protests, they defended Afghans' rights and many refused to participate in the festivities. One particular photograph circulated widely depicting three young Iranian men. One holds a sign written in English, with the word "racism" crossed through. Another holds a similar sign with "racism" crossed through, this time in Persian. Between the two, a third young man holds a sign that is not barred. Refusing the barred access, refusing to subscribe to the Symbolic demarcations, identifying with the Real, the sign reads "I too am Afghan."

notes

1 Throughout this essay, I capitalize Symbolic, Imaginary, and Real to represent their Lacanian heritage against their ordinary usage.

2 I have recently provided a general philosophical reading of Iranian cinema and its context that I cannot revisit here. See my *Iranian Cinema and Philosophy.*

3 A poor elderly woman gives him her sole valuable belonging, a necklace, which he falsely promises to give to Nasim.

4 While Noghreh and Jomeh are not the focal points, their names are not ironic either. Noghreh, whose life has no value, means silver. Jomeh means Friday, the holy day of Sabbath and rest.

bibliography

Bell, Derrick A. *Faces at the Bottom of the Well: The Permanence of Racism.* New York: Basic, 1992. Print.

Bogle, Donald. *Toms, Coons, Mulattoes, Mammies, and Bucks: An Interpretive History of Blacks in American Films.* New York: Continuum, 1989. Print.

Caputo, John D. *The Mystical Element in Heidegger's Thought.* New York: Fordham UP, 1986. Print.

Critchley, Simon. *The Ethics of Deconstruction: Derrida and Levinas.* 2nd ed. London: Verso, 1999. Print.

Derrida, Jacques. *Writing and Difference.* Trans. Alan Bass. Chicago: U of Chicago P, 1978. Print.

Erfani, Farhang. *Iranian Cinema and Philosophy: Shooting Truth.* New York: Palgrave Macmillan, 2012. Print.

Freud, Sigmund. *Totem and Taboo.* Trans. James Strachey. London: Routledge, 2004. Print.

Girard, René. *Violence and the Sacred.* Trans. Patrick Gregory. London: Continuum, 2005. Print.

Heidegger, Martin. *Being and Time.* Trans. Joan Stambaugh. Albany: State U of New York P, 1996. Print.

Heidegger, Martin. *Elucidations of Hölderlin's Poetry.* Trans. Keith Hoeller. Amherst, NY: Humanity, 2000. Print.

Heidegger, Martin. "Origin of the Work of Art." *Poetry, Language, Thought.* Ed. Albert Hofstadter. New York: Harper, 1971. 17–78. Print.

hooks, bell. *Black Looks: Race and Representation.* Boston: South End, 1992. Print.

Janicaud, Dominique. *The Shadow of That Thought: Heidegger and the Question of Politics.* Trans. Michael Gendre. Evanston, IL: Northwestern UP, 1996. Print.

Lacan, Jacques. *Le Séminaire de Jacques Lacan: XXIII: "Le Sinthome."* Paris: Seuil, 2005. Print.

Lacan, Jacques. *Seminar XI: The Four Fundamental Concepts of Psycho-Analysis.* Trans. Alan Sheridan. New York: Norton, 1978. Print.

Lacan, Jacques. "The Subversion of the Subject and the Dialectic of Desire." Trans. Bruce Fink. *Écrits.* New York: Norton, 2006. 671–702. Print.

Makhmalbaf, Mohsen. "Limbs of No Body: The World's Indifference to the Afghan Tragedy." *Monthly Review* 53.6 (2001): 29–58. Print.

Makhmalbaf, Mohsen, and Hamid Dabashi. *Conversations with Mohsen Makhmalbaf.* London: Seagull, 2010. Print.

Ricœur, Paul. *Lectures on Ideology and Utopia.* Ed. George H. Taylor. New York: Columbia UP, 1986. Print.

Schneider, Dan. "The Cyclist." *Cinescene* 2009. Web. 24 Aug. 2014.

Seshadri-Crooks, Kalpana. *Desiring Whiteness: A Lacanian Analysis of Race.* London: Routledge, 2000. Print.

Taylor, George H. "Racism as 'the Nation's Crucial Sin': Theology and Derrick Bell." *University of Pittsburgh School of Law Working Paper Series.* Working Paper 10. Apr. 2004. 269–322. Print.

Young, Julian. *Heidegger's Philosophy of Art.* Cambridge: Cambridge UP, 2001. Print.

Žižek, Slavoj. *Enjoy Your Symptom! Jacques Lacan in Hollywood and Out.* London: Routledge, 1992. Print.

Žižek, Slavoj. *Looking Awry: An Introduction to Jacques Lacan through Popular Culture.* Cambridge, MA: MIT P, 1991. Print.

[w]e are all the inheritors of sins committed by our parents, and of their [...] non-sins! [...] It's unavoidable.[1]

[...] Wittgenstein influenced me a great deal [...] It's the mystical aspect of Wittgenstein's thinking that especially attracted me.[2]

Il y a là un silence muré dans la structure violente de l'acte fondateur/Here a silence is walled up in the violent structure of the founding act.[3]

camil ungureanu

SACRIFICE, VIOLENCE AND THE LIMITS OF MORAL REPRESENTATION IN HANEKE'S *CACHÉ*

introduction

Jürgen Habermas argues in *The Postnational Constellation* that asymmetrical acts of sacrifice rooted in religious practice have lost their relevance for the moral-political domain: in secular modernity, community is to be built on equal rights, symmetry and reciprocity.[4] The Habermasian view echoes a narrative of Enlightenment opposing religious prejudice to secular reason, and prophesying the gradual disappearance of religion with its oft-violent offerings to the divine. Yet this theory of modernization has become questionable: even in Europe, the most secularized continent, religion has maintained its relevance in novel, often individualized forms, including in filmmaking, literature and philosophy.[5] Why, then, would sacrificial violence, which is so rooted in ancient religious practices, maintain its central relevance even for self-declared atheists such as Michael Haneke, and under which guises? Revisiting Haneke's *Caché* (*Hidden*, 2005) as a filmic transformation of the traditional bond between sacrificial violence, morality and community provides a powerful reflection on these questions. A late echo of myths of sacrificial fratricide (Cain and Abel, Remus and Romulus),[6] *Caché* is the story of two "brothers" – Georges, representative of the French community, and Majid, the Arab, the other – that revolves around a series of puzzles concerning sacrifice, victimhood, and different forms of violence: what is the interplay between individual and collective guilt and responsibility when the community (secretly) excludes and violently sacrifices some of its members? What is the symbolic significance of Majid's theatrical self-sacrifice, and of the "ghost director" sending accusing videos to Georges' family?[7]

Caché notoriously eludes clear-cut answers. One interpretative strategy of the film is to propose *prêt-à-porter* solutions to its enigmas. Yet what if Haneke's *methodical* avoidance of giving straightforward responses is not a European art director's characteristic affection for ambiguity but is crucial for understanding the stakes of the problematic of moral and cinematic representation itself, and of the significance of sacrificial experience? What if non-answering is part of an "adequate" answer itself? This question is not a cheap paradox: it is, I think, rewarding to probe into the significance of the filmic strategies of concealment by drawing on clues provided by Haneke's cinema and interviews. By focusing largely on the ethical dimension of Haneke's cinematic vision,[8] I argue that Haneke's *Caché* articulates a double logic of breaking with and retrieving the significance of the mysteries of sin, guilt, and the mystical experience so as to reflect on past injustices, the ethical bond amongst generations, and the difficulty of community building. On the one hand, guilt, moral responsibility, and the communal bond are characterized by a "mystical" dimension – a Benjamin-like "temporal index"[9] or a normative surplus that secretly connects different generations, and that is irreducible to full propositional enunciation and representation by a transparent moral reason and representation – e.g., as Habermasian idealized reciprocity. On the other hand, Haneke's *Caché* forsakes the inscription of sacrificial violence into a sacral narrative of redemption and community making. *Caché* is, I suggest, part of a broader dynamic of ethicization of religious experience: the holy aura of sacrificing the other disappears, and the sacrificed turns into a mere victim; and yet the self-sacrifice might still point to a possibility of moral transformation and the overcoming of violence.[10]

In the following, I start from examining why the identity of the accuser and the nature of responsibility and guilt remain partly enigmatic. Considering striking analogies between *Caché* and elements of Derrida's postsecular reflection on the hidden violence at the core of community building and on the absence of an ultimate origin of moral representation, I argue that, for Haneke, moral responsibility has a "mystical" or secret dimension beyond representation and discursive reason: Derrida's "formal" rhetorical figures of interruption[11] of any discourse claiming to have access to the *Grund* of representation in general corresponds to Haneke's filmic strategies of concealing the identity of the director and accusing gaze in the film.[12]

This interpretation sheds light on the meaning of Haneke's use of a postsecular or postreligious resignification of guilt and sin; this is a moral language distinct from, first, that of a self-sufficient reason able to shed full light on the issues of guilt and responsibility, and to regard them from the perspective of idealized symmetry and reciprocity (Habermas);[13] and, second, from that of conventional Christian discourse centred on the dogmas of original sin, guilt, and the fallenness of humankind.

Second, I deal with the question of the ambiguous moral significance of Majid's turning his own death into a spectacular self-sacrifice. To this end, I draw partially on Baudrillard's aestheticizing reinterpretation of the spectacularity of terrorist acts which tends to celebrate their violence, and build a contrasting comparison with Haneke's anti-aestheticizing construction of Majid's theatrical act. Majid's suicide under Georges' eyes is a disproportionate accusation against him; however, his act also has the symbolic value of unmasking – even if imperfectly – structural relations of injustice and violence concealed by the complacencies of bourgeois common sense and reasonableness. As if confirming Haneke's questioning of a transparent and linear frontier between filmic representation and reality, Majid's suicide in film uncannily anticipates Mohamed Bouazizi's real self-immolation in 2010 as a public dissent against political oppression – an act that was inspirational for the Arab Spring protesters.

the enigma of the "ghost director": guilt, responsibility and the "mystical" dimension of morality

Caché has at its centre the family of Georges Laurent (Daniel Auteuil) and Anne, his wife (Juliette Binoche); they begin to receive surveillance videotapes of their house accompanied by grotesque drawings of faces covered with blood. At the beginning nothing really happens in the videos, yet Georges and Anne become increasingly unsettled and distressed: why are they being so intimately observed and videoed, and by whom?[14]

The search for the author of the videos leads Georges – an intellectual who hosts a TV show about books – to an apartment on the outskirts of Paris. Convinced that "he knows who it is," Georges finds the apartment of Majid (Maurice Bénichou), a middle-aged man of Arab origins. It quickly turns out that Georges had known Majid as a child. Adopted by Georges' family, Majid had been his "brother" for a while. Majid now leads a modest and colourless life in Romainville with his teenage son. Majid freely admits that he has seen Georges on his TV show but, quite persuasively, manifests bewilderment at his charge concerning the videotapes and drawings. Georges vents his annoyance at his one-time "brother," yet he also admits that, when they were children, his lies – including that about "sacrificing" a rooster – were the trigger for Majid's removal from his parents' home.

In the subsequent encounter with his wife, Georges hides the truth about the visit, telling her that there was nobody at the apartment. However, rather uncannily, the visit to Majid turns up on a videotape sent by post to Georges' wife and to his boss at the TV station. What the video also exposes are the tears that a distraught Majid sheds immediately after Georges leaves the apartment. Anne confronts Georges with the proof that he was telling lies, yet Georges insists on his innocence, while also explaining his link to Majid: Majid's parents worked on the Laurent farm when he was a child, and his father esteemed them as good employees; however, after Majid's parents had vanished without trace in a political demonstration in Paris, he was adopted by Georges' family.

When, subsequently, Pierrot, the Laurents' child, fails to return home one evening, Georges and Anne go to the police. Without any proof, Majid and his son are turned into scapegoats: Georges has Majid and his son arrested on the suspicion of having kidnapped Pierrot, and they have to spend a night in jail. After a short while Georges pays a second visit to Majid. During this visit we witness the most troubling moment of Haneke's film. In front of an unrepentant Georges, Majid calmly takes a razor blade from his pocket and slits his throat open. After this ghastly episode, Pierrot is found and, in a puzzling closing scene, he is shown from afar – as if videoed by the ubiquitous enigmatic "director" – talking with Majid's son in front of a school.

These digital video images that are so central to Haneke's film are, paradoxically, unveiling *and* obscuring. They are taken by what I call a "ghost director"[15] so that the border between representation, fiction and reality is questioned: just as a ghost sees but cannot be seen, the "director" and his camera are all pervasive, but invisible. This notion of a ghost-like camera "eye" is true not only with respect to the videotapes made of the Laurents' house (as Georges walks directly by the exact location in which the camera had to have been placed) but also to the video in which he bullies Majid, clearly shot inside the very apartment where their interaction occurs. The invisible camera exposes the most intimate details about the current life of the protagonists and, what is more, appears to know long-buried-and-forgotten secrets about their lives. Yet the identity of this all-knowing and accusing gaze remains shrouded in mystery: how, then, to interpret the symbolic significance of the enigmatic "director"? According to a first line of interpretation, the "director" is to be identified as one of the film characters. This is the most natural and traditional hypothesis: it is in agreement with basic narrative conventions in filmmaking and storytelling; these conventions stipulate that in crime and mystery films the author of a misdeed or bizarre occurrence is one of its characters. These conventions also require that spectators come to know the crime, misdeed, or the secret origin of the trauma: the hidden is brought to light and often overcome towards the end of the movie. But *Caché* does not provide any unambiguous clues concerning the author of the accusation and the actual responsibility of the characters in the movie. Quite the opposite: Haneke goes to great lengths so as to convince the audience that none of the characters is the author of the videos/drawings. The most likely candidate is, no doubt, Majid: he has reason to bear a grudge against Georges; in addition, he was in the know as to the erstwhile events alluded to by the sent images. Yet he is insistently presented as innocent. Georges' allegations outrage and distress Majid – and we, as viewers, are persuaded by his reactions. The sincerity of his reactions is forcefully conveyed by images showing him crying in solitude, after Georges' departure.

A psychoanalytic interpretation provides a different version of this first line of reading: according to it, Georges himself is the "ghost director." Georges' personality is, from this perspective, split: incapable of dealing with a childhood trauma, Georges would unconsciously punish himself by sending the accusing videos and drawings to his own postal address. This interpretation is coherent *in abstracto*, but purely speculative; neither the film nor Haneke's own reflections on it contain any suggestion, however indirect, as to Georges' double personality.[16]

Finally, amongst the other film characters no one seems a plausible author of the accusation. Majid's grown son is introduced very briefly; he might know something; yet, faced with the accusation, he denies it flatly, and he is equally surprised and persuasive in his claims. And Pierrot, Georges' hardly present child, does not appear to have anything to do with the videos. In short: each and every film character is ruled out.

Is Haneke's invisible "double" a reference to an all-knowing, accusing God? The second hypothesis of a God as moral judge is prima facie plausible. The videotapes might be taken as gesturing towards an all-seeing and -knowing divine eye. The formal elements of the film – namely the use of long shots and motionless camera in order to enter the most hidden details of Georges' family life – seem to point to a transpersonal perspective – maybe an omniscient judge. But this reading is, in the final analysis, unpersuasive. The God-hypothesis is at odds with Haneke's unequivocal atheism, as well as with the patent lack, in *Caché*, of any suggestion whatsoever of God or divinity.

According to a third plausible interpretation, the anonymous "director" symbolizes an objective moral judge or perspective. The objectivity-hypothesis does convey a fundamental dimension of Haneke's directorial intention. Unlike *The Seventh Continent*, *Funny Games*, and *The Pianist*, *Caché* is one of Haneke's films that link his enduring interest in excessive acts of (self-destructive) violence with their historic-political background (consider *75 Fragments of a Chronology of Chance* and *The White Ribbon*). The idea of *Caché* itself has its origin in Haneke's watching of a TV documentary about a real yet purposefully hidden event, the so-called *Nuit noire*, when the French police arrested and drowned hundreds of peaceful Algerian protesters in the Seine.[17] The videos stand for a symbolic *j'accuse* against Georges' acts, but also against their objective historical background and "growing soil" – namely a relation of structural violence opposing the French state and majority to the others (Arab immigrants), as epitomized by the tragic happenings during the *Nuit noire*. As Haneke states, "linking the plot to politics kept the guilt from remaining at the personal level [...]"[18] In *Caché*, Haneke has Georges explain the broader setting of his relation to Majid in the following way:

> [i]n October '61 the FLN called all Algerians to a demonstration in Paris. They went to Paris. On October 17th, Papon, the police massacre. They drowned about 200 Arabs in the Seine. Majid's parents were probably among them. In any case, they never returned. When my father went to Paris to search for them, the police told him that he should be glad to be rid of these "jigaboos." My parents decided to adopt the boy, I don't know why. They must have felt responsible in some way [...]

The objectivity-hypothesis is, however, relevant for capturing only *one* crucial aspect of Haneke's moral concern. Conveying the idea that guilt and responsibility have a transindividual dimension does not explain why Haneke spends so much time and effort in weaving *unsolved* enigmas.[19] *Caché* is not merely a "whistleblower" refreshing public memory about the victims of the *Nuit noire*;[20] the *Nuit noire* is the springboard for a broader filmic reflection on the relation between violence, moral responsibility and the communal bond. A *fuller* interpretation of *Caché* takes into account the symbolic significance of the film's strategies of concealment in relation to Haneke's interest in the "mystical" dimension of cinematic and moral representation, as well as into the mysteries of "sin" and "guilt" marking the communal bond. To better clarify my suggestion that Haneke's "ghost director" points to a moral view of guilt and responsibility as having a "mystical" dimension, it is useful to make a brief detour into Derrida's postsecular view of the "mystical" foundation of authority and community, and underline striking affinities with Haneke's *Caché*.[21] Haneke's own references to the "mystical," the sin and the guilt are more persuasively understood by drawing on Derrida and his analogous strategy of unmasking hidden violence, rather than on Wittgenstein (whose usage of the "mystical" is explicitly invoked by Haneke). In "Force of Law: 'The Mystical Foundation of Authority'" Derrida is, just like Haneke, interested in unveiling the violence of modern-liberal communities – violence that is often concealed by common-sense or ideological complacencies. In so doing, Derrida's postsecularism consists in retrieving terms and experiences (faith, mystical, transcendence, etc.) that are traditionally considered "religious" beyond conventional religion.[22] For Derrida, the very foundation, construction and perpetuation of the modern-liberal community have a "mystical" dimension related to violence and responsibility. The term "mystical" does not refer here either to a direct and non-verbalizable experience of God or, from the positivistic perspective of Wittgenstein's *Tractatus*, to what goes beyond the "proper" use of language (i.e., the representation of reality). By the "mystical" foundation of authority, Derrida refers to the condition of absence of a transparent *Grund* of community, and the consequences of it. The very foundation of a modern community – that is tracing its borders, defining who-is-in-and-out, and adopting specific moral-political interpretations – involves a "mystical" moment of undecidability between illegitimacy and legitimacy, violence and justice.[23] Benjamin emphasizes this aspect with the term *rechtsetzende Gewalt* which Derrida translates into French as *violence fondatrice* (violence that founds): all law (in the broadest sense) is in part based on violence as there is no original law, but rather all law was instituted at some time and advances a specific interpretation. Inasmuch as the law presupposes the legitimacy of its own origin, it ultimately refers to an extralegal act, to an originating act of violence; and this *unnamable* violence constitutes the groundwork of the authority of law whenever the law (or statute or an individual judgment) appeals explicitly to the "legitimacy" of its own institution.

The "mystical," then, for Derrida, points to an abyss in the heart of an order that is supposedly well founded – the abyss of "vanished cruelties at the moment of constituting a state," of the "forgotten terror when a new law comes into force," and of the "events which remain historically uninterpretable or indecipherable."[24] This hidden or unnameable secret recurs in the performative character of moral-political activity; in calling it "mystical," Derrida follows Montaigne's referring to a covert violence at the core of community: "Here a silence is walled up in the violent structure of the founding act," one that – as Derrida rightly insists – also haunts and shapes the post-foundational community making.[25]

Derrida and Haneke meet with respect to the "mystical" silence and hidden violence built into the social order, and which mark the limits of moral representation of guilt and responsibility. They use either "formal"-rhetorical or -filmic means to convey the absence of an ultimate origin or "director" of (moral) representation. The existence of this "mystical" dimension of moral and filmic representation does not mean that we cannot or should not identify victims, their perpetrators, and take consequent action. Yet the content of guilt and responsibility is not grasped by a filmic representation claiming to have a transparent access to reality or immanent reason; in any community there are blind spots and silences over processes of exclusion and victimization. Community building creates victims to be mourned; the community and its members are haunted by them, and by an indeterminate yet exacting sense of (transgenerational) guilt and responsibility. Thus, as Haneke admits, "[g]uilt is the first question in all of Kafka's works. It's also true of all my films [...] It's inherent in our Judeo-Christian tradition, and especially in Central Europe. Actually, in all of the West."[26] We are, for Haneke, "children" and inheritors of sins and injustices committed by our ancestors: "[w]e are all the inheritors of sins committed by our parents, and of their [...] non-sins! [...] It's unavoidable."[27] Long-forgotten and -hidden acts of violence and exclusion are sometimes brought to light, even if their representation is always partial and truncated.[28] Other such acts are shrouded in a "mystical" silence, as they can remain unthematized and unverbalized, beyond even the current (dominant) moral imagination. These acts are not named and not even nameable, not least because the stories of the victims are at least partly irremediably lost; just like the "ghost director" haunting Georges and his family, the victims are bound to remain partly anonymous, and to transcend the horizon of our moral reason, powers and imagination. With their irremediable loss, what is hidden is meant to remain hidden: no image of idealized reciprocity can cure this open scar of the communal bond.[29] This reading can suggestively explain the symbolic significance of Haneke's willingness to preserve the enigma of an anonymous "director" unsettling comfortable moral beliefs, that is, of a ghost haunting a self-complacent Georges as representative of the French community.[30] It can, furthermore, explain the significance of Haneke's using the postsecular idiom of inevitable guilt and sin – namely of a moral language different from two opposite idioms: that of a self-sufficient moral reason able to shed a transparent light on the issue of guilt and responsibility, and to regard them from the perspective of idealized symmetry and reciprocity (Habermas); and that of conventional religion regarding the fallenness of humanity as the consequence of the original sin.

the enigma of majid's theatrical suicide: ethical ambiguity and haneke's refusal of aestheticizing and celebrating violence

Together with the videos and drawings, Majid's suicide puts Georges under suspicion. But what is the symbolic significance of Majid's surprisingly radical gesture?

Haneke carefully orchestrates the theatricality of Majid's act; in shooting the scene, Haneke does not spare the audience: the suicide is so graphically represented that Majid seems more to drown in his own blood than to die of his wound. The hyperrealism of the shots generates an effect of shock and terror in Georges and the audience. The theatrical effect of the suicide is augmented by its being ostentatiously performed under Georges' shocked look, and not in the darkness of Majid's solitude. This effect is further enhanced by the surprising nature of the suicide. Throughout the film, Majid is presented as leading a grey and uneventful life. So his radically violent act comes as an event that tears apart the narrative thread and the spectator's expectations: the suicide is neither announced nor motivated by previous clues; nor does it have a clear-cut justification in the film – it emerges as a disproportionate response to Georges' false accusations.

Majid's seemingly excessive reaction raises important questions: what's the ethical significance of Majid's counter-accusatory suicide, and is it fair at all? Is Majid a victim or is his suicide the result of excessive self-victimization? Does the suicide amount to a moral self-sacrifice or is it the result of a filmic staging that perpetuates Orientalist clichés about Arabs/Muslims (as moving between passivity or incapacity for real agency and extreme, irrational violence) under the mask of a progressive critique of structural violence?[31]

Haneke's filmic choices avoid, once again, unambiguous answers: Majid's act is as ostentatious as it is obscure. To get a better grasp of the significance of Majid's converting his own death into a theatrical act it is worthwhile to look briefly into Baudrillard's interpretation of spectacular terroristic suicides.[32] The point is *not* to replace our interpretation of Haneke's reflection on the absence of an ultimate origin or director of (moral and filmic) representation; while referring to Baudrillard sheds light on the spectacularity of violence, it does so as a *contrasting* comparison.

By drawing on Mauss's famous analysis of potlatch,[33] Baudrillard argues that the "new terrorism"[34] is to be understood as a mutually destructive "gift exchange" between the global capitalist System and the self-sacrificing terrorists.[35] In Baudrillard's bleak vision, the hegemonic capitalist System imposes a poisonous gift on everyone under the guise of determinate forms of work and consumer goods. The gift of the total System is a terror inflicted on everyone, and which reduces us to the status of things. This terror is so powerful and complete that it can be answered *only* negatively through the counter-gift of violent destruction. The terrorist counter-gift is paradoxical: it is the restoration, however briefly and violently, of exchange; yet the terrorist's death, being unanswerable, destroys at once a communication and social relationship. By "offering" suicide and death the total System is disrupted, and the social intercourse is annulled. The paradoxical gift exchange has an essential symbolic and spectacular dimension: since the relation of "physical" power between System and terrorists is downright asymmetric, the force of the terrorist act lies in its "symbolic and sacrificial" nature.[36] Thus, the terrorists' choice of the Twin Towers on 9/11 was "perfect," as the Towers encapsulated the symbolic "essence" and legitimacy of the total System represented by the United States. For Baudrillard, it is the symbolic gesture that brought down, in the first place, the Twin Towers. The force of the terrorists' gift of death is "far more than real":[37] by attacking the symbolic heart of the System, the counter-gift is able to undercut its real power.

Does Haneke's bleak vision of the symbolic conflict between the two "brothers" convey a Baudrillardian economy of violence and counter-violence? A Baudrillardian reading of *Caché* is, prima facie, plausible. Georges, who stands for the French community, may be seen as representing the *hegemon* or the System; and Majid, whose self-inflicted violence is meant to frighten and shock his "brother," may be regarded as personifying the terrorist. The French community is, according to this analysis, a totalitarian "iron cage"; its structural violence towards the other does not give him any other option than counter-violence and death.

The Baudrillardian reading has, however, a limited explanatory power: it relies on totalizing ideological certitudes and an aestheticization of violence (namely of dissolving the moral dimension of violence into jubilatory sensations)[38] that are absent in Haneke's film (and in Derrida's philosophy). Baudrillard turns the diversity and intricacy of global relations into a monolytic System, a "unique thought" that terrorizes its members, and US democracy into a totalitarian System that has "divine omnipotence and [...] absolute moral legitimacy."[39] If we accept this questionable ideological premise, Baudrillard's sympathy for terrorist violence may become less surprising. In replacing the dictatorship of the proletarian, terrorist violence becomes, in Baudrillard's aestheticizing vision, a source of generalized enjoyment. As Baudrillard claims with regards to 9/11, "[...] we have all dreamt of this event [...] everyone without exception has dreamt of it [...]"[40] A blow into the heart of the Behemoth, 9/11 is a universal source of (barely hidden) enjoyment, and a common dream come true.

The contrast between Baudrillard's exaltation of terrorist violence and Haneke's anti-aestheticizing filmic construction of Majid's suicide is, I believe, instructive. There is nothing in the film or in the director's own comments that calls for a sweeping generalization in Baudrillard's style. The bleak story of the two "brothers" unveils a structural violence and injustice between the majority community and the other (see above my reflection on mystical and morality in Haneke), but Majid's act is neither "enjoyable" nor is it celebrated as the only alternative to the "totalitarian" French system. Certainly, Baudrillard convincingly points out that, in conditions of stark asymmetries of material power, symbolic-demonstrative acts can become crucial: Majid's suicide and Baudrillard's terrorist acts have in common the relationship between spectacular violence and the struggle for recognition. But there are unbridgeable differences between terrorist acts (that are justified and condoned by Baudrillard) and Majid's suicide. The terrorists' counter-gift is plainly immoral, as it implies killing innocent people. In turn, Majid – a scapegoat committing suicide – has a moral significance that confers on it a sacrificial dimension: it is a desperate cry of blamelessness in front of repeated and groundless accusations; it stands for an attempt to shake up Georges' moral self-righteousness, and disrupt the logic of scapegoating always ready to be reactivated (as in the imprisoning of Majid and his son without any proof), and is part of a system of unequal power relationships between the dominant group and the Arab immigrants. Thus, Majid's act has a moral-symbolic import that is directed *both* at Georges as an individual and as a member of a community.

Majid's act can be placed closer to the spectacular bonze-style sacrifices for admirable ethical causes, rather than to Baudrillard's terrorists. Like the self-sacrifices of Tibetan monks, Majid's suicide conveys an ethical message: while Majid's suicide cannot be inscribed in a sacral story of salvation, his suicide may, as an interruption of a structural relation of injustice and as a call for recognition when communication fails, still play a role in a narrative of ethical transformation. Majid's gesture is an anguished call for recognition that disturbingly anticipates another Arab's self-sacrifice, a real and a public one this time: Bouazizi's setting himself on fire in 2010 in response to the direct repression of Ben Ali's authoritarian regime. Incidentally, Ali's regime was supported by the French state as well. Bouazizi's heroic act in response to direct persecution was hugely inspirational for the Arab Spring.

Yet Haneke's Majid is far from being a hero who elicits moral admiration. Haneke's strategy is to refuse the comfort of unilateral identification with and pleasure in Majid's violence.[41] The hyperrealism of filming the suicide generates an unbearable discomfort: we want to look away and close our eyes, but the suicide happens too quickly and unexpectedly. Haneke further introduces a significative informational lack as to Majid's justification and motivation for such a grave act. His theatrical suicide under Georges' eyes is excessive and disproportionate: Georges has a point in claiming that it is unfair to accuse him of something which occurred when he was six: how could he be accused of something he did at a time when he was not even responsible for his acts? Even if Georges' lies as a child have had an impact on Majid's life, he [Majid] should be seen as responsible for his own destiny as an adult, and for his own (failed) life. The suicide seems to have something of a revengeful act reflecting a personal failure as well – namely [of] an act of self-victimization.

On the other hand, Haneke blocks the identification with Georges. Georges feels wronged, and repeatedly claims his guiltlessness throughout the movie. He firmly believes he is in no way responsible: accusing him, Georges thinks, is unreasonable, if not plainly irrational. Georges explains the following about his childhood years:

> I didn't want him [Majid] in the house. He had his own room. I had to share. I was six years old! [...] I told lies about him. Afterwards he was sent away, sick, to a hospital or a children's home. I don't know which. I was happy. I don't feel responsible for it. *It's all absurd*!

But not even Georges' loving wife believes him. She questions him repeatedly, and so does the audience under the impact of the "ghost director." While it is unfair to overburden Georges either with Majid's death or with the hidden "sins" of the French towards Arab immigrants, he destroys any trust and communication with his "brother," and turns him once again, in a gesture that is resonant of the *Nuit noire*, into a scapegoat for his son's disappearance.[42] Georges fails to acknowledge that responsibility has a historical and collective dimension, namely that Majid's suicide is not only directed at him as an individual but also that it has a broader moral-symbolic significance.

In sum, Haneke undercuts the self-complacent concealing or justification of violence on both sides. The moral goal of Haneke's portraying of structural *and* reactive violence is anti-Baudrillardian: it aims not at the aestheticizing exaltation of violence against the System but at unveiling and questioning an economic circle of violence and counter-violence (see above).[43] Haneke's strategy of concealment undercuts an interpretation that converts violence into something immediately accessible, transparent, and ideologically justifiable. Like Derrida, Haneke's *Caché* challenges the comfort of common sense (the peaceful, bourgeois life of Georges' family), but also the aestheticizing celebration of violent reversals. Haneke refuses, further, the release or enjoyment of final reconciliation and of overcoming the trauma of past violence.[44] Instead, like Derrida's moral philosophy, Haneke's film calls forth an uncomfortable and open interrogation, an ethos of questioning of past and present violence as well as of our share and limits in determining guilt and responsibility. Divided between identifying with and putting themselves at a distance from Majid and Georges, spectators are called to interrogate themselves and their complacencies, and accept secret and unpleasant complicities as well as a sense of guilt and responsibility for concealed forms of violence. In Haneke's and Derrida's vision, experiences of guilt and responsibility also have a secret or "mystical" dimension that defies full verbalization, codification and "directorial" control. The relations of violence and domination hidden behind the facade of the normal order remain always insufficiently thematized given the structural limits of moral powers, knowledge and representation. As the "tradition of the oppressed"[45] is not a mere exception to the reign of the ethical norm, the question of the "mystical index" of the moral life of community "cannot be settled cheaply."[46] It is an open wound in the core of communal life.

notes

I would like to thank Bogdan George Popa, Russell Kilbourn, Alexandra Popartan, Ivan Pintor, and an anonymous reviewer for comments on a draft of this article.

1 Haneke qtd in Cieutat and Rouyer 149.

2 Haneke qtd in Cieutat 146.

3 Derrida, "Force of Law" 942/943.

4 Habermas, *Postnational Constellation* 101; idem, *Reason and Rationality* 166.

5 Bradatan and Ungureanu.

6 See also Kline.

7 This article develops and modifies an argument that I sketched briefly in Ungureanu, "Final Remarks." Therein I use the term "postsecular" so as to interpret Haneke's relation to Christianity, and to draw a comparison with Bruno Dumont's *The Life of Jesus* (1997).

8 The formal-cinematic aspects of Haneke's film have been largely discussed, not least by Haneke himself. Haneke's formal choices corroborate my interpretation of his view of the limits of moral representation (see below).

9 I have in mind Benjamin's famous passage:

> The past carries with it a temporal index by which it is referred to redemption. There is a secret agreement between past generations and the present one. Our claim was expected on earth. Like every generation that preceded us, we have been endowed with a *weak* Messianic power, a power to which the past has a claim. That claim cannot be settled cheaply. (Benjamin 254)

10 This paradoxical relation to the religious heritage justifies the talk of Haneke's postsecular ethics, namely of an idiom that is different both from conventional religious ethics and from a

secular ethics based on an immanent reason. This interpretation differs from the view that the film is a postcolonial "morality tale" (amongst others, see Grossvogel). While the political background of the narration is postcolonial, Haneke's directorial intention is more general (see below).

11 Derrida's use of rhetorical figures (e.g., figures of interruption, obscurity) is not merely formal. Digression, ellipsis, for instance, are used by Derrida to suggest something fundamental about the language and representation, namely the impossibility to have access to presence, as well as the absence of an ultimate frontier between fiction and reality, non-literal and literal meaning. For an example of Derrida's use and reflection of a figure of speech as ellipsis questioning the traditional view of it as merely "formal," see Derrida, "Ellipsis" 371–77.

12 My analysis is complementary to interpretations emphasizing the ethical import of Haneke's reflections on cinematic representation; see Wheatley, *Michael Haneke's Cinema*; idem, *Caché/Hidden*; Brunette. For a congruent reading focused on the relation between representation and memory, see Kilbourn.

13 Habermas uses the language of postsecularism in his late writings. However, morality remains for him *within* the domain of a self-standing reason and rational representation. In contrast, there is an affinity between Derrida and Haneke in that they retrieve religious language ("mystical," "sin") beyond dogma and conventional religion in order to reflect on the limits of moral and/or filmic representation. For a detailed discussion of postsecularism, see Ungureanu, "Uses and Abuses" 1–19.

14 Haneke's formal choices (e.g., the digital texture of the video) contribute to the destabilization of the "immediate control of reality" and of the transparency of (moral) representation. See Haneke qtd in Cieutat and Rouyer 151. *Caché* interweaves the reflection on cinematic and moral representations and their "mystical" blind spots; therein consists a further correspondence between Haneke and Derrida: they use rhetorical or filmic strategies to question the transparent border between representation, fiction and reality (see below). For a discussion of Haneke's formal-cinematic choices, see, for instance, Romney; Kilbourn.

15 Derrida is well known for reflecting on the way the figure of the ghost – neither alive nor dead – questions the idea of a controllable and transparent border between fiction, representation and reality. See Derrida, *Spectres of Marx*.

16 An alternative Lacanian–Žižekian interpretation regards the enigma of the ghost director and the irruption of Majid's violence as "manifestations" of the Real appears to be more promising. However, I do not pursue this interpretative path since I am not persuaded that the Lacanian–Žižekian analysis captures Haneke's deep ethical interest and refusal to aestheticize violence (that is, to dissolve the moral problematic of violence into jubilatory sensations). Resorting to some elements of Derrida's reflection on hidden violence, "mystical" and morality have more explicative power, and are more congruent with Haneke's directorial intentions (see below). In contradistinction, see Žižek for a characteristic example of an analysis of religion, revolution and cinema that ends in a suspension of the ethical, and the celebration of revolutionary violence as a flight into the Real. A good critique of Žižek's view is contained in Sharpe and Boucher. For an alternative way of using psychoanalytical insights, see Mamula chapter 5, dedicated to Haneke and Chris Marker.

17 See also Alain Tasma's *Nuit noire, 17 octobre 1961* (2005).

18 Haneke qtd in Cieutat and Rouyer 149. See also Wheatley, *Michael Haneke's Cinema*; idem, *Caché/Hidden*; Brunette; and for an alternative interpretation focused on the issue of "secrecy," see Yacowar.

19 With the exception of radical libertarians or individualists, it is generally accepted that imperfect obligations emerge by virtue of membership in a family or community: the admittance of a collective dimension of responsibility (of the Germans towards Jews; of the French towards the victims of the *Nuit noire*) does not point to unfathomable mysteries.

20 For more details on these events and the origin of Haneke's movie, see Kline.

21 The point of introducing aspects of Derrida's view is not taking *Caché* either as a mere illustration of an abstract thesis or as advancing a fully fledged philosophical argument; it is to intimate that there are enlightening correspondences between elements of Derrida's conception of the

"mystical" and of the absence of an ultimate foundation of representation and Haneke's strategy of concealment of the "director" and origin of moral accusation and representation in *Caché*. For clarifying methodological reflections on the interactive relation between film and philosophy, see Mulhall.

22 Derrida famously speaks of "religion without religion." See Derrida and Vattimo.

23 Derrida, "Force of Law" 920–1045.

24 Ibid. 990/991.

25 Ibid. 942/943.

26 Haneke qtd in Cieutat 147.

27 Haneke qtd in Cieutat and Rouyer 149.

28 As I have pointed out, Haneke's reflection on the limits or blind spots of the cinematic and the moral representation go hand in hand. For Haneke, "our perception of the world is naturally fragmented" (Haneke qtd in Cieutat 140); Haneke also speaks of the "impossibility of description" (qtd in Cieutat and Rouyer 152). See also Haneke, "Violence and the Media."

29 The excluded (like the victims of the *Nuit noire*) are not sacrificed victims to be inscribed into a sacral history of redemption; they are victims to be mourned. For Derrida and Haneke violence loses both its sacral aura and its positive function in community building: the loss of the victim is irremediable and unredeemable (for a complication of this image with respect to Majid's figure that has an ethical-sacrificial dimension, see below).

30 Here I refer only to those elements of Derrida's conception that help me build an analogy with Haneke's film and which, incidentally, are also convincing to me. Overall, however, Derrida's moral conception is based on an inflationary understanding of sacrifice. The very structure of the concept of duty is, for Derrida, "sacrificial-Abrahamic." In Derrida's hyperbolic rhetoric:

> [a]s soon as I enter into a relation with the other, with the gaze, look, request, love, command or call of the other, I know that I can respond only by sacrificing ethics, that is, by sacrificing whatever obliges me to also respond, in the same way, in the same instant, to all the others. I offer a gift of death, I betray, I don't need to raise my knife over my son on Mount Moriah for that. Day and night, at every instant, on all Mount Moriahs of this world, I am doing that, raising my knife over what I love and must love, over those to whom I owe absolute fidelity, incommensurably. (Derrida, *Gift of Death* 68)

For elements of a critique of this overburdening notion of duty linked to a catch-all notion of sacrifice, see Ungureanu, "Derrida's Tense Bow"; idem, "Bourdieu and Derrida."

31 Andrei Apostol suggested to me this interpretation in a private conversation. By pointing out the ambivalence of the representation of Majid's suicide, my reading goes in a different direction (see below).

32 Baudrillard's name is mentioned at a cocktail party at Anne's publishing firm (Osterweil 38; Kilbourn 187). Osterweil and Frey relate Baudrillard's social theory to Haneke's films, yet in a different sense, with a focus on the theory of image and representation (Osterweil; Frey). However, I think that drawing attention to the "elective affinities" between Derrida and Haneke is more fruitful: as I have pointed out, they are both interested in problematizing the strict opposition between representation, fiction, and reality, while rejecting the view of a totalizing fictionalization.

33 In potlatch, a form of gift-giving found in the northwest of North America and in Melanesia, one leader "offers," destroys and ostentatiously sacrifices objects, slaves, a banquet, or indeed anything, to a rival leader. The latter is obliged to accept and then to return the gift through exceeding the gifts given to him in the previous exchange. Social relations between individuals, groups and tribes are defined through such escalating and competitive exchanges that can take on violent, spectacular, and excessive forms. See Mauss.

34 I take the phrase "new terrorism" from Baudrillard's *Spirit of Terrorism* 25.

35 In Baudrillard's work terrorism first emerges as a theme against the background of the Baader-Meinhof and Red Brigade terrorists in the late 1960s and 1970s. See Baudrillard, *Symbolic Exchange*. For more recent analyses, see his *Carnival and Cannibal* and, most importantly, *Spirit of Terrorism*.

36 Baudrillard, *Spirit of Terrorism* 12.

37 Ibid. 17.

38 Charles Taylor accuses Derrida of a celebration or aestheticization of violence beyond its morally problematic character. This is what Taylor calls, in his *magnum opus A Secular Age*, Derrida's "neo-Nietzschean anti-humanism" (327, 726, 695). But I think that this is a misrepresentation of Derrida's view based on the opposition between justice and violence that follows an academic fashion rather than Derrida's own texts. In contrast, Derrida and Haneke have in common the interruption of the celebration and aestheticization of violence. See also Ungureanu, "Aestheticization of Politics."

39 Baudrillard, *Spirit of Terrorism* 9.

40 Ibid. 6.

41 Grossvogel speaks of Haneke's "Brechtian exercise in distancing" (Grossvogel 41).

42 For a suggestive interpretation of the loss of communication in Haneke's film and its relation to *Code Unknown*, see also Mamula chapter 5.

43 See also Haneke's useful reflections in his "Terror and Utopia of Form." Note that Kline makes use of René Girard's well-known theory of violence and the sacred in interpreting Haneke's movie, but he does not propose a plausible interpretation as to why the authorship of the videos remains ultimately unknown (Kline). From my perspective, the Girardian reading has the merit of pointing to the centrality of the issue of sacrificial violence in relation to community building, and to a violence that is "hidden" at the origin of community. But Girard's line of argumentation, based on the scapegoat mechanism as concealing the truth of the unlimited original violence, diverges from Haneke's ethical concerns, and does little to explain his strategies of concealment of the ultimate origin or director of the filmic and moral representation: Majid's ethical self-sacrifice is not meant to cover a hidden truth, but to unveil it (see later). A Girardian reading of Majid's sacrifice (not discussed by Kline) may become more convincing if one regards it as a late ethical echo of a Christic self-sacrifice as a way of overcoming the economic circle of violence and sacrifice, but is undermined by the familiar Eurocentric gesture of conferring a world-historical relevance to Christ's sacrifice.

44 The meaning of the final scene that brings together Georges' and Majid's sons is a matter of speculation. It could be read as suggesting either that the next generation inherits the faults and responsibilities of their parents, or that there is the *possibility* of a dialogue and reconciliation. It is, however, clear that Haneke's film does not provide any warrant of reconciliation or closure of the trauma of violence and counter-violence.

45 Benjamin, *Illuminations* 257.

46 Ibid. 276.

bibliography

Baudrillard, Jean. *Carnival and Cannibal, or the Play of Global Antagonism*. Trans. Chris Turner. London and New York: U of Chicago P, 2010. Print.

Baudrillard, Jean. *Symbolic Exchange and Death*. Trans. Ian Hamilton. London: Sage, 1993. Print.

Baudrillard, Jean. *The Spirit of Terrorism and Requiem for the Twin Towers*. Trans. Chris Turner. London: Verso, 2003. Print.

Benjamin, Walter. *Illuminations: Essays and Reflections*. Trans. Harry Zohn. New York: Harcourt, 1968. Print.

Bradatan, Costica, and Camil Ungureanu, eds. *Religion in Contemporary European Cinema: The Postnational Constellation*. New York and London: Routledge, 2014. Print.

Brunette, Peter. *Michael Haneke*. Urbana and Chicago: U of Illinois P, 2010. Print.

Cieutat, Michel. "Interview with Michael Haneke: The Fragmentation of the Look." Trans. Robert Gray. Brunette 139–47. Print.

Cieutat Michel, and Phillipe Rouyer. "Interview with Michael Haneke: You Never Show Reality, Just its Manipulated Image." Trans. Peter Brunette. Brunette 148–56. Print.

Derrida, Jacques, "Ellipsis." Derrida, *Writing and Difference* 371–77. Print.

Derrida, Jacques. "Force of Law: 'The Mystical Foundation of Authority'." *Cardozo Law Review* 11 (1990): 920–1045. Print.

Derrida, Jacques. *The Gift of Death*. Trans. David Willis. Chicago and London: U of Chicago P, 1994. Print.

Derrida, Jacques. *Spectres of Marx*. New York and London: Routledge, 1994. Print.

Derrida, Jacques. *Writing and Difference*. London and New York: Routledge, 2001. Print.

Derrida, Jacques, and Gianni Vattimo, eds. *Religion*. Cambridge: Polity, 1998. Print.

Frey, Mathias. "*Benny's Video*, *Caché*, and the Desubstantiated Image." *Framework* 47.2 (2006): 30–36. Print.

Girard, René. *Violence and the Sacred*. Trans. Patrick Gregory. Baltimore: Johns Hopkins UP, 1977. Print.

Grossvogel, D.I. "Haneke: The Coercing of Vision." *Film Quarterly* 60.4 (2007): 36–43. Print.

Grundmann, Roy, ed. *A Companion to Michael Haneke*. London: Wiley-Blackwell, 2010. Print.

Habermas, Jürgen. *The Postnational Constellation: Political Essays*. Trans. Max Pensky. Cambridge, MA: MIT P, 2001. Print.

Habermas, Jürgen. *Reason and Rationality: Essays on Reason, God and Morality*. Ed. Eduardo Mendieta. London: Polity, 2002. Print.

Haneke, Michael. "Terror and Utopia of Form: Robert Bresson's *Au hasard Balthazar*." Grundmann 565–74. Print.

Haneke, Michael. "Violence and the Media." Grundmann 575–79. Print.

Kilbourn, Russell. *Cinema, Memory, Modernity: The Representation of Memory from the Art Film to Transnational Cinema*. London: Routledge, 2010. Print.

Kline, Jefferson. "The Intertextual and Discursive Origins of Terror in Michael Haneke's *Caché*." Grundmann 551–62. Print.

Mamula, Tijana. *Cinema and Language Loss: Displacement, Visuality and the Filmic Image*. New York and London: Routledge, 2013. Print.

Mauss, Marcel. *The Gift: Forms and Functions of Exchange in Archaic Societies*. London: Cohen, 1966. Print.

Mulhall, Stephen. *On Film*. 2nd ed. London: Polity, 2008. Print.

Osterweil, Ara. "'*Caché*'. Review of *Caché*." *Film Quarterly* 59.4 (2007): 35–39. Print.

Romney, Jonathan. "*Hidden*. Review of *Caché*." *Sight and Sound* 16.2 (2006): 63–64. Print.

Sharpe, Matthew, and Geoff Boucher. *Žižek and Politics: A Critical Introduction*. Edinburgh: Edinburgh UP, 2010. Print.

Taylor, Charles. *A Secular Age*. Cambridge, MA: Belknap, 2007. Print.

Ungureanu, Camil. "Aestheticization of Politics and Ambivalence of Self-Sacrifice in Charlie Brooker's *The National Anthem*." *Journal of European Studies* (Spring 2015) (forthcoming).

Ungureanu, Camil. "Bourdieu and Derrida on Gift: Beyond 'Double Truth' and Paradox." *Human Studies* 36.3 (2013): 393–409.

Ungureanu, Camil. "Derrida's Tense Bow." *The European Legacy* 18.6 (2013): 727–39.

Ungureanu, Camil. "Final Remarks: What is the Use of Postsecularism? Conceptual Clarifications and Two Illustrations." *Religion in Contemporary European Cinema: The Postsecular Constellation*. Ed. Costica Bradatan and Camil Ungureanu. New York and London: Routledge, 2014. 199–218. Print.

Ungureanu, Camil. "Uses and Abuses of Post-Secularism: An Introduction." *Democracy, Law and Religious Pluralism in Europe: Secularism and Post-Secularism*. Ed. Ferran Requejo and Camil Ungureanu. London and New York: Routledge, 2014. 1–17. Print.

Wheatley, Catherine. *Caché/Hidden*. London: Palgrave, 2012. Print.

Wheatley, Catherine. *Michael Haneke's Cinema: The Ethic of the Image*. London: Berghahn, 2009. Print.

Yacowar, Maurice. "*Caché* and the Private/Public Secret." *Queen's Quarterly* 113.2 (2006): 224–34. Print.

Žižek, Slavoj. *The Puppet and the Dwarf: The Perverse Core of Christianity*. Cambridge, MA: MIT P, 2003. Print.

jorge bastos da silva

BODIES OF ESTRANGEMENT

mel gibson, sacrifice and history

violence in gibson's oeuvre

Mel Gibson's output as a filmmaker is not impressively large but, for better or worse, it has never left moviegoers and critics indifferent. Apart from his directorial début with *The Man without a Face* (1993), the fairly conventional, mildly sentimental tale of a disfigured man who befriends a boy and helps him with school, the three feature films he has directed so far have been greeted with outrage by some and with enthusiasm by others.

Braveheart (1995) fuelled patriotic feeling in Scotland and, according to Lin Anderson (21–23), is likely to have helped win the referendum which brought forth the re-establishment of the Scottish Parliament in 1999. The film offered a vindication of Scottish identity and a proud commemoration of one of the nation's most distinguished heroes. For a number of viewers south of Hadrian's Wall, however, its depiction of the English as ruthless colonialists sounded predictably offensive and historically false. *The Passion of the Christ* (2004), most notably, gave rise to a controversy which has made it into one of the films most thoroughly discussed – on ethical, historical and theological grounds if not so much, perhaps, in terms of its aesthetic or cinematic qualities – of the last couple of decades. While many viewers have deplored its discrepancies with the Gospel narratives or found its depiction of physical violence unwarrantable, congregations have crowded into pre-booked theatres to watch the movie as part of their religious devotions.

Two issues stand out amid the criticisms levelled at the film. In the first place, the contention has been made that "Gibson did not undertake the necessary homework" (Perry and Schweitzer 10) – that is, he either neglected to study or unwisely dismissed as irrelevant modern biblical exegesis and official documents of the Catholic Church that exonerate the Jews as a whole from supposed deicide and explicitly undermine centuries-old anti-Semitic assumptions. This double problem is often connected with Gibson's belonging to an uncompromising branch of Catholicism that rejects the Second Vatican Council as unsuitably "liberal" and ecumenical.[1]

The second major cause for criticism lies in Gibson's use of violence. While the majority of critics resented what has been described as a "relentless and violent assault on the senses" (Deacy and Ortiz 127), some were prompt to point out that "[t]he criticism of the movie as too violent does not ring completely true for those familiar with the Christian church in its worship" (Johnston, "Dynamic Icon" 63). The undeniable brutality of entire sequences of *The Passion* notwithstanding, in this article I will submit that, far from being gratuitous, violence is integral to Gibson's vision and artistic purposes.

On the whole, the criticisms outlined above amount to the charge that *The Passion* is unsatisfactory, if not outright flawed, aesthetically as much as theologically and historically, and that it provides viewers with an artistic experience that is ethically and spiritually inadequate. My contention is that Gibson's film exacerbates certain aspects of the biblical story for reasons pertaining to a pessimistic view of human nature that can be recognized through the study of his oeuvre as a whole. My aim, therefore, is neither to "exonerate" Gibson nor to join the host of his detractors, but to attempt sympathetically to interpret what is at stake in the bulk of his work.

As far as its impact is concerned, *Apocalypto* (2006) stands almost inevitably as an anticlimax. Following hard upon rather unpleasant revelations concerning Gibson's beliefs and private life, the film has been perceived as strange and ahistorical. Its mixed reception can probably be seen as the result of Gibson's bold decision to further develop some of the strategies put forward in *The Passion*, such as the use of dead languages and the depiction of crude, albeit ritualised, violence, while trying to deliver something of an action movie with blockbuster ambitions. One purpose of my essay is to argue for a balanced assessment that places all three of Gibson's movies within a frame of authorial consequence. To treat Gibson as an *auteur* entails the recognition of a degree of imaginative consistency underlying the body of work he has created in several capacities (in addition to directing, Gibson co-authored the script for *The Passion* and *Apocalypto*; he produced both those films as well as *Braveheart*, in which he also had the main acting role).

Such an interpretive stance involves an acknowledgement that, beginning with *Braveheart* through *The Passion* and on to *Apocalypto*, a certain personal vision unfolds of the nature and significance of human events – a vision that is articulated through the choice of recurring cinematic techniques and visual-thematic motifs. I do not mean to contest what critics have written about *The Passion* in the long polemical aftermath of its première, nor is it my concern to judge whether the author's beliefs have been misplaced. Rather, my argument enjoys the benefit of hindsight – now that we can appreciate the ultimate coherence of what is in effect a trilogy on historical subjects – to highlight the most significant ways in which Gibson's vision is cinematically achieved. Depending on such a vantage point, which most academic (and indeed polemical) writing so far published on *The Passion* has lacked, my assessment of the three films allows me to examine his understanding of history and to suggest that sacrifice is a visual-thematic hallmark of his fiction.[2]

sacrifice and the deputization of guilt

In the animation film *The Miracle Maker* (2000) – released by Icon Productions, which Gibson founded and co-owns – we find the story of Jesus evoked according to the common denominators of Christian teaching (as Jesus approaches, John the Baptist hails him: "Behold! The lamb of God who takes away the sin of the world") as well as couched in terms of religious orthodoxy and political prudence. Jewish authorities voice their concerns about doctrinal matters and a possible uprising instigated by Jesus. The events of Palm Sunday are illustrative in this respect. Whereas Jesus is welcomed enthusiastically into Jerusalem by the common people, members of the Sanhedrin are uneasy, yet Caiphas scolds them and puts their minds at rest: "You know nothing! Nothing at all! Don't you realize that all the might and anger of Caesar can be aimed at one man? At this 'magician' from Nazareth! Let one man die, and all the people will be saved."

The High Priest's intuition of the imperatives of political expediency is a perfect example of the scapegoat mechanism. This has been described by René Girard in the context of his wide-ranging investigations into the problem of evil (cf. *The Scapegoat*; *Violence and the Sacred*). Girard allows us to see sacrifice as a social device by means of which communities are purged of impurity and sin through what we may call *the deputization of guilt*, its transference onto an individual (sometimes a group) that must either be cleansed or eliminated, like tearing a rotten limb from the body of the people. As it informs ritual practice and is embedded in emblematic narratives, sacrifice is central to the fabric of commonality. Voluntarily or not, the scapegoat is a cardinal agent of social cohesion. He affords a sense of justification and belonging.[3] His presence denotes that at the heart of social relationships lies a fundamental piety. In practice, this intimation can coexist with a fine piece of realpolitik such as Caiphas'. His speech in *The Miracle Maker* corresponds almost verbatim to the passage in the Gospel of John (11.47–53) which Girard sees as the clearest statement of the principle that one man must die for the sake of all the others (*Scapegoat* 112–14).[4]

In his own films Gibson goes beyond the stock characters of the action hero and of the scapegoat more fully to explore the meanings of sacrifice, both verbally and graphically. In so doing, he at once establishes sacrifice as the cornerstone of the progression of history as he sees it, and casts a shadow both upon humanistic assumptions regarding the possibility of nonconflictive social relationships and upon the values of secularism which have for the most part underpinned Western modernity since the time of the Enlightenment.

To take Gibson as an *auteur*, that is, to assume a coherence of purpose and of values across the three above-mentioned films, sets upon us the task of describing the physiognomy of their family resemblance. The following features may be briefly enumerated: *Braveheart*, *The Passion* and *Apocalypto* inculcate a sense of history as liturgy, or, to put it another way, as fundamentally dependent on defining acts of ritualization; they betray a distrust of the institutions of power, positing instead the primacy of the individuals' integrity and the merits of spontaneous affection between them and their natural or chosen community, be it family, clan or nation; they engage in the representation of violent action in hyper-realistic mode and (increasingly, from *Braveheart* to *Apocalypto*) by experimenting with exotic languages which estrange the viewer from the enactment; they share an authorial vision at the centre of which lies the ultimately religious question of death and transcendence (equated either with the resurrection of the individual or with the continuity of a family or an ethnic group).

Given such a context, the cinematic realization of Gibson's vision is overlaid in terms of political and ideological dramatization. Even as they explore different civilizational backgrounds, all three films depict peoples in conflict: Celts (Scots and Irish) vs. English in *Braveheart*; Jews and Romans in *The Passion* (or, seen through the prism of religion, Jewish, Proto-Christian and Pagan affiliations); the Mayas and other Mesoamerican peoples in *Apocalypto*. Moreover, all films present stories of imperialism and resistance, dramatically compounded by acts of sadism, arbitrary policies, feats of courage, and ties of solidarity. Given the diversity of cultural contexts evoked, one suspects that the director is hinting that all worldviews and all forms of social life are either founded upon or otherwise centrally define themselves by means of acts of sacrifice, either of their own members, of enemies or ideological adversaries, or of a divine figure. Some contemporary philosophers would certainly concede the point. In a recent book, Simon Critchley confutes the assumption that modernity itself is tantamount to secularism, stressing instead:

> I do not see the relation between religion and politics in terms of some purported passage or even progress from the pre-modern to the modern, where religion would be that unwelcome pre-modern residue in modern political life. Rather than seeing modernity in terms of a process of secularization, I

> will claim that the history of political forms can best be viewed as a series of *metamorphoses of sacralization.* (10; see also 84)

While Critchley's point is obviously not commensurate with the one famously made by Ernest Renan in his essay "What is a Nation?," it is nonetheless worth noticing a tacit analogy with the latter's understanding of what it is that constitutes that modern political construct par excellence: "A nation is a great solidarity created by the sentiment of the sacrifices which have been made and those which one is disposed to make in the future" (*apud* MacMillan 81–82). This quasi-definition (there are nuances in Renan's argument which lie outside my compass at present) makes it clear that conflict and its ritualization are indelible components of nation building.

themes of power and conflict

The emphasis on situations of national or ethnic conflict can be seen as a function not only of Gibson's interest in history but also of his apparent suspicion of formal institutions. In all three films, one finds an indictment of power as self-serving and corrupt. On the whole, of course, the plots hardly allow for moral ambivalence, as they are largely set in a good-vs.-evil framework (that there is no real indeterminacy is corroborated by the probable impact of *Braveheart* on Scottish patriotism, as mentioned above). But the stories specifically target those in power as cruel and devoid of scruples. Of Edward the Longshanks, the first thing we are told and shown in *Braveheart* is how he treacherously invited the Scottish nobles to talk of a truce and had them all hanged – a vision of horror for young Wallace. Rather surprisingly, Pilate is granted a measure of conscientiousness and sympathy in *The Passion*, but the indignity and inhumaneness of professional soldiers – willing, sadistic oppressors – is tangible in all three movies and nowhere as plain as in this. King Herod, on the other hand, is depicted as decadent and despicable, not unlike the pitifully ineffective Prince of Wales and his effeminate entourage in *Braveheart*. Finally, in *Apocalypto* the King and Queen of the Maya preside over the killing and beheading of prisoners as acts of atonement to the gods. The sacrifice is carried out by the High Priest with unmistakable gusto.

An important subset of figures of power is indeed the priests. In this case, a development is noticeable across Gibson's films. *Braveheart* is punctuated by rituals of many kinds: we witness burials, weddings, Wallace being knighted, his trial and execution; furthermore, battles and truces are, to an extent, also ritualized events. Apart from the wedding of the Prince of Wales at the start of the film, though, priests are always seen on the side of the Scots – absolving the fighters before the battle at Stirling, performing funeral rites and weddings (significantly, Wallace and Murron are secretly married by a priest in the forest at night to avoid the outrage of *prima nocte*).

In *The Passion*, on the other hand, it is the priests who demand that Jesus be crucified; they effectively exact the order of execution from a reluctant Pilate. And when Jesus is being scourged by the Roman soldiers, many of those present look away in disgust and horror. Significantly, the script draws a distinction between "punire" and "castigare," making it clear that such flagellation is abnormal, that it is being performed with excessive zest and zeal. Most rabbis stare sternly on, as Satan walks among them.

In *Apocalypto*, the role of the priesthood is similar: they capitalize on mass hysteria in order to perpetuate a morally corrupt aristocracy. Turning the anxiety and gullibility of the common people to their advantage, the High Priest rehearses the concept of a manifest destiny of sorts. Addressing the people from the top of the pyramid, he proclaims:

> These are the days of our great lament. The land thirsts. A great plague infests our crops. The scourge of sickness afflicts us at whim. They say this strife has made us weak. That we have become empty. They say that we rot. Great people of the banner of the sun, I say we are strong. We are a people of destiny. Destined to be the

> masters of time. Destined to be nearest to the gods. Mighty Kukulkan! whose fury could scorch this earth to oblivion – let us appease you with this sacrifice. To exalt you in your glory. To make our people prosper. To prepare for your return.

Then, turning to the terror-stricken victim that is brought to the post: "Warrior, unafraid and willing! With your blood you renew the world! From age to age. Thanks be to you" – and he sticks the knife into the victim's chest and takes out his heart to show it to the cheering crowd, announcing that it is "The heart of god!" He then places the heart on embers for the augur to examine. The whole procedure is plainly opportunistic. Sacrifice seems like a foregone conclusion for Jaguar Paw, but it is prevented by an eclipse – and both in sacrifice and in the suspension of sacrifice the manipulative nature of the power of king and priests is perceptible.

In *The Passion* and *Apocalypto*, therefore, religious ceremonial is adjudged corrupt, implicitly (inasmuch as it is not actually stated on the verbal level) but with the visual obviousness of enacted drama. There is evident condemnation of ecclesiastical power and, strangely enough, perhaps, for someone with Gibson's Catholic background, clear misgivings about priestly intercession. Meanwhile, the indictment of formal or ritual mediation throws into relief one paradox of sacrifice which applies to Wallace, Jesus and Jaguar Paw alike: in some respects, slaughtering is enshrining; heroes are made *and* unmade through sacrifice.[5] Moreover, they survive it, either literally or symbolically, thereby ensuring the salvation of others, the continuity and regeneration of that community which is meaningful to them and which, to an extent, defines itself through bonds of blood. In the case of *Braveheart*, one may go so far as to say that Wallace's sacrifice is instrumental in turning the Scots from an ethnic group into a nation. Wallace is betrayed by the elder Bruce and other noblemen into the hands of Longshanks. Later, when Robert the Bruce takes up the standard of liberty that was Wallace's, he addresses the men on the battlefield with the following words: "You have bled with Wallace! Now bleed with me." And they charge to cries of "Wallace!" Robert holds the thistle-embroidered cloth given to Wallace by Murron which represents Scotland (cf. Anderson 84, 92–93). The film ends with the sound of Gibson's voice – Wallace, as it were, summing up his legacy from beyond the grave, stating that the Scots "won their freedom". Additionally, the fanciful notion that the future King of England is Wallace's son plays upon the logic of displacement and substitution with a vengeance. It also coheres with the theme of fertility vs. the wasteland that structures much of the action and imagery of *Apocalypto*.

As noted above, *The Passion* suggests an economy of expiation and atonement which has aroused critics' reservations. Commentators have objected that "[t]he degree of violence expended on the body of Jesus helps marginalize the rest of his life and teachings, and allows only the briefest, final moment for the resurrection" (Morgan 89). There certainly is some unintended irony in the fact that more notable resurrections occur in *Braveheart* and *Apocalypto*. Besides, a comparison with *The Miracle Maker* is instructive and appears to add strength to that line of criticism. It is only after four-fifths of the total length of *The Miracle Maker* that one sees traces of physical violence, as Jesus appears carrying the cross with blood trickling down his head and robe. This is followed by Jesus' crucifixion, his death and the ensuing prodigies, the deposition from the cross, burial, and finally resurrection. All this is covered in less than fifteen minutes, and in fact the resurrection and the sequences showing Jesus coming to the apostles after his death and appointing them their respective missions take up more time than the preceding Stages of the Cross, the final message of the film clearly being one of hope. Moreover, it is worth noticing that, unlike *The Passion*, in *The Miracle Maker* Jesus' suffering is not offered as a spectacle at all. Apart from the soldiers who surround him, on his way to Calvary Jesus is very much alone, there being no grieving mother, no distressed followers and no moved bystanders. However, after he rises again he is shown repeatedly to be in close contact with the apostles.

In turn, *Apocalypto* essays variations on the topic of substitutionary sacrifice. One such variation hinges upon the symbolic identity of the protagonist, Jaguar Paw, and his basic, vital connection with the life of the jungle. At a certain stage of his run back from the Mayan city, Jaguar Paw is chased by a jaguar on account of a perceived threat to its cub (incidentally, a good example of *agape*). As the jaguar is on the verge of catching him, and just as Jaguar Paw is about to be struck down by an enemy, their paths intersect, so that the jaguar kills the Mayan pursuer and ends up being killed by the other warriors. It effectively saves Jaguar Paw by dying in his stead. Arguably, it stands for the victimization of the jungle and its people – and for their resilience and their ability to fight back.[6]

Resurrection can thus be construed as either real or figurative: it operates by transference to Bruce in the case of Wallace; it is literal for Jesus; it involves a complex interplay of substitutionary and balancing equivalences for Jaguar Paw. In each and every case it is connected with the affirmation of a community and warrants its continuity in time. Sacrifice, either carried out or (in the case of Jaguar Paw) eluded, is associated with the glorification of the hero, the fulfilment of a personal destiny and the justification of the oppressed. *Apocalypto* is especially rich in this respect. In addition to the aspects mentioned above, it is worth noticing the predicament of Jaguar Paw's family. When the Holcane warriors attack, Jaguar Paw hides his wife and son in a deep chasm in the ground. Although they are safe from the aggressors, Seven and Turtles Run are unable to climb out and they are in danger of death when it starts raining heavily and the pit is shown to be the point of convergence of the waters, a natural sinkhole. Jaguar Paw has unwittingly left his family in a place which becomes reminiscent of a *cenote*. *Cenotes* are deep pits or caves with water into which the sacrificial victims' mangled bodies were thrown by the Mayas.[7] The situation of Seven and Turtles Run is in effect symmetrical with Jaguar Paw's on top of the Mayan pyramid, and it parallels the moments of katabasis in Jaguar Paw's forced pilgrimage – his passage through a tunnel on the way to the execution, then his falling on an open mass grave, his plunge into a waterfall and getting caught in quicksand (this provides him with camouflage that makes him as black as the jaguar).[8] The pit is an alternative netherworld in which the salvation of Jaguar Paw's family is represented by the birth of a new child in the womb of the jungle. Because it offers rebirth instead of annihilation, the near-sacrifice imposed by the jungle contrasts with the actual sacrifice – which amounts to genocide and nothing more – on the altars of the Mayan gods. The film closes with Jaguar Paw turning his back on both the Mayas and the Spaniards who are arriving on boats: "We should go to the forest. To seek a new beginning," he says as he carries his newborn son in his arms, and he tells Turtles Run to follow.

Hence, insistence on situations of ethnic or national conflict underlies the fundamentally agonistic (in both senses of the word) take on ethics and politics that we come to recognize as characteristic of Gibson's filmography. Power tends to be depicted as the ability or the ambition to take advantage of others, namely through a mechanism of surrogate victimage involving either aggression or manipulation or both; and the persistence of morality depends on the integrity of the individual who takes a stand against such assault. The showiness of the vicious contrasts with the composed, unassuming behaviour of the upholder of the values of continuity and renewal, often in garb as well as in demeanour. The exponent of righteousness may be subjected to ruthless abuse of his body and his dignity, but he is remarkable for a certain assured tranquillity which reflects inner peace.

sacrifice, aggression and *agape*

Villains are notorious not only for their viciousness but also for their lust – lust for power and for flesh. The meekness of the good involves a completely different kind of sensuality which is compatible with the spirit of self-giving.

Melanie J. Wright has commented shrewdly on one particular moment in Gibson's re-enactment of the *via dolorosa*: "With a rasping breath," she remarks, Jesus "reaches out towards the cross, which is close by. His cherishing touch suggests a tactile pleasure is to be found in its surfaces [...] Jesus strains forward and embraces the cross: it is a moment of sensuality and intimacy, before the deathwards journey resumes" (167). Similar overtones may be detected in *Braveheart*. Wallace's execution stands out so much in the texture of the film that the viewer is apt to forget that it is neither the only nor the first instance of sacrifice. Wallace's return to Scotland and his encounter with Murron after a number of years are marked by a pungent display of abnegation by a female character who remains unnamed. The English lord puts an end to the joy of a wedding party by bursting in with soldiers to claim his right of *prima nocte*, granted by Longshanks as a way of luring noblemen of a certain type into moving to Scotland. The (in fact) wrong of *prima nocte* satisfies lust on the personal and represents oppression on the political level (the lord may be said to invade the wedding party). The groom is ready to fight, but the bride prevents him; and there is a dignified, if sad, sensuality – a kind of appeasement of herself and others – in the way she conciliates her husband and removes one soldier's dagger from his neck in slow, concentrated gestures which resemble Jesus' "intimacy" with the cross. Like Jesus, the bride embraces her fate in an attitude of quiet triumphalism, imbued with an assurance of the moral superiority of the martyr, thereby endowing sacrifice with a particular meaningfulness. Clearly, the bride stands for compassion and resignation – for *agape*. Conversely, *eros* is on the side of the aggressor. This contrast is in keeping with the overall dualistic set-up of Gibson's films.

The demands of *agape* figure prominently in all three movies. They range from acts of radical self-denial and anxiety for the loved ones to God's teardrop for the death of his son at the end of *The Passion*. The relationship between fathers and sons is indeed an important topic, and so are weddings and marriages. Young Murron's gift of a thistle to the grieving Wallace defines the character of a relationship that will retain traces of innocence and shyness even after their wedding night. By contrast, *eros* is associated with rape (even if legal, as *prima nocte*), with decadence in the case of King Herod's court, and with the lewd relish of the Maya High Priest in the kill. It is clearly depicted as abusive and unjust. Furthermore, while *agape* furthers a sense of collectivity and continuity, *eros* thrives on the exclusion or the oppression of some individuals. It may not be too far-fetched to suggest that there is a graphic correlation between the emotions of *eros*, as setting apart person from person, and tearing the body asunder, on the one hand, and *agape* as the process of *re-membering*, of retrieving a sense of togetherness and simultaneously of redeeming the integrity of the self, on the other. The two, of course, can and do coexist as facets of one and the same story or event. *The Passion* shows us Jesus' suffering touching some of his executioners, who are disturbed and perhaps converted from their inhumaneness to feelings of compassion, and intercuts the crucifixion with the Last Supper, in which he institutes communion – to be followed, of course, by the risen body after death.

An antithetic argument is inscribed into the films from the very start. The titles of the movies are clearly charged, pointing to the extreme, imminently spiritual character of the situations depicted. Moreover, Gibson makes use of epigraphs which encapsulate a set of judgments upon history, and indeed a sense of historical justice. *The Passion* opens with a title-card quoting from Isaiah 53: "He was wounded for our transgressions, crushed for our iniquities; by His wounds we are healed." This is followed by a date: "700 BC" – a symptomatic detail which suggests a teleology of history: centuries before the birth of the Christ it was possible for the wisest, or perhaps for the inspired, to anticipate the events of the Passion. In a similar fashion, at the start of *Apocalypto* the viewer is offered an aphoristic statement from the historian Will Durant: "A great civilization is not conquered from without until it has destroyed itself from within." In the case of *Braveheart* one does not find an epigraph as such, but Gibson makes use of a device which amounts to one. The film opens with Robert the Bruce's voiceover, cautioning: "Historians from England will say I am a liar. But history is written by those who have hanged heroes." The claim is typical of Gibson's narratives in so far as they rely on their own ability to construct meaningful, and indeed moral, renditions of historical events while dispensing with strict adherence to the cognitive methods of history proper.

It is revealing that *Braveheart* begins with so blatant a dismissal of history as a discipline of inquiry based on the judicious examination of evidence from the past. In effect, regardless of the quotation in *Apocalypto* or of the claims to literal rendering of the Gospel narratives made on behalf of *The Passion*,[9] these films amount to self-authorizing narratives (in that they depend on, and rather spectacularly convey, a sufficiently coherent understanding of the situation of the individual and of communities in history) more than rely on a proven commitment to documentary fidelity or textual accuracy. Gibson's oeuvre foregrounds the conviction that human experience is patterned in accordance with mythical, anthropological assumptions and archetypal narrative structures whose seemingly universal validity is suggested by the presentation of cross-cultural analogues in successive films. In other words, his work reflects the belief that the history of peoples and of individuals is plotted, and that its plot points to transcendence.

To view history as having sacrifice as its centre is to view history as a surface where the reification of religion takes place, to postulate a religious rationale (not necessarily orthodox, i.e., in accordance with mainstream theology or pastoral convention) for the array of human events. Such vision amounts to a sublimation of history, that is to say, to the detection of a meaning or a *telos* that bears upon the transcendence of history proper, upon the (ultimately personal) realm of spirituality. Gibson never sets aside the historical scaffolding, but while history provides the flesh, it is never the spirit of his artistic vision. Which means that those who judge *The Passion* by criteria of historical accuracy are not necessarily wrong, yet they subscribe to an epistemology that is different from Gibson's more "inspirational" stance.

Indeed, Gibson's worldview as reflected in his films would appear to be ultimately anti-historical in so far as the science of history rests upon the interpretation of evidence which is intrinsic to the circumstances and events lived by human societies in time; conversely, Gibson's plots invariably suggest an interpretive grid that looks beyond the actual and the circumstantial while pointing to an externality situated in the domain of ideology – or faith. At the same time, it is through history (even if it is finally discarded), through his kind of history making, that the tangibility of truth is perceived – as an imaginative reconstruction, that is, which does not fear to face the reproach of the "positivistic" or the factually minded.

Neither the procedures involved in this position nor the cultural status of its products are unique. Referring to works like Erich Maria Remarque's *All Quiet on the Western Front* and Margaret Mitchell's *Gone with the Wind* as formative of the memory of important historical events, Astrid Erll notes:

> Fictional media, such as novels and feature films, are characterized by their power to shape the collective imagination of the past in a way that is truly fascinating for the literary scholar (and somewhat alarming for the historian) [...] Historical accuracy is not one of the concerns of such "memory-making" novels and movies; instead, they cater to the public with what is variously termed "authenticity" or "truthfulness". They create images of the past which resonate with cultural memory. (389)

"Authenticity" and "truthfulness," it is important to add, are not primarily aesthetic qualities but rather conditions of a consensus which obtains between author and audience on the basis of an assurance of shared assumptions. They depend on a persuasion regarding a largely unspoken worldview which is distinct from the pursuits (admittedly also grounded in precepts of interpersonal authentication) of historiographic inquiry.

the composition of sacrifice: verbal and visual

In Gibson's films, the point of sublimation of history is the scene of sacrifice. As purveyor of trans-historical significance and (for some viewers) in the striking crudity of its visual realism alike, the scene of sacrifice is *in excess* of the meaning of the plot. This quality of excess is all the more evident as a pattern can be discerned across Gibson's historical pictures. The scene of sacrifice is made up of a relatively constant set of visual and narrative components. One aspect is obviously the stridency of the suffering that has been so much remarked upon, especially with respect to *The Passion*. No matter how elaborate the surrounding elements happen to be, the rawness adopted for the depiction of the actual immolation (with the partial exception of *Braveheart*, where the execution of Wallace is not shown in all its gory detail) underlines the corporeality of the human condition – arguably, as a somewhat morbid strategy for highlighting the transcendental implications of solidarity and sacrifice. The corporeal embeddedness of moral sublimity (or pseudo-sublimity, in the case of *Apocalypto*) is expressed in the symbolism of the heart, which is evoked in the title of the first film and is central to the ritual of the Mayas. As for *The Passion*, Jesus says as the flagellation is about to begin: "My heart is ready, Father. My heart is ready"; and Mary calls him "Flesh of my flesh, heart of my heart."

On the other hand, in all three films sacrificial victims are executed with their arms outstretched.[10] The pervasiveness of this posture may be taken as revealing of the centrality of the story of Christ in the director's imaginary.[11] The posture of outstretched arms and exposed torso makes it clear that the victims are defenceless in the hands of their executioners. At the same time, it allows the director to explore the situation of the victims in a particular way. *The Passion* and *Apocalypto* feature point-of-view shots which emphasize the helplessness of the victims by bringing their experience closer to the audience.[12] A direct interpellation of the spectatorial experience is at work when the audience is offered an immersive view which subjects the visual field to the gaze of the victim, a strategy presumably capable of eliciting stronger sympathetic response. For a moment, it is as if a portion of the sacrifice were being performed on each and every member of the audience.[13] The striving for the personalization of suffering provides a new context for Susan Sontag's remark: "No 'we' should be taken for granted when the subject is looking at other people's pain" (6). It is possible to speculate that this amounts to an important, specifically cinematic instance of *catharsis*.[14] Furthermore, just as they visually present the victims' ordeal by facing the audience with an immediacy of affliction (reinforced by auditive impressions such as heavy breathing), those shots convey a judgment on the situation, for as they associate the perspective of the viewer with that of the lying victim they evince the fact that the world is upside-down (the theme of cosmic disarray is concurrently pressed on the viewer of *Apocalypto* by the eclipse). The composition in *Braveheart* is simpler, where the subjective shot is limited to the vision of Murron in the crowd and we do not get the inverted view.

On a larger scale, the emphasis on corporeality engenders a staging of sacrifice in which both the slaying and the slain may undergo transfigurations. In *Braveheart*, even if the magistrate remains solemn and hieratic, or alternatively affects a countenance of compassion, executioners wear masks. Wallace is "purified by pain." We watch him being hanged and racked, faced three times (in a Christ-like manner) with the temptation to ask for mercy, and beheaded. Robert the Bruce narrates the rest in voiceover: "After the beheading, William Wallace's body was torn to pieces. His head was set on London Bridge, his arms and legs sent to the four corners of Britain as a warning." A pointed depiction of Jesus' flesh being savagely torn from his torso is provided in *The Passion*; he bleeds, he is nailed to the cross, and, finally and most importantly, he resurrects, the nail hole in his right hand plainly visible. In *Apocalypto*, not only the Holcane warriors but the people of the village too are adorned with tattoos and piercings, scars and elaborate hairdos. There is, however, a gradation, for the garishness of the Mayas is more extreme. The figures of priests are overwrought with jewellery (a visual indication of their complicity with the royal family) and zoomorphic masks in a grand totemic display that is obviously meant to fill the common people with awe (whereas for the moviegoer it may simply make the beastliness of their function all the more vivid). Some of the priests have their skin dyed yellow, red and green. As for those who are consigned to sacrifice, a grim transfiguration takes place even before death and mutilation: as if to match the flamboyant look of the priests, their bodies are dyed blue by the crowd as if grotesquely anointed.

Strategies amounting to the prefiguration of the sacrifice are another important ingredient in the composition of all three films. Prefiguration serves the purpose of intensification of the drama as the action signals forward to the climactic moment. Prior to Wallace's execution, jesters mime the several torments and desecrations. Jesus faces his fate with full awareness of the physical suffering and the humiliation, and the viewer is also forewarned of the horrific nature of crucifixion by witnessing the hesitation of Pilate and the anguish in the faces of Mary and Magdalen. Besides, *The Passion* is a special film in this respect, because few spectators – at least in the West – are unfamiliar with the Crucifixion. They may be assumed to be picturing the end from the very start. As for *Apocalypto*, the anticipatory function is discharged through the concourse of several factors. The film opens with a tapir hunt in which several men of the village are engaged. In contrast to Maya ritual, the sole purpose of the kill is to secure food. A knife through the heart finishes off the tapir after it has been caught in a trap. The heart is the first organ to be handed out and it is prized as a token of accomplishment. Later, as the captives reach the city of the Maya, severed heads can be seen on spikes and in large pots. The frantic chanting and dancing of the populace may be deemed ominous. More decisively, the captives themselves begin to adumbrate their fate when they see murals representing the slaying of men covered in blue pigment.

There is a verbal contribution to the build-up of anxiety through mention of the topic of fear in all three films. In the foreshadowing of the sacrifice the visual aspect is nonetheless paramount, just as it is in the graphic enactment of the sacrifice itself. After *Braveheart*, where the smashing of heads and the hacking-off of limbs in the field of battle abound but the gruesome details of Wallace's dismemberment and evisceration are not fully acted out on screen, Gibson is consistent in his choice of a narrative style that pre-empts *telling* (namely the description of violence) in favour of *showing*. That he strives for realism is obvious. That this realism has proved disturbing to viewers is deserving of commentary. Gibson's directorial style may be said to depend upon two basic strategies. On the one hand, it involves offering the audience a bewildering spectacle of violence. On the other hand, it involves the use of dead and remote languages.

Both strategies may be supposed to aim at defamiliarizing the figures and events portrayed for the viewer. They contravene the soporific character of conventional, expected depictions (e.g., syrupy or sentimental representations of Jesus). They substitute a strong, at times almost expressionistic, vision for the redundancy of complacent and deflated perceptions. Arguably, this drive is all the more valuable as the film industry very often deals with the theme of sacrifice in terms of caricature, as can be seen in Steven Spielberg's *Indiana Jones and the Temple of Doom*; of trivialization, as in Norman Jewison's apologetic, pop-kitsch *Jesus Christ Superstar*; or of bold but blatantly unrealistic recontextualization, as in the comic book world of Sam Raimi's *Spider-Man 2*, where the hero becomes a Christ-like figure.

In fact, we are able to locate the aporia of artistic realism when we become aware that verisimilitude (and hence one particular index of credibility) has to do with abiding by or satisfying the audience's expectations and worldview. The premises of mimesis match the premises of spectatorship – there is certainly a protocol of representing and a protocol of viewing – and this is something that Gibson's films deliberately and significantly challenge.[15] How much stylization or aestheticization is needed to achieve an effect of naturalism is a question that must ultimately be addressed. One hint may be found in the fact that, in *The Passion*, it is Gibson's own hand that hammers in the first nail through Jesus' flesh (cf. Levine 146). The imputation is clear. As artistic object, the film is not independent from the author, it is rather a testimony of his personal commitment; the author is implicated in a very material way, he partakes of the offence and of the guilt. Christ's redemptive agency, therefore, must also operate on Gibson's behalf.

A second instance of the complication of visual messages which is allowed to erupt amidst the stark presentational realism that dominates *The Passion* (and another feature which is connected with the imagery of the body) is the androgynous appearance of Satan. Satan provides a visual articulation of the spiritual allegory of the film along lines that are absent from *Braveheart* and that only surface in the occurrence of the eclipse in the case of *Apocalypto*. Such characters and events suggest the metaphysical entanglements of human history. Satan's androgyny, in particular, is, apart from the tear from Heaven, the most striking figurative departure from the Gospels. Moreover, the picture of Satan carrying his–her grotesque offspring constitutes a monstrous icon of motherhood, an almost burlesque parody of Mary's suffering for her son, of her com-passion. The presentation of Satan as an anti-*Pietà*, regularly pitted against Mary by the editing, is revealing of the aesthetic insufficiency of the very realism that constitutes the fundamental texture of the film.

Again, a shift is noticeable in the order of the films as far as languages are concerned. There is very little speech in *Braveheart* that requires translation, although the characters occasionally speak Latin, French and Gaelic in addition to English. In *The Passion* they speak Aramaic and Latin, and in *Apocalypto* they speak Mayan. This is not simply a matter of verisimilitude or historical picturesqueness, and it is certainly more than a veering towards ever more pronounced exoticism. The contrast of languages is at once a function of the characters' personal and ethnic identity, and it contributes to the viewer's recognition of the situations depicted as defined by acts of violence (such as looting and colonization) and heroism (based upon a sense of being and belonging that entails availability for self-sacrifice). The clash of languages mirrors the clash of peoples: it manifests the mutual incommensurability of the alterities in conflict. This is the thematic significance of the use of Latin or Mayan. But, more importantly perhaps, the remoteness of the languages constrains ordinary viewers to rely on subtitling. The near-opacity of the verbal constituent implies a focus on the visual.[16] It is correlative with the physicality and the visual concreteness of the filmic presentation, the intensity of which often seems to be designed to shock the viewer into alertness.

Gibson's films (quite literally) take pains to emphasize the perverseness and brutality of the extremities of human existence. They do so by adopting a mode of cinematic realism which goes beyond the degree of violence usually deemed to be acceptable in the art of cinema. This breach of artistic decorum is congruent with Gibson's depiction of history as the interplay between unbearable, yet sometimes inescapable, circumstances and the chances of redemption and regeneration. The marked physicality of the presentation is responsible for a presumed effect of defamiliarization for the viewer as a result of which the uncanny and the sublime – the feeling of estrangement, perhaps even of revulsion, giving rise to the ability to see anew – are made to converge. At the centre of this dialectics lies the act of sacrifice, either of self or of others. The consideration of transcendence translates formally into the scene of sacrifice as a recurring motif that stands out conspicuously in the sequential narrative. The dramatic and symbolic privileging of sacrifice denotes Gibson's readiness to subject historical interpretation to a moral and aesthetic framework. To the extent that his films have documentary value, they do so at least as much regarding Gibson's personal vision as regarding the historical or pseudo-historical situations they ostensibly mean to portray.

notes

1 On Gibson's upbringing and his family's values, see Pendreigh 25–28; Clarkson 15–17, 30–38, 194–201.

2 The attention paid by critics to the imaginative continuities and the reciprocal imbrications of Gibson's three films has been scarce. Mitchell and Plate (345) and Ortiz (117) are exceptions.

3 If one may resort to a pun that has become familiar, atonement entails at-one-ment.

4 In the context of Christianity, however, Girard's general points on sacrifice as a pillar of the social imaginary need to be qualified in light of Easter. David Bentley Hart aptly remarks that

> Christ is condemned to death by the duly appointed authorities of his age, whose verdicts are no more than proper exercises of political prudence and responsible governance. And the crucifixion is an expression of a particular sort of social equilibrium; it is a perfect epitome of the legal, religious, and political rationality by which human society sustains and justifies itself. Yet God's verdict entirely reverses that of Christ's judges [...] Easter reveals that divine justice is on the side of the particular, the rejected, the victim we are willing to offer up to the greater good. (486)

5 This ambivalence is close, but not exactly identical, to the one Girard phrases like this: "Because the victim is sacred, it is criminal to kill him – but the victim is sacred only because he is to be killed" (*Violence* 1).

6 One may hazard the interpretation that one element of Maya mythology in particular is layered into the story. According to Karl Taube, "[t]he name of the ancient sun god was *Kinich Ahau*, Sun-Faced Lord, a powerful being closely identified with the jaguar. It seems that this god transformed into a jaguar during his nightly journey through the underworld" (53). It may be deemed paradoxical, however, that Jaguar Paw is spared ritual sacrifice because of a solar eclipse.

7 The rain god Chaach of Maya mythology, on whose behalf it is believed that the bodies of the slain were ritually placed in *cenotes*, is also connected with the jaguar (see Meletinsky 195).

8 The descent into the underworld is a motif shared by many strands of mythology. It is connected with initiation or immortality (namely metempsychosis) or both. According to Mircea Eliade, "to descend into hell amounts to undergoing 'initiation death', an experience that may found a new mode of being." The cave is the place of divine epiphany par excellence, "the place where, after a period in hiding, there is the apparition of a saviour god, a prophet or a cosmocrat" (36, 38; my translations). For examples of this motif in film, see Holtsmark.

9 In the documentary *By His Wounds, We Are Healed: Making* The Passion of the Christ, included in the *Passion* DVD, Gibson asserts that there is "very little deviation from the synoptic Gospels."

10 This was noticed of Wallace in *Braveheart* by Pendreigh (213–14) even before the release of the other two movies.

11 In the case of *Apocalypto*, this displacement of the visual idiom of the Crucifixion is paralleled by the appropriation of a Christian referent in the title.

12 Mark Goodacre points out the originality of this strategy in the context of Christ biopics (43).

13 According to Robert K. Johnston's assessment, Gibson's goal in *The Passion* "was to deglamorize events that have become idealized by providing a visceral experience of their horror" (*Reel Spirituality* 154).

14 Through such shots, it may be argued as well, *The Passion* replicates the schemata of the *imitatio Christi* by means of its own technical devices, and opens up new territories to the "revered gaze" which Alison Griffiths connects with a tradition of seeing the Crucifixion that harks back to medieval iconography.

15 The question is discussed by Stephen Prince with regard to the presentation of violence in *The Passion*.

16 As has already been noted by commentators of *The Passion* (see Apostolos-Cappadona 107–08; Wright 167) and as acknowledged by Gibson in the documentary *By His Wounds, We Are Healed*.

bibliography

Anderson, Lin. Braveheart: *From Hollywood to Holyrood*. Edinburgh: Luath, 2004. Print.

Apostolos-Cappadona, Diane. "On Seeing *The Passion*: Is there a Painting in this Film? Or is this Film a Painting?" Plate 97–108. Print.

Clarkson, Wensley. *Mel Gibson: Man on a Mission*. London: Blake, 2005. Print.

Critchley, Simon. *The Faith of the Faithless: Experiments in Political Theology*. London: Verso, 2012. Print.

Deacy, Christopher, and Gaye Williams Ortiz. *Theology and Film: Challenging the Sacred/Secular Divide*. Malden, MA: Blackwell, 2008. Print.

Eliade, Mircea. *De Zalmoxis à Gengis-Khan. Études comparatives sur les religions et le folklore de la Dacie et de l'Europe orientale*. Paris: Payot, 1970. Print.

Erll, Astrid. "Literature, Film, and the Mediality of Cultural Memory." *Cultural Memory Studies: An International and Interdisciplinary Handbook*. Ed. Astrid Erll and Ansgar Nünning in collaboration with Sara B. Young. Berlin: De Gruyter, 2010. 389–98. Print.

Girard, René. *The Scapegoat*. 1986. Trans. Yvonne Freccero. Baltimore: Johns Hopkins UP, 1989. Print.

Girard, René. *Violence and the Sacred*. Trans. Patrick Gregory. Baltimore: Johns Hopkins UP, 1979. Print.

Goodacre, Mark. "The Power of *The Passion*: Reacting and Over-Reacting to Gibson's Artistic Vision." *Jesus and Mel Gibson's* The Passion of the Christ: *The Film, the Gospels and the Claims of History*. Ed. Kathleen E. Corley and Robert L. Webb. London: Continuum, 2004. 28–44. Print.

Griffiths, Alison. "The Revered Gaze: The Medieval Imaginary of Mel Gibson's *The Passion of the Christ*." *Cinema Journal* 46.2 (2007): 3–39. Print.

Hart, David Bentley. "Death, Final Judgment, and the Meaning of Life." *The Oxford Handbook of Eschatology*. Ed. Jerry L. Walls. Oxford: Oxford UP, 2008. 476–89. Print.

Holtsmark, Erling B. "The *Katabasis* Theme in Modern Cinema." *Bucknell Review* 35.1 (1991): 60–80. Print.

Johnston, Robert K. "*The Passion* as Dynamic Icon: A Theological Reflection." Plate 55–70. Print.

Johnston, Robert K. *Reel Spirituality: Theology and Film in Dialogue*. 2nd ed. Grand Rapids, MI: Baker, 2006. Print.

Levine, Amy-Jill. "Mel Gibson, the Scribes, and the Pharisees." Plate 137–49. Print.

MacMillan, Margaret. *The Uses and Abuses of History*. London: Profile, 2010. Print.

Meletinsky, Eleazar M. *The Poetics of Myth*. 1998. Trans. Guy Lanoue and Alexandre Sadetsky. New York: Routledge, 2000. Print.

Mitchell, Jolyon, and S. Brent Plate. "Viewing and Writing on *The Passion of the Christ*." *The Religion and Film Reader*. Ed. Jolyon Mitchell and S. Brent Plate. New York: Routledge, 2007. 343–47. Print.

Morgan, David. "Catholic Visual Piety and *The Passion of the Christ*." Plate 85–96. Print.

Ortiz, Gaye W. "'Passion'-Ate Women: The Female Presence in *The Passion of the Christ*." Plate 109–20. Print.

Pendreigh, Brian. *Mel Gibson and his Movies*. London: Bloomsbury, 1997. Print.

Perry, Marvin, and Frederick M. Schweitzer. "The Medieval Passion Play Revisited." Plate 3–19. Print.

Plate, S. Brent, ed. *Re-viewing the Passion: Mel Gibson's Film and its Critics*. New York: Palgrave, 2004. Print.

Prince, Stephen. "Beholding Blood Sacrifice in *The Passion of the Christ*: How Real is Movie Violence?" *Film Quarterly* 59.4 (2006). 11–22. Print.

Sontag, Susan. *Regarding the Pain of Others*. London: Penguin, 2004. Print.

Taube, Karl. *Aztec and Maya Myths*. 1993. London: British Museum P, 2009. Print.

Wright, Melanie J. *Religion and Film: An Introduction*. London: Tauris, 2007. Print.

filmography

Braveheart. Dir. Mel Gibson. Icon Productions/Ladd Company, 1995. DVD.

Apocalypto. Dir. Mel Gibson. Icon Productions/ Touchstone Pictures, 2006. DVD.

The Miracle Maker. Dir. Stanislav Sokolov and Derek Hayes. Ffilmian S4C Films/British Screen/ Icon Entertainment International/BBC Cymru Wales, 2000. DVD.

The Passion of the Christ. Dir. Mel Gibson. Icon Productions, 2004. DVD.

PART TWO

sacrifice, transcendence, self-transcendence

FAITH, SACRIFICE, AND THE EARTH'S GLORY IN TERRENCE MALICK'S *THE TREE OF LIFE*

george b. handley

introduction

This essay attempts to read Terrence Malick's 2011 film *The Tree of Life* as ecotheology. More specifically, I argue that the film expresses a Judeo-Christian ecotheology that understands human experience and human meaning within an evolving physical cosmos that is subject to ongoing chaos and contingency. Such a universe, of course, has raised some difficult questions for monotheistic theologies that embrace the idea of God's omnipotence. Judeo-Christian theology, for example, has more often as not simply bypassed these questions by ignoring or denying the complexity, temporal depth, and violence of the earth's story. How, for example, can one reconcile the idea of providence or believe in the meaning of human suffering when life itself is subject to and even dependent on chance and violence or when human experience takes place in such a small fragment of geological time? In order to sustain faith in providence in such a universe, Malick's unique contribution is to suggest that one must be willing to absorb the insults of accident and sacrifice the human drive to control and master one's own destiny. In his invocation of Job, his allusions to Dostoevsky's *The Brothers Karamazov*, and his debt to Kierkegaard, Malick suggests that the recompense for this sacrifice is an intensification of appreciation for existence itself, unadorned by expectation, and a revelation of what Dostoevsky calls the earth's "glory" (289). The paradox is that the earth's glory is only made available once one accepts that the will of God cannot easily be distinguished from nature's indifferent and indiscriminate whims; God becomes possible, in other words, in a universe where he doesn't seem necessary and where biology itself appears miraculous. The film's ecotheology blurs the distinctions between the earthly and the heavenly and between the finite and the infinite and in so doing points to the substance of our experiences in these bodies and in this life and the beauty and strangeness of this earth, rather than to a world to come, as the site of human hope.

the tree of life and theology

The importance of theology in Malick's films is not self-evident, so before getting directly into a theological reading of the film it will first be helpful to understand the debates about Malick's intentions in *The Tree of Life* and about his engagement with theological themes. Some critics, such as David Sterrit and Rob

White, for example, acknowledge the theological obsessions of the film but consider them naive and simplistic and overshadowed by its exceptional aesthetic accomplishments.[1] On the other hand, Brent Plate as well as various online sources indicate fascination and praise for the film's theological achievements.[2]

Part of the confusion seems to stem from the perplexing question of where *The Tree of Life* fits within the broader context of Malick's oeuvre, which includes films with little or no theological treatment, or at the least implicitly existentialist contexts, such as *Badlands* (1976) and *Days of Heaven* (1978). It would be an overstatement, however, to argue that *The Tree of Life* is the first of Malick's films of theological or, specifically, of ecotheological import. Both *The Thin Red Line* (1998) and *The New World* (2005) address the question of what one critic calls the "wonder of presence" in the face of the indifference of natural beauty, specifically as it is juxtaposed with the unfolding of historical events that involved catastrophic levels of human suffering (Jones 25). What Robert Sinnerbrink says of *The New World*, for example, could easily be said of both *The Thin Red Line* and *The Tree of Life*:

> [I]t aesthetically discloses the sublimity of nature understood as elemental earth, that which underlies and supports any historical and cultural form of human community. Acknowledging this unity with nature is what makes possible the kind of plural co-existence or marriage between worlds that *The New World* evokes through mythic history and cinematic poetry [...] Nature is both the deeper ground of cultural reconciliation and the hidden source of a utopian community that could found a new world; but this experience of nature remains a poetic evocation, a moment of aesthetic sublimity celebrated fleetingly on film. (191–92)

This is to suggest, then, that Malick's films are interested in understanding the natural ground of human experience – which is often imagined to be a kind of spiritual unity with the cosmos – as well as the cultural and moral failures that have led to human indifference to the environment. Indeed, as Sinnerbrink and other critics have pointed out, Stanley Cavell had picked up on the role of the natural world in Malick's earliest films, as early as 1979 ("Foreword"). Building on Cavell's critique, James Morrison and Thomas Schur remark that Malick demonstrates how film

> recalls (because it enacts) the rift between people and nature that follows speech: film names things. The image resembles the physical world, but it neither imitates nor reproduces it – thus to watch a film is to bear witness to our banishment from the mythical garden. (67)

As I intend to demonstrate, this banishment, however, is not as simple as it might sound. Nature's role in the violence and tragedy of human experience is also what foments life. Malick doesn't lament this darker side of ecology but rather integrates it into his vision of spirituality. That is, his films resist nostalgia for a benevolent and harmonious nature that is no more (indeed that never existed) as well as a yearning for a spiritual world beyond this earth that is yet to come. Robert Silberman's observations about *The Thin Red Line* pertain to *The Tree of Life*. He notes a transition away from seeing nature "as fortification and as property" and a turn to "a spiritual version of landscape as a site of devastation, death and possible transformation" (171). That is, while conforming to the shape of the Judeo-Christian Fall, Malick's return to paradise is not an escape from but a prodigal return to earthly conditions.

Malick is indebted to Martin Heidegger's notion of the work of human "worlding" over and against the raw earth (*Being and Time*).[3] However, as Martin Donougho argues, "[Malick's] films constantly show the crossing of nature and culture, animal and human, as we shall observe, which lends the event of 'worlding' a very different color" (363). That difference lies in his portrayal of the activity of the human imagination, often portrayed in his use of voiceovers, as less tragic than environmental discourse usually admits. Instead of seeing nature and culture as oppositions, Malick sees their relationship as inherently interdependent. As we will see, the voiceovers in *The Tree of Life* are even more overtly theological than they had been in *The Thin Red Line* or *The New World*, often directly addressing deity in a series of interrogatory questions. The net effect is that the possibility of God emerges out of the dialectical struggle between the human work of worlding and the resistant ontology of the earth. We see his characters imagining, making, and remaking themselves in relationship to the earth and its myriad and particular forms and thus probing the possibilities of providence.[4] These subtextual conversations – queries by individuals who stand confronted by the mystery of physical existence – reflect a view that the earth and biology itself provide the context of human and divine becoming. In its portrayal of an intense and profound human consciousness and the margin of freedom this consciousness grants against determinism, *The Tree of Life* provides a version of Judeo-Christian theology that is more sympathetic to a process theology where all agents are interrelated and have an indeterminate future.

In this sense, Malick probes film's potential to be a kind of poetic reinvention or remaking of the world, that is, as a kind of cosmology. Based on his reading of the film, for example, Plate argues:

> Cinema is part of the symbol-creating apparatus of culture, yet it also aspires to more: to world-encompassing visions of the nomos and cosmos. Cinema allows us to see in new ways, through new technologies, re-creating the world anew, telescoping the macrocosmic past and far away, and bringing these visions to bear on the microcosmic structures in the here and now. (535)[5]

Cinema as cosmology, however, depends on a conception of divine creativity that is similarly poetic in that it engages in repurposing rather than in creating *ex nihilo*. Process theologian Catherine Keller believes that this is particularly evident in the account of Job where we see "chaos bewitched [...] charmed rather than compelled" (146), transforming, in the words of Deleuze and Guattari, "chaotic variability" into "chaoid variety" (qtd in Keller 146). She explains: "Art is not chaos but a composition of chaos" so that it constitutes "a chaosmos, a composed chaos – neither foreseen nor preconceived. We may readily imagine Elohim's creativity as closer to art than to science" (171).

Keller's process theology is indebted to a Deridean reading of Genesis that resonates with Malick's film. She argues that early Christianity "systematically and symbolically sought to erase the chaos of creation" (xvi). Specifically, it banished the idea that life relied on pre-existent and continuing chaos within the order of the universe. That is, Christianity established the dogma of creation *ex nihilo* out of fear of the ongoing challenge posed by chaos and disorder. This dogma, however, has not been easy to reconcile with the existence of evil and the meaning of innocent suffering. It has perhaps also challenged Christianity's ability to accept the Huttonian and Darwinian implications that human existence and the diversity of all life are indebted to eons of death, violence, and change. The question of nature's relation to grace, of course, is an old theological debate that asks whether or not natural process is in need of redemption from a deity who stands outside of the world or whether divinity is somehow part and parcel of the unfolding of evolutionary and geological time. The powerful argument of process theology and of related attempts within Judeo-Christian ecotheologies to accept science is that chance and accident are seen as partners rather than opponents of God's creative work.[6] While there are other forms of ecotheology that do not embrace the evolutionary story and deep time quite so directly, they are arguably less effective in orienting the spiritual and ethical concerns of believers toward the earth. As I will argue in my reading of the film, however, Malick makes clear that in order to make the earth more central to our understanding of heaven we must be willing to rethink our assumptions about human self-determination and divine providence.

malick's debt to job, kierkegaard, and dostoevsky

The Tree of Life revisits the chaotic events of the earth's creation and seeks to understand their relationship to one family's story. Malick invokes Job at the film's opening to announce his intention to come to terms with these seemingly disjointed stories in a Judeo-Christian context. He suggests that the transcendent and hopeful meaning of the human story can only be forged in the toughest of contexts – that of the vast and complex and seemingly indifferent universe of chaos and deep time. The film frames the family's tale between the tales of Job and Abraham, as I will demonstrate, and highlights the role of sacrifice as the means by which a cosmic order is instituted. What must be ritually sacrificed is any human expectation of a divinely sanctioned earthly reward. Just as Abraham must sacrifice his son, one must return any manifestation of God's benevolence to God since they cannot be earned, expected, or, ultimately, possessed.

At the outset of the film, we read the words of God's terrifying interrogation of Job: "Where were you when I laid the foundations of the earth?" In the biblical text, this question initiates God's litany of creation's wonders that is intended to diminish Job's sense of self-importance but also to remind him of his lack of secure autonomy within the matrix of the creation (see Job 38–42). Placed within the vast expanse of the ongoing death and rebirth of all life forms, Job reevaluates his place in the cosmos and, consequently, the meaning of his own sufferings and losses.

William Brown offers a new ecotheological reading of Job that resonates with Malick's aims. By reading the story from the perspective of our contemporary understandings of chaos, evolutionary deep time, and biodiversity, Brown sees it as an injunction to live more gently on the earth. Specifically, Brown argues that what we find in Job offers no "cozy cosmos" but rather one that "is terrifyingly vast and alien" (129). Brown notes: "Job comes to realize that the world does not revolve around himself, nor even perhaps around humanity. Creation is polycentric" (133). This exposure to previously unimagined diversity and immensity brings Job to accept that he, like all of creation, is an alien and that he is not central, even if also free. He learns to

> affirm his own life in extremis, to embrace his identity as Homo alienus and his connection with all aliens, to revel in his freedom, wild thing that he is, and to step lightly on God's beloved, vibrant Earth. God's challenge to Job to "gird up your loins" and be catapulted into the margins of life, to take the plunge into the depths of chaos and come up for air, to muster the courage to start a new family, is now fulfilled. Such was Job's baptism, his terrifying and edifying immersion into Nature. (140)

Catherine Keller similarly reads Job as an under-appreciated ecotheological text. In Keller's view, understanding the problem of human evil and suffering essentially begins by responding to the divine mandate: "*Look at the wild things*" (Keller 129). To redress the human suffering caused by chance would also have to involve examining the totality and diversity of life that "a universe of open-ended indeterminacy" makes possible (140). While traditionally read as a theodicy, these authors transform Job's story into an ecotheology whereby human injustice and suffering are contextualized within the much broader framework of all living things, all processes of death and transformation.

Malick similarly wants to represent both the limits and the potentiality of human agency within the restraints of the biological and physical universe. His God is at best distant but, based on the persistent interrogations of Malick's characters, is always relevant and never definitively absent. Malick's God, like Job's, must be sought, contended with, interrogated, but eventually loved, even against all reason. *The Tree of Life*'s long visual sequences of cosmic creation, of dinosaurs, and of microscopic complexity rivals *2001: A Space Odyssey* for its audacity in insisting on a story that stretches well beyond the short range of human memory and experience. It is, in this sense, a film with a biocentric impulse. However, in its juxtaposition of these sequences with a deeply intimate and phenomenological representation of one family's experience that appeals to our human compassion, it seeks to understand the meaning of intimate human experience within the context of life's diversity. Through careful montage, the film dialectically moves between an imagined biocentric cosmos and one that is anthropocentric – personal, particular, and located in the microcosm of Waco, Texas, in the 1950s.

The logic of this montage is, perhaps, counterintuitive to much of contemporary environmentalism, since it seems to suggest that the significance of human experience is directly challenged by the immensity and diversity of the physical universe. For Malick, nature does not merely offer pastoral comfort, but it is, also, a chief cause of an alienation that we must endure. We hear at various points in *The Tree of Life* several reverse interrogations of the kind the Lord gives to Job. "Where were you?" queries the mother upon losing her son. As the eldest son observes the mentally ill and incapacitated who rely on the mercy of others, he asks: "Can it happen to anyone?" Again, the son asks, after his friend drowns in the neighborhood pool: "Where were you? You let a boy die. You'll let anything happen. Why should I be good, if you aren't?"[7] Curiously, following this moment in the film is a scene portraying DDT being sprayed in the streets, a provocative reminder of the unseen and, at the time, misunderstood toxins that would cause damage to the environment and to human health.[8] But the montage also raises the ecotheological question: why bother worrying ourselves about environmental damage, let alone something like ecological restoration, if the universe is already so capricious as to take life with indifference? Why, given the immense complexity of life-forms and interdependencies that challenge our autonomy, should we believe in our capacity to predict and control the consequences of our environmental choices? The universe appears unmanageable, unpredictable, and alien to human happiness and comfort and in this sense seems to totter toward a justification of human indifference, even nihilism.

But Malick is determined to move us from Job's chastisement to Job's inexplicable joy. In the film, the preacher offers a sermon on Job and suggests, echoing biblical rhetoric about human vanity, that we "wither as autumn grass and, like a tree, are rooted up." Thus, "the tree of life" is not just biblical reassurance of eternal life but also the emblem of human belonging to a world of death and change, prompting the preacher's question: "Is there some fraud in the scheme of the universe?" He then poses a series of theological quandaries:

> Does he alone see God's hand who sees that he gives, or does not also the one see God's hand who sees that he takes away? Or does he alone see God who sees God turn his face toward him, or does not also he see God who sees him turn his back?

In other words, is God manifest more by absence or by presence? Does not God take as much as he gives?

Malick's intentions here are made clearer when we realize that these questions are directly lifted from a discourse by Kierkegaard on Job that explores the reasoning behind Job's perplexing conclusion, "the Lord gave and the Lord took away, blessed be the name of the Lord!" (121). Kierkegaard's discourse elaborates on Job's capacity to overcome the world, to maintain a faith that is steady in the face of life's violent changing circumstances. Kierkegaard walks us through the reasoning of a man who loses everything and who still wishes to believe in and even praise God, not despite bad things that have happened but – in a tougher theology – *because* of losses God has directly caused. Under such circumstances, Kierkegaard reasons that a man might conclude that human error led to his losses. While these explanations provide an illusion of sufficiency and clarity, for Kierkegaard they "are sufficient to make [one's] soul indifferent to everything" (120). This is centrally important to understanding the film: to remain alive to the world, to see and experience it in all its sensuousness, is to accept it as both given *and* to understand that, as a gift, it is unearned and can be taken away. Moreover, one must abdicate the need to make such providence reasonable. Kierkegaard insists, and Malick seems to agree, that the benefit of the acceptance of an irrational justice of God is that it shields us from delusions of our own power and autonomy. Kierkegaard warns: "above all learn from Job to become honest with yourself so that you do not deceive yourself with imagined power, with which you experience imagined victory in imagined struggle" (123). Malick underscores that one must, in short, come to accept a radical gap between action and consequence, between what one wills and what one gets.

The preacher adds his own answer to the questions cited from Kierkegaard, providing us insight into Malick's own adaptation of Kierkegaard's theology: "We must find that which is greater than fortune or fate. Nothing can bring us peace but that" (*Tree of Life*). The sermon implies that one errs if one lives according to principles that are based merely on expected outcomes or the illusion of control. God, ultimately, is ambiguous, uncannily absent and yet ubiquitous; fortune and misfortune alike are one's constant and unpredictable companions; time and chance, as the preacher in Ecclesiastes says, happen to all and joy is only real when one can accept God in such a whimsical universe. If this seems irrational, it is more irrational still to deny the reality of change so as to protect the idea of divine sovereignty or, for that matter, to determine God's inexistence merely on the basis of his apparent inability to conform to individual expectation or desire.

Mr O'Brien follows the preacher's sermon with a sermon of his own about the pervasive injustice of the world, concluding that "the world lives by trickery" and warning the boys against trying to be "too good." His is a philosophy of strategy and negotiation rather than of submission. Job and Abraham, however, find their margin of freedom from the inevitable march of suffering not through trickery but through radical and willful submission to *what is*, like Kierkegaard's knight of faith. Job cannot guarantee through his own righteousness what his circumstances will be, and Abraham cannot speak the irrationality of what has been asked of him. It would appear in both cases that the test is of something more profound. What is asked of them is a kind of active willing of misfortune that becomes a sacrifice of what will be or has been taken away. Kierkegaard, of course, insists that this kind of radical integrity is not infinite resignation, or the passivity of Christianity that Nietzsche criticized; it is, instead, a taking up of the knife, believing that God will nevertheless provide; that is, to accept that all has been taken and still believe all will be restored. It is active acceptance, even willing what has happened; it is the capacity to accept the actual as well as to courageously anticipate the possible.

For Kierkegaard, rational explanations of what happens function as illusions that allow us to avoid having to see experience directly in all of its radical unpredictability and contingency. Sacrifice, on the other hand, is a way of anticipating what experience requires. It is interesting to note what Derrida has argued in relation to this question. For him, sacrifice is properly understood not as substitution but as "the putting to death of the unique in terms of its being unique, irreplaceable, and most precious" (58). Or as he also puts it, it is "raising one's knife over someone and putting death forward by giving it as an offering" (72). Ultimately it is a matter of accepting the terrible truth that "conceptual thinking" has its limit; it must confront "its death and finitude" (68). He further argues that what appears to be Abraham's exceptional story of sacrifice and suffering is in fact quite common. This is because, as an individual, I cannot be answerable to others in programmatic or generalized ways. I can only answer experience one moment, one person, one context at a time, and each time that I do, I bypass all other alternatives. I cannot expect to love or even make decisions without sacrificing the many others I might have loved or the other commitments I can now no longer make because of each decision I have already made. Kierkegaard's knight of faith, Derrida argues, "decides, but his absolute decision is neither guided nor controlled by knowledge. Such, in fact, is the paradoxical condition of every decision: it cannot be deduced from a form of knowledge of which it would simply be the effect, conclusion, or explicitation" (77).

Derrida insists that every human choice is haunted by what is made unavailable to us as soon as a choice is made. We choose to love one person, one family, or maybe we love many, but in any case we will never devote ourselves to all. Derrida's revision here of Kierkegaard suggests that ethics are always embedded in choice by the fullest range of possible actions, making the angst of Abraham's land of Moriah "our habitat every second of every day" (69). We shield ourselves from the difficulties of such broad contexts, however, by pretending that our decision making and our choices can follow a script and can arrive at expected consequences. To feel the sorrow of loss is a form of sacrifice. It is sacrifice to love any gift, whether that gift be the fruit of human love or the experience of natural beauty. All attachments, all sorrows, and all experiences are radically delimited by choices that ever narrow and delimit the course of an individual life. This paradox heightens the need for and value of rituals whereby we enact the sacrifices of choice and expose our interconnectedness to others and to the physical universe. In this way, we see and take responsibility for the choices we have eliminated. The implication here is that the only adequate idea of God is one who reigns over a universe of infinite possibilities and yet who therefore remains a secret.

This is perhaps the reason why Malick insists that before God can be experienced as benevolent and giving he must be sought after in the incidents of loss and suffering. Jack's search for God is initiated by the loss of his brother, the one who has died in the years between childhood and adulthood, and he seeks him in all deviations, all losses, and all disruptions of hope and expectation for a frictionless life. God remains abeyant in the film, despite the unrelenting search, but Malick's insistence on an elusive and uncanny God allows for a collapse of difference between heaven and earth, between the mother as mother and the mother as Mother Mary, between the trees of Waco and the Tree of Life. Indeed, at times, we do not know when we are in heaven or on earth in this film or when we are dealing with particular human lives or with allegories of human experience. Art's contingent order that emerges from chaos is recompense for loss; it imagines a restoration, a making sacred of the loss of God in the world. Malick provides an enigmatic and brave scene at the end of the film of milling people that includes our protagonist family hugging on the sands of some imaginary edge of the world or perhaps at the threshold of heaven. The implication is that to imagine and hope for the restoration of all things, of lost siblings and children, is to sacrifice or make holy, as the etymology of the word implies, that which is mundane and accidental. There is suddenly little distinction between such metaphysical hope of reunion and the simple act of filmic representation of ordinary life on screen. Both are acts of imagined restoration and imbued with a sense of the holy.

The film opens with an opposition between what is defined as "the way of grace" and "the way of nature" (*Tree of Life*). Initially, at least, the parents seem to be embodiments of these two positions. The father prizes strength of will and individual autonomy over any willingness to accept chance or misfortune, which he sees in his wife as a kind of passive naivety and ultimately as a weakness. Although a religious man, he does not teach his sons meekness and radical humility but instead insists that "it takes fierce will to get ahead in this world." This presumption of radical individual autonomy is, of course, central to the American mythos of self-determination, which Malick suggests is at odds with a Jobian creation theology. In one sequence, the father lectures to his eldest son, saying:

> Twenty-seven patents your father has. It means ownership. Ownership of ideas. You gotta sew 'em up. Get 'em by the nuts [...] You make yourself what you are. You have control of your own destiny. You can't say, "I can't." You say, "I'm having trouble. I'm not done yet."

These words are interspersed with images of the father in the courtroom, losing the battle for his patents and thus losing the very power he teaches is within the son's controlling grasp if he can just muster enough fortitude to weather life's mishaps. In a theological context, the father's philosophy of self-determination cannot account for any deviation from his plans except either as a form of failure or injustice. It is not coincidental then that he teeters on the edge of abuse and maniacal control of his wife and sons when their actions and even his own career inevitably diverge from his plans. Already a frustrated musician, the father loses his job. The son's voice is immediately heard to say: "Why does he hurt us? Our father." The double entendre echoes as both a genealogical and theological question. The existence of evil and suffering emerges as a particularly acute problem within a universe where ultimate control of outcomes is possible. But this is neither the universe Malick depicts nor the world in which the family lives.

For Malick, God is only possible in a universe where he doesn't appear to be necessary. Holiness, in other words, shouldn't have to stand out as some kind of exception to the facts of physical life. To paraphrase Annie Dillard, extrascientific belief in God is no less rational than trying to explain the bare fact of the extravagance of a giraffe (146). Her argument is that the question regarding the meaning of biology already and inevitably postulates a metaphysics. If we imagine that the universe points to the necessity of God and therefore the inevitability of benevolent control of events, we are never confronted by the challenge of having to imagine transcendent meaning freely. Belief in a cosmos of the more secret God, however, becomes a genuine and courageous choice as Kierkegaard suggests, rather than mechanistically predetermined by order or logic or by knowledge. Freedom is possible in a universe of indeterminacy; it is, as Kierkegaard so powerfully argued, fraught with anxiety, caught as we are between the actual and the possible.

The tough part of this theology means having to absorb the shock, even the insults, of physical existence. The youngest son has died, and we don't know what from, but we do know that Malick's own youngest brother committed suicide in his early twenties and that the film's portrayal of the death is at least consistent with a suicide. And it is the mother's voice, not initially the father's, who informs us of the theology of the film. The way of grace is expressed as St Paul's notion of charity as we hear the mother explain at the film's outset: it "accepts being slighted, forgotten, disliked, accepts insults and injuries" whereas the way of nature "finds reasons to be unhappy when all the world is shining around it, when love is smiling through all things." The way of grace is the capacity to suffer long, to bear all things, to withhold judgment and to wait upon the Lord. It is mistaken to assume, as the father wants to believe, that the mother's acceptance of grace is a sign of passivity and weakness. As noted above, upon losing her son, we hear the mother reversing God's interrogation of man and asking: "Lord. Why? Where were you?" But significantly at the film's conclusion, the mother has gone well beyond mere passive Christian resignation. She has assumed the role of proactively sacrificing her own child, moving from the position of Job, who maintains his integrity in loss, to Abraham, who raises his knife and wills the terrible things the Lord asks of him. In this moment, the exceptional circumstances of Abraham's story become universal, as Derrida has insisted. Death must be taken and given as a gift, as that which sweetens life, and in biological terms, as that which moves life forward. We see what appears to be a figurative representation of how grace has transformed the mother's heart. With arms upraised, she says: "I give him to you," she says. "I give you my son." Like Kierkegaard's Job, she has overcome the world because, with "the image of sorrow expressed in [her] countenance," she can pronounce the name of the Lord blessed and thus "still witnesses to joy" (122).

The mother's theology neither requires nor yearns for causal explanations or for the need to make God's grace rational or based on desired circumstances or outcomes – even though all the while it hopes for, even anticipates, restitution. The film represents restoration as an imagined space, hoped for and expressed in all music, art, and literature, where all things are reunited after the great dispersal of human bodily experience. And by so doing it stanches the flow of pain and the toxic spread of blame that a tighter, more rational theology might inspire. Because she cedes the need to control, to definitively delineate the good from the bad, she is able to glory so fully in the joy of existence and the beauty of the earth. There is no question that the many scenes in the film showing her at play with her children depict her as the portal through which Jack must pass to learn to see the glory of this earth. She shows Jack the way to accept the interdependency of joy and woe – to paraphrase William Blake's "Auguries of Innocence," to accept sorrow and beauty as necessary partners of experience and coefficients of human meaning, and bring heaven and earth together and to see a Blakean world in a grain of sand, eternity in an hour (506).

By contrast, the father comes belatedly but perhaps redemptively to a similar conclusion, once he has sacrificed his own need to control the outcome of events in his life. The youngest son has already died in the film's opening sequence, thus shattering the father's illusions of mastery. The father also loses his job. In his humiliation, we hear him recalibrating his theology:

> I wanted to be loved because I was great. A big man. I'm nothing. Look at the glory around us. Trees and birds. I lived in shame. I dishonored it all and didn't notice the glory. I'm a foolish man. (*Tree of Life*)

This embrace of the glory of the earth, of a kind of existential joy that is independent of circumstance, is the ecotheological turn in the story; it is the Jobian praise of God and of the world after the humiliations of loss and the Abrahamic faith that all will be restored, even if all is taken away.[9] These lines have resonance with another work of theological import, Fyodor Dostoevsky's *The Brothers Karamazov*, thus underscoring the seriousness of Malick's theological ambitions. These lines are almost directly lifted from the Pevear and Volokhonsky translation of the novel, a moment in the novel where Dostoevsky provides a biography of Alyosha's model and spiritual guide, Zosima, modeled after hagiographic literature of nineteenth-century Russia. Zosima tells the story of his own spiritual development by recounting the story of his brother who was an atheist until he learned of his impending death and discovered God. As he was dying, Zosima's brother no longer feared death: "Why count the days," he says to his family, "when even one day is enough for a man to know all happiness. My dears, why do we quarrel, boast before each other, remember each other's offenses? Let us go to the garden, let us walk and play and love and praise and kiss each other, and bless our life" (Dostoevsky 289). Zosima's brother here implies that a return to the garden is a matter of perception, not circumstance. We see in the film an attempt by Malick to portray in long, seemingly uneventful but tender scenes this kind of exultation in life itself, an exultation embodied in child's play and in the mother's unmistakable gift for *joie de vivre*. Zosima's brother stares outside the window on his deathbed, exulting in the trees and birds and here echoes the words of Jack's father:

> None of us could understand it then, but he was weeping with joy: "Yes," he said, "there was so much of God's glory round me: birds, trees, meadows, sky, and I alone lived in shame. I alone dishonored everything, and did not notice the beauty and glory of it all." (289)

There is insufficient space here to recount the development of Dostoevsky's theology, but it is important to note that his famous portrayal of Ivan Karamazov's rejection of Christian theology, based on a powerful argument about the suffering of innocent children, emerged from a growing awareness of the deterministic and overly logical character of radical socialist ideology. Specifically, Dostoevsky objected to socialism because it insists on finding human and political culprits for all forms of human injustice. While sympathetic to these concerns, enough to provide what many consider to be one of the most powerful arguments against Christianity within his novel, Dostoevsky nevertheless insists that Ivan's

> convictions are [...] a synthesis of contemporary Russian anarchism. A denial not of God, but of the meaning of His creation. All socialism has arisen and begun with the denial of the significance of historical reality

and has proceeded to a program of destruction and anarchism. (Qtd in Mochulsky 584)

Socialism and atheism, for Dostoevsky, were forms of hatred toward human freedom. That is because they detest the very symptoms of the kind of free and open-ended indeterminacy that Catherine Keller insists theology must embrace (Mochulsky 621). In other words, even if we could choose a different universe of no unnecessary or human-caused suffering, such a mechanistic and predictable world would foreclose the possibility of human freedom and the persistence of chaos in the workings of the world that continue to make life, freedom, and even beauty possible.[10]

After this story, Zosima recounts his admiration for the book of Job, as if in anticipation of contemporary rereadings of Job as an ecotheological text. He states that in this story "the passing earthly image and eternal truth here touched each other. In the face of earthly truth, the enacting of eternal truth is accomplished" (Dostoevsky 292). God turns Job's attention to the inherent goodness of the world, of all that is, according to Zosima, "And Job, praising God, does not only serve him, but will also serve his whole creation, from generation to generation and unto ages of ages" (292). When presented by the question of how it is possible to love new children after his former had been taken away, Zosima explains that "the old grief, by a great mystery of human life, gradually passes into quiet, tender joy," that the gift of death, suffering, and change is a heightened joy at the cumulative memories restored by encountering the earth's glory (292). Innocent children will die but that does not stop other innocent children from still being in need of love, nor do innocent deaths change the sacrificial nature of love, since according to Derrida to love one or to love a few, I must sacrifice the need to love all.

Dostoevsky intended the entire novel, and particularly Zosima's story, to be a response to Ivan's challenge regarding the suffering of innocent children, but more specifically he hoped Zosima's biography might point the reader away from the need for scholastic proofs or defenses of the reality of God and instead envelop the reader within the affirmation of mystical experience.[11] Dostoevsky invokes Schiller's "Ode to Joy" in the novel and suggests that "'ancient Mother Earth' [is] the divine fire, that which gives life and joy to all God's creations" (Mochulsky 611). This almost pagan sense of earthly power is dark too, however, since it is the power of destruction, of death and violence, and the grounds for the experience of chaos. To love the earth and to love earthly experience, earthly glory, and earthly beauty is to accept the responsibilities of human freedom and the paradoxes of a benign God who both gives and takes away. Indeed, after hearing Zosima's life story, Alyosha emerges from the monastery:

> Night, fresh and quiet, almost unstirring, enveloped the earth. The white towers and golden domes of the church gleamed in the sapphire sky. The luxuriant autumn flowers in the flowerbeds near the house had fallen asleep until morning. The silence of the earth seemed to merge with the silence of the heavens, the mystery of the earth touched the mystery of the stars [...] Alyosha stood gazing and suddenly, as if he had been cut down, threw himself to the earth. He did not know why he was embracing it, he did not try to understand why he longed so irresistibly to kiss it, to kiss all of it, but he was kissing it, weeping, sobbing, and watering it with his tears, and he vowed ecstatically to love it, to love it unto ages of ages. "Water the earth with the tears of your joy, and love those tears [...]" rang in his soul. (Dostoevsky 362)

He is infused with an all-encompassing will to forgive all, to love all, to accept all, and this feeling connects him to everything and to everyone: "It was as if threads from all those innumerable worlds of God all came together in his soul, and it was trembling all over, 'touching other worlds'" (362). This is what Dostoevsky, adapted from the writings of St Tikhon who influenced him, considered to be a kind of cosmic ecstasy – the most profound experience of love – that is found in contemplation of the world and of our plain and unadorned human existence in it. Love is what transforms the world into paradise, for Elder Zosima, because "the beauty of nature proclaims the glory of the Creator," even and especially when such beauty comes with the price of suffering and the experience of abandonment (Mochulsky 634).

Malick's "way of grace," in other words, is the way of Kierkegaard's Job and Dostoevsky's Zosima and Alyosha. It is the transformation of this earth into an experience of paradise, here and now, and the acceptance of the inherent value of what *is*, instead of the maniacal and rational focus on what must or should or even could be. It is to blur the distinctions between the tree of life as the heavenly symbol of eternity and the trees of everyday living as symbols of biological process. This is no simplistic formula for ignoring life's insults and losses; joy is a call to love nature and exult in the chance to be alive, even though that also means accepting the inevitability of terrible suffering and, of course, death. Dostoevsky's great theme is that we can only find the deepest joys in the midst of our greatest sorrows, that we can only understand the gift of life in the context of death and loss. Jack's mother is tempted by anger and blame following the news of her son's death, but in confronting this pain and owning it as the privilege of experience instead of assigning rational responsibility for it to agents either human or divine she transforms it and all of earth itself into a meaning of deep holiness.

Jack's first voiceover expresses that he has only been able to approach God because of loss and because of witnessing his mother's grace in accepting it: "Brother, Mother: It was they who led me to your door" (*Tree of Life*). The images of thresholds, door frames, window frames that emerge in the film suggest this liminal arrival to the possibility of God, perhaps most subtly suggested by the hint of a release of tension in grown Jack's face with which the film ends. Of course, the image itself is ambiguous, as is any definitive triumph we can glean from the movie. The film enacts a path back to God and to restitution in imagined scenes of reunion; we are relegated to having merely to *imagine* restitution and reunion with all lost lives, all dispersed human stories. But the artistic imagination is already compensation since it brings us into the realm of possibility. The brother and mother are simultaneously biological relations and spiritualized into the hope of restitution by Jesus and Mary. The implication here is that one errs spiritually and one does unspeakable harm to the world, not because one is indifferent to others or to the physical environment but because one keeps trying so hard to make oneself self-sufficient, to be the "big man" Malick's father wanted to be. And in so doing and in inevitably failing, one finds culprits – human, divine, or natural – and acts out violence upon them.

conclusion

As many environmental philosophers have argued, seeing nature not as dead matter that lies outside of or as background to human agency but as mutually alive and co-dependent with us is vital to any environmental ethic.[12] For this reason, environmentalism has often resorted to a kind of reinvented paganism, dressed in the language of science. Instead of adopting a neopagan spiritualism, Malick's originality lies in injecting new spiritual breath into the biblical stories. He revisits our assumptions about biblical narratives, specifically assumptions about the Bible's inadequacy in the face of the earth's story. He turns the table on the environmentalist logic that has so long been critical of anthropocentrism for failing to truly reckon with nature. Such criticism, though warranted by our arrogant and indifferent degradation of nature, has failed to admit the implicit metaphysical underpinnings of biocentrism, which is frequently offered as the preferred alternative to the Judeo-Christian tradition. Arguing that a biocentric universe is preferred to an inflated sense of human significance and centrality might make more room for nature, but it offers no balm for the reality of human suffering. It only raises the questions: why should we love or care for nature if it lies at the root of all our suffering? Why should we believe that the world is inherently valuable? How can we know it and understand it except by the lights of our limited human understanding? Why should we do the cultural work to rise up to our moral responsibility if we have also convinced ourselves that human culture gets in the way of ecologically sound living and understanding?

Instead, Malick highlights the very human work – the poetic, world-making work of art – that is needed to imagine the complexity, depth, and violence of natural history within a cosmological context that still manages to accommodate human existence and suffering as meaningful.[13] Rather than repressing or denying chaos and its threat of dissemblance of human order and meaning, Malick's film transforms it into a necessary and integral component to a providential cosmos. And rather than repressing or denying the vital importance of human imagination in finding our place in the universe, he shows its indispensability especially to the work of expanding our understanding of the earth and of the universe. Given a new form and order in this way, nature comes spiritually alive and thus provides reason for metaphysical hope beyond death. But since one can never be sure what portion of that spiritual life is one's own imagining nor, for that matter, what portion of environmental history is anthropogenic, metaphysical hope will always be human, that is, imagined and not determined by biology alone.

To fail to see our biological contingency is as dangerous as failing to see the liberties of the imagination. We can see secular representations like Malick's film as articulations of a postsecular cosmology that accepts providence within an indeterminate and open universe.[14] As demonstrated in the film, acceptance requires a sacrifice of one's need to dictate and control outcomes in what turns out to be one's rather unplotted life. At its most challenging, this includes the sacrifice of what we love and more profoundly the acknowledgement that all love is already sacrifice. For us as viewers, the aesthetic experience of the film provides a contingent sense of order, a worlding of imagined possibility, by which we can conceive of the meaning of our own sacrifices. Despite its biocentric impulses, this world we experience in the film is still human made. This is a paradox that we need not lament but rather acknowledge as our plight. Our environmental problems require that we acknowledge nature's otherness, but they also require that we recognize that nature's otherness is something *we have imagined*. What Malick argues for, then, is not biocentrism per se but a biological tempering of our anthropocentrism. The film's inevitable artistic failure to represent an authentic otherness of nature nevertheless teaches us that the universe we live in is only as real to us as we can imagine and that we therefore share collective responsibility to imagine well the meaning and value of its reality.

notes

1 Sterrit, in fact, argues that the film exhibits a "shortage of theological sophistication" (52) and depicts a kind of "bloodless version of suffering" that is too easily reconciled to faith (57). Michael Atkinson argues similarly that the film is wrought with simplistic theology: "Malick attempts," he writes, "in several ways to suggest a replay of the story of Job that just seems half-hearted" (79).

2 Plate believes that Malick's film is "simply the latest in a millennia-old project, shared by cultures across the world, of visually reconciling the microcosmos with the macrocosmos, finding our local lives situated within the grand scheme of things" (528). Plate suggests specifically (and rightly, in my judgment) that Malick is engaged in thinking through the implications of Darwinian evolution – one particularly biological meaning of "the tree of life" – and the monotheistic meaning of this same symbol in biblical cosmology. For online sources, see Parker et al.; Leary; Horton.

3 Malick, for example, studied philosophy as an undergraduate at Harvard and later, as a Rhodes Scholar at Oxford, focused on Heidegger, Kierkegaard, and Wittgenstein. His translation of Heidegger's *Vom Wesen des Grundes* was published as *The Essence of Reasons* in 1969.

4 In this respect, I am in agreement with Morrison and Schur who insist that Malick's voiceovers provide something quite different from the traditional privileged access to the internal world of

a character since these internal dialogues are so often abstract and unanswered questions and since they are often not even clearly cognizant to the characters in question (27). They are more like rhetorical stances adopted temporarily by characters as experiments of possibility or a subscript of inner and otherwise unspoken psychology.

5 For this reason it is particularly disappointing that Sterrit would criticize *The Tree of Life* for what he considered to be a missing sense of

> the boundless contingency of the human spirit, faced with unyielding pain as well as needed solace, and greater recognition of the power we humans have to remake and rejuvenate the myths, philosophies, and theodicies we invent to make sense of ourselves. (57)

He seems to have missed the audacity and self-consciousness of Malick's cosmological ambition, as I will attempt to show.

6 For other examples of this kind of ecotheology, see Miller; Cunningham; Brown.

7 Plate's otherwise excellent treatment of theology in the film nevertheless argues unpersuasively that no character ever directs their questions to deity. This would seem to ignore these direct questions the mother and son pose to God in direct retort to the citation from Job with which the film begins. These are, of course, ambiguous, since there can be human substitutions (Was the father responsible for the drowning? Did he not get there in time?). Perhaps Plate means only to describe God's indirect presence and relevance in the film, but there is little doubt that Malick intends to open the question of the significance and communicability of the human voice directed to deity.

8 This scene also overtly identifies the location as Waco, which appears to be autobiographical, since it is where Malick and his two brothers were raised.

9 It is not clear what the cause of the son's death is, but as noted above Malick himself lost a brother to suicide – a brother who, like the boy in the film, played and eventually studied guitar. Notice of the death is brought by telegram, which is not inconsistent with what might have happened in the case of Malick's brother who was in Spain at the time of his death. See Biskind 248–49.

10 Dostoevsky's critique of atheism and of socialism has been met with many responses that have sought to defend notions of spirituality and human freedom within an atheological context. See, for example, Dworkin.

11 In response to a letter requesting to know what Dostoevsky's rejoinder to Ivan's Grand Inquisitor would be, the author explained his plans for the serial novel:

> I have not as yet shown an answer to all these atheistic theses, and one is needed. Exactly so, and it is in precisely that now my anxiety and all my concern lie. For this 6th book, The Russian Monk [the chapter cited above about Zosima's life] which will appear on August 31, was intended as an answer to this whole negative side. (Mochulsky 590)

Mochulsky explains that "The Russian Monk was conceived as a theodicy [...] Ivan Karamazov's logical argumentation is opposed by the Elder Zosima's religious world outlook. Euclid's reason negates; mystical experience affirms" (591).

12 See, for example, the 1967 essay by Lynn White, "The Historical Roots of Our Environmental Crisis" that initiated the field of ecotheology. Or for a more recent example, see David Abram's *The Spell of the Sensuous.*

13 Restoration ecologist William Jordan has argued that until we come to terms with the negative side of nature's destructive and indifferent processes, that is until we develop adequate theodicies by which to make moral sense of the world, we will not be capable of engaging in the hard work of restoring it to health.

14 Although it has various definitions, I mean here by postsecular the resurgence of interest in religion and the sacred in the context of postmodern secularism. It may be the case that Malick's religiosity has nothing postmodern or secular about it, but because it emerges in this film in the context of acceptance for the secular scientific understandings of the universe, it arguably qualifies as a form of the postsecular.

bibliography

Abram, David. *The Spell of the Sensuous: Perception and Language in a More-Than-Human World.* New York: Vintage, 1997. Print.

Atkinson, Michael. "The Tree of Life." *Sight & Sound* 21.8 (2011): 79. Print.

Biskind, Peter. *Easy Riders, Raging Bulls.* New York: Simon, 1998. Print.

Blake, William. *The Complete Poems.* Ed. Alicia Ostriker. New York: Penguin, 1978. Print.

Brown, William. *The Seven Pillars of Creation: The Bible, Science, and the Ecology of Wonder.* Oxford: Oxford UP, 2010. Print.

Cavell, Stanley. "Foreword to the Enlarged Edition." *The World Viewed: Reflections on the Ontology of Film.* Cambridge, MA: Harvard UP, 1979. ix–xix. Print.

Cunningham, Conor. *Darwin's Pious Idea: Why the Ultra-Darwinists and Creationists Both Get it Wrong.* Grand Rapids, MI: Eerdmans, 2010. Print.

Derrida, Jacques. *The Gift of Death.* Trans. David Wills. Chicago: U of Chicago P, 1995. Print.

Dillard, Annie. *Pilgrim at Tinker Creek.* Norwich: Canterbury, 2011. Print.

Donougho, Martin. "Melt Earth to Sea." *Journal of Speculative Philosophy* 25.4 (2011): 359–74. Print.

Dostoevsky, Fyodor. *The Brothers Karamazov.* Trans. Richard Pevear and Larissa Volokhonsky. New York: Farrar, 2002. Print.

Dworkin, Ronald. *Religion without God.* Cambridge, MA: Harvard UP, 2013. Print.

Heidegger, Martin. *Being and Time.* Trans. John Macquarrie and Edward Robinson. New York: Harper, 1962. Print.

Horton, Michael. "Review of 'The Tree of Life.'" *Out of the Horse's Mouth.* White Horse Inn, 20 June 2011. Web. 18 Aug. 2014. <http://www.whitehorseinn.org/blog/2011/06/20/review-of-the-tree-of-life/>.

Jones, Kent. "Acts of God." *Film Comment* 42.2 (2006): 24–26, 28. Print.

Jordan, William R., III. *The Sunflower Forest: Ecological Restoration and the New Communion with Nature.* Berkeley: U of California P, 2003. Print.

Keller, Catherine. *The Face of the Deep: A Theology of Becoming.* New York: Routledge, 2003. Print.

Kierkegaard, Søren. "The Lord Gave, and the Lord Took Away; Blessed Be the Name of the Lord." *Eighteen Upbuilding Discourses.* Ed. and trans. Howard V. Hong and Edna H. Hong. Princeton: Princeton UP, 1990. 109–26. Print.

Kubrick, Stanley, dir. *2001: A Space Odyssey.* Metro-Goldwyn-Mayer, 1968. Film.

Leary, M. "Tree of Life as Biblical Theology." *The Other Journal: Filmwell* 3 Sept. 2011: n. pag. Web. 15 Aug. 2014. <http://theotherjournal.com/filmwell/2011/09/03/tree-of-life-as-biblical-theology/>.

Malick, Terrence, dir. *Badlands.* Warner Bros., 1976. Film.

Malick, Terrence, dir. *Days of Heaven.* Paramount Pictures, 1978. Film.

Malick, Terrence, trans. *The Essence of Reasons.* By Martin Heidegger. Evanston: Northwestern UP, 1969. Print.

Malick, Terrence, dir. *The New World.* New Line Cinema, 2005. Film.

Malick, Terrence, dir. *The Thin Red Line.* 20th Century Fox, 1998. Film.

Malick, Terrence, dir. *The Tree of Life.* Fox Searchlight Pictures, 2011. Film.

Miller, Kenneth R. *Finding Darwin's God: A Scientist's Search for Common Ground between God and Evolution.* New York: Harper, 1999. Print.

Mochulsky, Konstantin. *Dostoevsky: His Life and Work.* Trans. Michael A. Minihan. Princeton: Princeton UP, 1967. Print.

Morrison, James, and Thomas Schur. *The Films of Terrence Malick.* Westport: Praeger, 2003. Print.

Parker et al. "Hot Topics: The Tree of Life." *London School of Theology.* London School of Theology, n.d. Web. 15 Aug. 2014. <http://www.lst.ac.uk/hot-topics/the-tree-of-life>.

Plate, Brent. "Visualizing the Cosmos: Terrence Malick's *The Tree of Life* and Other Visions of Life in the Universe." *Journal of the American Academy of Religion* 80.2 (2012): 527–36. Print.

Silberman, Robert. "Terrence Malick, Landscape and 'What is this war in the heart of nature?'" *The Cinema of Terrence Malick: Poetic Visions of*

America. Ed. Hannah Patterson. London: Wallflower, 2007. 164–78. Print.

Sinnerbrink, Robert. *New Philosophies of Film: Thinking Images*. New York: Continuum, 2011. Print.

Sterrit, David. "Days of Heaven and Waco: Terrence Malick's *The Tree of Life*." *Film Quarterly* 65.1 (2011): 52–57. Print.

White, Lynn. "The Historical Roots of Our Ecological Crisis." *The Ecocriticism Reader: Landmarks in Literary Ecology*. Ed. Cheryll Glotfelt and Harold Fromm. Athens, GA: U of Georgia P, 1996. 3–14. Print.

White, Rob. "Bad Blood." *Film Quarterly* 65.1 (2011): 4–5. Print.

russell j.a. kilbourn

"WHEN I SWALLOW HIS HEART AND LUNGS, JESUS IS PLEASED" *the transmediation of sacrifice in* the journals of knud rasmussen

I have never witnessed shamanism. I have only heard about it. One way of making it visible is to film it.

Zacharias Kunuk (2006, http://www.isuma.tv)

transmediation: (nothing) lost in translation

Film, as it is transformed by digital video technology, persists as the dominant narrative medium into the twenty-first century, remaining, too, "one of the most powerful media" for ensuring "the continuation of older myths, even as it alters them."[1] In this essay I consider the Isuma "Fast Runner" trilogy in terms of its transmediation of both sacrifice, on the one hand, and communion, on the other. I focus on the second, central film in the trilogy, *The Journals of Knud Rasmussen* (2006),[2] for its elegiac yet resolutely un-Romantic treatment of these themes. Such transmediation is achieved through the seemingly incongruous yoking of state-of-the-art digital video with the codes of an oral memory based in the film's representation of manually reproduced material forms and repeated, even ritualized, practices. Sacrifice signifies here initially in symbolic or specifically theological senses, the latter exemplified in a Christian context in Jesus' paradigmatic act of self-sacrifice. At the same time, however, these Inuit narratives also embrace a more colloquial metaphorical notion of "self-sacrifice." Communion, as a form of symbolic sacrifice, on the other hand, signifies both as the ritualistic attenuation of the Last Supper, commemorating the Christian sacrifice, and also in relation to such etymologically linked concepts as community and communication. The treatment of sacrifice and communion in the Isuma films, in other words, is symptomatic of what S. Brent Plate calls the "transmediation" of specific religious themes in contemporary cinema (6–8).

"Transmediality" has emerged in contemporary media studies as part of a discourse that takes account of the operations of contemporary media forms in an increasingly globalized and digitized cultural context. "Mediality," for instance, refers to the condition of medium specificity; a "set of characteristics that define a medium, i.e., the specific technical, textual, but also cultural conditions of various media."[3] "Transmediality" therefore refers to those aspects of a post-adaptive text which, according to Eckart Voigts-Virchow, "re-appear after the transcoding or, to put it in more Darwinian terms, those elements that survive in adaptation" (141). Transmediality names those aspects of a text that are subject to translation, transposition, adaptation, remediation, etc. – which are *not* as it were "lost in translation" (142).

On a fundamental level, as a function of its transmediation of sacrifice and communion, *The Journals of Knud Rasmussen* is about *language*, and the difficulty or impossibility of translation from one language, or medium, to another, where the partial failure of translation, transposition, adaptation, leads to the production of new forms and therefore meanings. The film's story connects self-reflexively with its form, even as it connects with larger questions of the transmutation and survival of certain religious themes in contemporary visual culture. Plate analyses the transmediation, if not the transvaluation, of religion in cinema, beginning from what he calls their shared nature as modes of mediation:

> As mediations, the framing and projecting activities of religion-making and filmmaking take the world "out there" and bring it "in here," to our temple, to our table, to our theatre. Through the medium of film, space and time are re-created by activities such as cinematography and editing, just as consecration rites and the mythological forces of religions reform the material "stuff" of the world, offering a new, ideal world, projected for a community's pleasure and, indeed, for their very survival. Film, like religious myth and ritual, offers windows onto other worlds. (3)

As Plate recognizes, however, just as the relation between the quotidian world we inhabit on a daily basis and any other possible worlds is more complex than this model might suggest, both film and religion, as modes of mediation between subject and world, do not act neutrally but actively shape and determine the meanings they convey, reinforcing Marshall McLuhan's precept that the "medium is the message."[4] This recognition acquires renewed significance for a filmmaker grappling with the exploration of specific indigenous cultural or religious themes via the latest filmmaking technologies.[5] Transmediation is thus the most precise term for what the Isuma team has achieved in a film such as *The Journals*:

> From cultures in which orality is the primary mode of communication, to highly literate book-bound cultures, to contemporary multi-mediated cultures, religion is morphed by, adapts to, and affects the media with which it is engaged. Indeed, myths, rituals, and symbols are only existent *as* media [...] And, in its existence as media, religion must change in order to stay the same. That is, for religious traditions to continue through history they must be translated, or better, *transmediated*, put in a new form. (Plate 5–6)

The new form's meaning, moreover, derives directly from its material and "mediatic" difference from pre-existing forms. As Plate implies here, the very fact that something gets translated suggests that there is something *there* to be translated or transcoded, carried across the barrier between media forms (6).

sacrifice, communion, community

What is the relation between sacrifice and the Christian ritual of communion? In a reading of Gabriel Axel's 1987 film *Babette's Feast*, Clive Marsh enlarges upon the meaning of communion:

> A celebration of communion [...] in the Christian tradition, is a place where the presence of God and the availability of the grace of God are guaranteed [...] [A] celebration of communion is a symbolic shared meal which enables people to participate in the presence of a loving, gracious God [...] The bread and wine relate to the body and blood of Jesus [...] the expenditure of whose life Christians claim to be an action in which God's own self was somehow being given. Communion recalls that past event, but also celebrates the presence of a God who continues to operate in a Christ-like way. Participation in communion in the present, then, signals a preparedness on the part of

> Christians to participate in the action of such a self-giving God.[6]

What becomes of this sacrament in the context of 1920s Inuit culture as reconstructed in the film? What of its metaphorical, if not to say sacred, connotations, outlined here? Both sacrifice and communion are dependent in their meaning upon deeply engrained traditions of binary thought. By the same token, the Inuit transmediation of sacrifice and communion alike is dependent upon the deconstruction of such interrelated binaries as body vs. mind or spirit, on the one hand, and starvation vs. conversion, on the other. The first is a southern ("Western") binary, imported into this Inuit cultural context in a manner to be elaborated upon below. The second, however, depends upon the first – starvation is to body as conversion is to spirit – and is a pairing specific to *The Journals*. At the centre of the film's story is this linking of survival (having enough food to eat) to spiritual conversion from shamanism to Christianity: trans-cultural blackmail of the worst kind. Marsh reminds us that in Christian understanding, as in René Girard's theory of sacrifice, Jesus' death is regarded as a "sacrifice to end all sacrifices" (212). In this respect (as in others), "Christian faith and thought was modifying sacrificial practice within the Jewish tradition from which Christianity emerged. But without attention to Judaism (and not only as a 'past' religion) Christianity will not rightly be understood" (212). It could therefore be argued that, as represented in the film, Inuit faith and thought, whose cultural origins have nothing whatsoever to do with Christianity, are shown to be modifying – transmediating – Christian sacrificial practice in a manner ironically analogous to the Christian appropriation and re-signification of Old Testament narrative elements. Moreover, in spite of the film's apparently preferred message, the two cultural traditions, Christianity and shamanism, historically can be seen to co-exist, up to a point, in symbiosis. Marsh goes on to argue that: "it is therefore necessary [...] to understand something of Jewish sacrificial tradition in order to read communion aright" (212). Joseph Martos, in his introduction to Catholic sacraments, identifies "three types of sacrificial offerings," from pre-Christian times, over against which the sacrament of communion can be compared: gift offerings, shared offerings, and sin offerings.[7] "Gift offerings" allow people to acknowledge "dependence on a transcendent reality for things they possessed and enjoyed" (235), a concept of the communion as Eucharist, or thanksgiving, that falls somewhat outside this essay's ambit. "Shared offerings" imply the "need for union with a transcendent reality" for right living, which aligns with the film's representation of the taboos that structure the daily lives – and deaths – of the Inuit in the film (235). This is seen in the lengthy sequence of Avva's explanation to Rasmussen (and to the viewer) of why there is evil in the world – although these taboos are more representative of the need for union with an all-too-immanent quotidian reality – the weather, disease, famine, the natural world – to ensure survival. "Sin offerings," finally, allow people to acknowledge "past disregard of the transcendent reality and their disobedience of the transcendent order" (235). Marsh elaborates:

> Most dimensions of the sacrificial tradition attend, of course, to the vertical axis: the relationship between the human and the divine. Sacrifice in the context of worship could, however, never be a vertical affair only. Horizontal relations are always also in view. Public worship can never be a merely private practice: a matter between the believer and his/her god. (213)

It is in this sense, argues Marsh, that communion can be thought of as "shared sacrifice":

> Shared offerings highlight this feature of worship directly. The two dimensions are also neatly preserved in the ambiguity of the word "communion" itself. Communion is always and at once communion with god and communion between participants. The two dimensions cannot be separated. (213)

In Benedict Anderson's well-known formulation, a nation is "*imagined* because the members of even the smallest nation will never know most of their fellow-members, meet them, or even hear of them, yet in the minds of each lives the image of their communion."[8] While this is not the place in which to make an argument for the Inuit in the film as comprising a "nation," the Igloolik Inuit, and Avva's family in particular, might be said to constitute an ideal example of this kind of human community whose members are bound together in relations of both physical and "spiritual" proximity. At the same time, on the level of the production of the film itself, the Isuma team exploits the latest digital video technology, transmediating pre-existing media, to fashion a wholly new kind of community. As I argue elsewhere,[9] this key feature of the film's production is reflected self-reflexively within the diegesis, from the very opening scene, in which a group of Inuit in 1912 participate in the collection of their own ethnographic data, including the gramophonic recording of traditional songs, the writing of their names in the syllabary invented for them by white missionaries, and the taking of a group photograph. Here my aim is to examine a less overt, more complex form of transmediation that extends and complicates the interpenetration of style and story that already characterizes the film as a whole.

Sacrifice operates in *The Journals* by means of interrelated semantic and formal elements, in ironic counterpoint to the thematic and narrative focus on the impact of the introduction of Christianity upon traditional Inuit culture in the 1920s. The film thematizes the ever-present threat of famine and even starvation, tying it inexorably to the parallel threat of catastrophic spiritual transformation. In the process, however, the film maintains a resolutely critical stance with respect to both the ethnographic perspective of the outsider, which it ironically incorporates, and to its own preferred Inuit perspective. *Atanarjuat*'s conclusion exemplifies Girard's precept that "sacrifice is primarily an act of violence without risk of vengeance."[10] In the shift to a locatable historical setting, sacrifice also manifests in *The Journals* on the collective level of the fate of the group as a whole, but with completely different stakes. The internecine conflict in the earlier film gives way to a potentially apocalyptic clash of cultures, with the Inuit put into the position of sacrificing not one of their own or some substitutive animal victim, but their traditional way of life. As in *Atanarjuat*, there is a shift from literal to metaphorical sacrifice, where the latter must be appreciated in all of its tangible force. Retributive violence, whether real or metaphorical, is absent from *The Journals*, and violence, or rather sacrifice, manifests in the diegesis as sacramental transformation, as counter-balance to the imminent threat of hunger and starvation.

What is the nature of the traditional shamanistic culture that the film sets in opposition to the modernizing and assimilationist force of conversion to Christianity that drives the narrative? Among certain northern North American peoples, a shaman is "a tribal medicine man or wizard,"[11] the key figure in any so-called "primitive religion holding that gods, demons, ancestral spirits, etc. work for the good or ill of humankind through the sole medium of the shamans."[12] To this extent, unlike *Atanarjuat*, *The Journals* represents an Inuit world in the throes of radical change, determined by what Michelle H. Raheja calls "a binary opposition between Inuit and 'southern' communities."[13] A principal feature of this underlying opposition, ironically, is the Inuit freedom from the kind of hierarchically binaristic thinking outlined above, in the context of visual representation as reproduction of an extra-cinematic reality. In other words, to the extent that non-Inuit outsider culture for much of the twentieth century was characterized by what Elizabeth Mittman and Mary R. Strand call the "transcendental anchor" of a metaphysical worldview,[14] Inuit culture is determined otherwise, according to a wholly other logic in which the natural and spiritual worlds are coterminous, co-existing on the same plane of visibility. Visibility, after all, is the precondition for representability, the Inuit spirit world appearing within the frame, as part of the *mise-en-scène*, alongside – and seemingly of the same value as – everything else. Therefore, while in its story *The Journals*, perhaps unavoidably, exploits specific oppositions – Inuit vs.

whites; shamanism vs. Christianity; traditional vs. imported technologies; etc. – it does so in order to quietly deconstruct the very thinking that underpins such binaries in the first place, even as the film, on the visual level, remains caught up in the binaries informing the photographic image since its inception in the nineteenth century.

It can be argued that the film stretches the truth, changes history to suit a certain agenda; indeed, contemporary scholarship shows the relation between Inuit shamanistic culture and Christianity to be much more complex and complicated than the film allows.[15] I would counter the argument that the film's version of events misrepresents or simplifies "history", however, with J. Edward Chamberlin's claim that "[t]he remedy for the dispossession of Aboriginal historical discourse may ultimately lie less in recovering the realities of the past than in encouraging the imagination of those who will shape the stories in the present."[16] This is an argument that Isuma co-founder and cinematographer Norman Cohn, for one, shares.[17] *The Journals* is a "post-cinematic" film in so far as it exemplifies the new norm of digital, post-celluloid cinema. "Post-cinematic," therefore, refers to both the total *diffusion* of the cinematic as culturally dominant, but also its *transcendence* via new digital technologies, which by now affect *every* phase of our engagement with cinema – production, post-production, distribution, reception and evaluation – to the extent that even when we view non-digital films today, we do so by and large through digital means. Indeed, *The Journals* constitutes a meditation on the very nature of the post-cinematic moving image, of which it is a distinctive example. This intensely self-conscious, self-reflexive tendency is nothing new in the history of film, but it is arguable that even more is now at stake in the face of its structural disavowal. The distinction between celluloid and digital invokes the indexical and iconic nature of the cinematic image, in so far as one can still have faith in the prior presence of the pro-filmic event in the age of digital video. In Peircian semiotics, the cinematic image bears an *iconic* and therefore mimetically grounded dimension that has no relation to the *symbolic* – and genuinely arbitrary – nature of the word as sign. The illusion of the ongoing *presence* of the pro-filmic referent, therefore, is a key point in an analysis of Isuma's use of the medium; that is, the degree to which high-density digital video is *not* put in the service of spectacular and costly special effects, whether during or post-production, but is rather exploited almost exclusively as a capture medium, recording what has been put in front of the camera, or has made its way there, whether or not by the filmmakers' intentions.

While Isuma's intended audience is primarily Inuit, the advent of HD digital video opens new avenues of address. Norman Cohn explains:

> As video artists in the first decades of a medium whose distinctive character finally reveals itself in high-definition, we have responsibilities to a second, universal audience of which Inuit are a part. We explore changes in storytelling made possible by [the] unique properties video brings to narrative representation [...] As agents in our own lives, and spectators of others, we recognize authentic meaning only in emotions experienced in "real time;" that is, not the fake and fractured time of conventional filmmaking but the three-dimensional time of real life.[18]

The advent of digital technology in the 1980s and 1990s significantly altered the conditions of production, not to speak of the reception, of film narrative. When engaging critically with *The Journals* it is crucial to consider the relations among the spectator, the unique context or conditions of production, and the film in itself, as a distinct semiotic object. Sylvie Jasen, for instance, stresses the significance of Isuma's emphasis upon exhaustive and at times redundant behind-the-scenes research and preparation in order to re-create the lived authenticity of Inuit culture *c.*1922.[19] As Cohn confirms, their technique consisted of shooting hundreds of hours of footage and several takes for each scene, with perhaps a few minutes or seconds ending up on screen in the final edit, with other sequences cut altogether. This is an increasingly typical approach in the digital era of more affordable cameras and computer editing software.

sacrifice, authenticity, intertextuality

Since the release of *Atanarjuat, The Fast Runner* in 2001, Isuma Production's[20] use of digital video has been central to its creation of a transnational indigenous art cinema. Utilizing the latest in handheld digital video technology in order to record their careful reconstructions of pre-contact Inuit culture, *The Journals* exemplifies what anthropologist Faye Ginsburg calls the "Faustian dilemma" faced by indigenous filmmakers in Canada and elsewhere: "on the one hand, they use new technologies for cultural self-assertion, on the other they spread a technology that might ultimately only foster their own disintegration."[21] *The Journals* self-reflexively interrogates the intersection of indigenous self-representation and new media forms – especially high-definition digital video technology – grounding this exploration in its auto-ethnographic quasi-documentary re-creation of traditional Inuit ways. Cultural and epistemological conflicts play out in the form of a series of binaries – pre- vs. post-contact Inuit culture; orality vs. literacy; shamanism vs. Christianity; etc. – each of which is complicated and critiqued even as the seeming inevitability of destructive cultural transformation is dramatized.

The Journals adapts portions of the Greenlandic ethnographer's record of a 1922 expedition to Canada's Arctic to gather data on the Inuit and their culture, centred on the figure of the shaman. Why would Kuñuk and Cohn choose the account of a white explorer and ethnographer, no matter how sympathetic, as the film's entry-point into the last days of Inuit shamanism? Rasmussen's function in the narrative points to the very purpose of ethnography to study and document every aspect of the culture of a specific ethnic group.[22] The better part of the film is not about Rasmussen (Jens Jörn Spottag) or a southern or outsider perspective at all, however: "What we were researching was what was not written," explains Kunuk, speaking of the process of adapting the journals. In a complex, elliptical narrative the film focuses upon the faces, bodies, lives and identities of the Inuit characters, portrayed, as in Isuma's other films and videos, by non-professional Inuit actors. The story ultimately focuses on the relation between Avva (Pakak Innukshuk), the last great Inuit shaman, and his daughter, Apak (Leah Angutimarik), the only one of his children to share in his shamanistic powers. As in the other films, the actors wear seemingly authentic costumes, use authentic tools and other props, within real Arctic locations with real weather and natural light. This aesthetic, many years in development in Isuma's early TV and video work, first achieved a more global audience with the 2001 release of *Atanarjuat*. That film's story, set in a mythic pre-historic time, traces the effects over two generations of an Inuit community of an initial, initiatory act of violence. Seemingly lending itself to discussion in terms of Rene Girard's analysis of productive violence in so-called primitive cultures, in the end the form and function of sacrifice in the film is transformed, as the need to eliminate harmful retributive violence is achieved not through the application of redemptive violence (i.e., sacrificial ritual), but through the deliberate disavowing of any kind of violence against other human beings.

Atanarjuat concludes with the eponymous hero deflecting rather than perpetuating the violence that manifests the "evil" produced through the initial breaking of a taboo. In the film's climactic scene, rather than seeking vengeance by killing the villainous Oki, as he seems prepared to do, Atanarjuat merely overpowers him, intoning "the killing stops here!" Atanarjuat thereby breaks the vicious cycle of retributive violence, which included Oki's act of parricide, and which had threatened the community as a whole. But the reason he was able to manipulate Oki into a vulnerable position in the first place is because the latter had caught and eaten an enchanted Arctic hare, which rendered him placid and well disposed toward his archenemy. The hare is sent through supernatural means by Qulitalik, Atuat's grandmother's absent brother, who twenty years before left the community with his family rather than risk exposure to the retributive violence that had been unleashed by the stranger's murder of the tribe's rightful chief. The hare functions in the narrative as the sacrificial victim in lieu of the deserving human one, who is subsequently exiled from the community, thereby fulfilling the primary social function of sacrifice, as outlined by Girard: "If left unappeased, violence will accumulate until it overflows its confines and floods the surrounding area. The role of sacrifice is to stem this rising tide of indiscriminate substitutions and redirect violence into 'proper' channels" (10) – in this case the acts of hunting, killing and consuming Arctic wildlife for survival. Hence, the substitution of the hare for the human perpetrator-victim, who nevertheless in the end undergoes the metaphorical death of banishment, guaranteeing the survival of the community.

The Journals is considerably more complex in its structure, invoking and transforming the significance of sacrifice in a way that gestures outside the story's limits toward a future beyond the film that may or may not correspond to contemporary Canadian Inuit reality – the very context of the film's production. *The Journals* also ends with a scene of "banishment" in which formerly valued members of the community are sent away for ever – only here these individuals are not human but spiritual beings. The banishment nevertheless bears the value of a sacrificial act. The film's full title is *A Series of Events Reported in The Journals of Knud Rasmussen*, and principal plot elements are adapted from Rasmussen's account. The main action unfolds in Arctic Canada in 1922 during the Greenlandic explorer's Fifth Thule Expedition. The British, in the person of Captain William Parry, had made first contact one hundred years earlier, in 1822, with authority over the Arctic territory passing from Britain to Canada in 1880.[23] A concerted program to convert the Inuit to Christianity was already well underway in the 1920s (Davis 208), and it is no accident that the one "missionary" character in the film is Nuqallaq's (Natar Ungalaaq) father, Umik (Samueli Ammaq), displaying all the zeal of a recent convert. *The Journals* therefore depicts a moment of change if not more catastrophic than first contact then of a different order of catastrophe: the advent of Christianity and the demise of traditional shamanism in Inuit culture. In the film, at least, the threat of death by starvation, on the one hand, and cultural – or spiritual – death, on the other, exist in clearly indirect relation: the choice between remaining true to traditional Inuit ways and facing a slow death, vs. embracing a new life under the sign of the cross and gaining access to the food cache.

intertextuality and love

Underlying its attention to language and representability, the key to understanding the transmediation of sacrifice and communion lies in the film's complex treatment of love. The Christian sacrament of communion, outlined above in relation to a very different film (*Babette's Feast*), is predicated upon a model of communal love or bonding around the central metaphor of consuming the god's sacrificial body and blood; the shared meal in effect binds the community together in affirmation of the symbolic function of Christ's offering of *himself* as sacrificial victim. *The Journals* explores these ideas in combination with other modalities of love, ranging from Inuit forms of communal bonding, at one extreme, to Western Romantic love as embodied in the lyrics of a nineteenth-century opera, at the other. The transformation of the model of communion, and its focus on the body, stands in the midst of these radically different conceptions of love.[24]

Following Rasmussen's statement that "I came to hear songs and legends if you will share them, and to learn about your beliefs," the shaman Avva challenges him to first "sing us something in your language." Rasmussen agrees and launches into "M'apparì tutt'amor," the Italian version of the aria from *Martha*, an 1847 romantic comic opera by German composer Friedrich von Flotow.[25] This bridges to a second Trading Post scene, eliding extra-diegetically with the original Enrico Caruso recording, an ironic reminder of the gramophone scene in *Nanook of the North*, which was, of course, silent. While it is interesting that the historical Rasmussen was a frustrated opera singer, proving that the Isuma team did their homework, more revealing is the ironic intertextual resonance of this opera's themes, as evidenced in the lines we hear (in Italian) in the film: "She appeared to me, purest of love. / I discovered with my eyes this vision of delight. / Lovely was she that my hungry heart, in a snap to her did fly. / Martha, Martha, you have left me, / And my heart with yours has vanished. / Peace and quiet, gone now forever, I will surely die of pain." Caruso's version of this aria is heard once more over the post-credits sequence, in which, in extreme long shot, a tiny dog sled travels toward a waiting group of people – perhaps Avva going to re-join the Christianized Inuit after divesting himself of his shamanistic powers; an incongruous juxtaposition of formal elements that nonetheless manages to convey an elegiac sadness. The aria's hyperbolic romanticizing of death over lost love (*Martha* is a *comic* opera) could not contrast more starkly with the fate of the Inuk Allakariallak, who is said to have died of starvation some two years after "the character of Nanook had achieved fame in the US and Europe."[26] This story, even if apocryphal, informs the plot of the Isuma film, wherein cataclysmic cultural change is driven to a significant degree by hunger.

The implications of the *Martha* intertext extend to the film's representation of the immaterial world on the levels of *mise-en-scène* and soundtrack, facilitating its quiet critique of different conceptions of love. These range from, on the one hand, Western European ideals of Romantic love vs. the commemoration of divine grace in the communion ceremony to, on the other hand, utterly non-Romantic Inuit notions of communal well-being above and beyond individual survival. The latter bear comparison to the Christian sacrament in their basis in "embodied" cultural memory (objects, social practices). The film's critique of Romantic love manifests, for instance, in Big Piita's tearful confession to Nuqallaq that he "lost [his] beautiful wife to [...] a killing sickness, just before I sailed from home. She should have been with me." This tallies with the historical Peter Freuchen, who lost his first wife, an Inuit woman, to the Spanish influenza in 1921, one year before the time in which the film is set. Nuqallaq responds: "I lost my first wife, too. She ended her own life. Then I found a new wife to make me happy again. Be cheerful. There's a lot of nice women here for you." What Nuqallaq's pragmatism doesn't reveal is that his "true love" is none other than Apak, with whom he has, as we say today, a "history." Ironically, Apak also has her "true love," her first husband, who was killed when an outsider tried to take her for himself. Her subsequent marriage, to a man she doesn't love, arranged by her father as a way of avoiding further bloodshed, leaves her with a single avenue to not so much love as sexual pleasure (although there is no hard line between these things): her dreams.

The dream scenes, in which Apak, in extreme close-up and grainy black and white, has sex with her dead husband, stand as unique stylistic moments in which cinematographer Cohn's background as video artist is manifest. Looking like something one could watch looped on a monitor in an urban art gallery, these scenes represent a marked intensification of the film's overall art video aesthetic. Of course, her spirit-helper is not the only one who knows of these dreams; as meetings with both her father and Nuqallaq make clear, everyone knows, and so the impossible visibility the film grants to the dreams gains some justification in terms of this communal understanding of one woman's most intimate, inner life.

As if in ironic contrast to Apak's dreams, the *Martha* aria ("M'appari tutt'amor" [She appeared to me, full of love]) manifests both intra- and extra-diegetically, on a soundtrack otherwise characterized (like *Atanarjuat*) by traditional Inuit songs, performed live to camera, as well as the dirge-like hymns sung by the Christianized Inuit in Igloolik – what drove Avva and his family away in the first place. It is his daughter Apak who stands at the juncture of these various forces, Inuit and non-Inuit, as she is the one to whom in the second Trading Post scene, to the strains of Caruso, Therkel Matthiasen gives a morsel of salted food, and who in the end must kneel to accept the sacrament of prohibited organ meat while the Christianized Inuit drone tunelessly around her. She is driven to this after her confession of having concealed a miscarriage that, she claims, has brought misfortune upon her family. It is Apak's struggle, as much as her father's, upon which the film focuses. This is not merely a matter of young marriageable woman as object of exchange in a patriarchal culture; she is, after all, the only character to whose interior life the viewer is granted visual and auditory access in the greyscale dream sequences in which she has sex with her dead husband. Whether her miscarriage is the result of a kind of immaculate oneiric conception is left to the viewer to decide.

"we follow our ancestors' rules because they work"

Following Avva's long monologue in direct address to camera (to be discussed below), the off-screen Rasmussen asks: "The rules you follow: eat this but not that, touch this but not that – what is the meaning of doing each thing just one way?" In other words: what is the function of ritual and *taboo* in your culture? Avva's non-answer – why is there "evil" in the world? – is the old question of the justification of faith in the good (or in gods or a "God") in the face of bad weather, illness, famine, and suffering. From the Book of Job to Milton's *Paradise Lost*, the literary genre of *theodicy* describes a text whose purpose is to justify faith in God, or to "justify the ways of God to man."[27] That is, if there is a God who is good and loving, why is there so much evil and suffering in the world? The emphasis, in the film's representation of *Inuit* culture, is on observing *taboos*: a fixed set of cultural prohibitions guaranteeing continued communal stability and harmony. Avva attempts to answer Rasmussen's unanswerable question ("What is the meaning of doing each thing just one way?"): "All our customs come from life and turn toward life," he explains ... "Our world is good and Inuit have our place in it." For indigenous Inuit society, unbeholden to the myths of Providence and Progress, change is bad: this is, after all, a culture that by the end of the nineteenth century had not changed substantially in three millennia. Avva's final answer to Rasmussen – "We follow our ancestors' rules because they work" – could double as the self-justification of a Hollywood producer, highlighting the irony that, in a second-order sense, the Isuma filmmakers are themselves breaking taboos, flouting the rules of narrative continuity, recognizable psychological motivation, and a readily legible diegetic world. Kunuk does not follow his cinematic ancestors' rules, in other words, but the "rules" of an alternative cinematic tradition, a transnational art cinema. The meaning of sacrifice and communion are determined in this transmediated context.

Towards the end of *The Journals*, Inuit Christian priest Umik makes explicit the connection between breaking taboos and taking communion: animal organ meats become the body and blood of Christ in an Inuit appropriation of transubstantiation. According to Greenlander Gretel Ehrlich: "[b]lood on the ice is not a sign of death but an affirmation of life. Eating meat becomes a sacramental experience" (qtd in Davis 210). This idea, however, is altered significantly in *The Journals*' representation of the Inuit's historical acceptance and appropriation of specific Christological tropes. To quote one of the hymns sung by the Inuit converts: "I cross over through my mouth. When I swallow his heart and lungs, Jesus is pleased." Historically, the ambivalent import of such appropriation is received negatively; throughout the film, however, cultural appropriation always cuts both ways. As noted above, *The Journals* opens with a scene of a number of Inuit in 1912 organizing themselves to have their photo taken, in a long slow fade from colour to the sepia tones of early photography. As they stare into the lens, whose transcendent point of view is identical to that of both the film camera and the viewer, the image freezes into an approximation of an early ethnographic photo, but with the difference that the subjects of the photo are also its authors.[28]

The opening scene inaugurates the film's ironic engagement with the history of photographic and cinematic ethnographic representations of the Inuit, dating back to Robert Flaherty's 1922 *Nanook of the North.*[29] Unlike that early pseudo-documentary, however, *The Journals* represents the Inuit's appropriation of the colonizing ethnographic gaze. But at what price? This gaze manifests in the film in more than one way, and never in a straightforward reinscription of the colonizing gaze of ethnographic photography. According to Jasen, the film places emphasis "not on the filming producing a *record* of the past but on the actors *reenacting* their past and thus learning the traditional practices through their bodily performance in the present" (10).[30] For Fatimah Rony, contemporary "ethnographic cinema is above all a cinema of the body," meaning that "the focus is on the anatomy and gestures of the indigenous person, and on the body of the land [s/he] inhabit[s]."[31] This corporeality is self-consciously emphasized; the Isuma films balance often extreme close-ups of the actors' faces with long takes of their fur-clothed bodies moving through the high Arctic spaces as figures against a blank canvas. The corporeal nature of Inuit film, its emphasis on the body in various senses, can be linked furthermore to the question of the materiality of the medium: the practical and aesthetic (as much as ontological) differences between video and film as distinct narrative media. According to Angela Krewani, this distinction is muddied in the Isuma film's hybrid textuality:

> *The Fast Runner* integrates structural elements of video art, such as the handheld camera, the detailed movements and actions and the imprecise and shifting framing of the images. With a deconstructive intent, Kunuk applies the stylistic devices of the medium [of] film and stretches them into the shifting visual aesthetics of video art [... offering ...] a different visual semantics.[32]

In *The Journals*, Rony's precept is also literally true, with animal body parts at the centre of the network of ironic sacramental references and complex thematization of the clash of traditional Inuit spirituality with a Western Christological metaphysics. The prospect of cultural destruction must be met with a sacrificial gesture, whether individual or collective, an element of both the narrative and of Inuit history at once appropriated *and* imposed from outside, necessitating an extremity of cultural adaptation. One could say that *The Journals*, beginning with its title, is an ironic response to the truism that even the best-intentioned anthropologist or ethnographer inevitably affects and changes the culture that s/he wishes to document and understand in its authenticity. In making *Nanook of the North* Flaherty failed to "acknowledge his own role as an agent of change in the lives of the Inuit" (Rony 110). What of the Isuma team as Inuit auto-ethnographers? In a key early scene *The Journals* offers a fascinating twist on Rony's contention that contemporary "ethnographic cinema is above all a cinema of the body," meaning that "the focus is on the anatomy and gestures of the indigenous person" (111). In *cinema verité* style, Avva delivers an eighteen-minute monologue to the off-screen Rasmussen,[33] in which he recounts his birth, childhood, his consecration as a shaman (*Angakut*), and the introduction of his "spirit-helpers." Visible throughout in the shot's narrow depth of field, behind and to one side of Avva, is what appears to be a young Inuit woman, wearing a more ornate than usual hooded fur costume; one of Avva's three principal spirit-helpers, she sits, virtually motionless, looking straight ahead, for the duration of this sequence. In this film the bodies of spirits look the same as human bodies: Avva's "spirit-helpers" are represented by actors wearing special costumes, placed in the shot as elements of the *mise-en-scène*, with no special effects whatsoever – a deceptively significant formal choice. These non-human, "spiritual" entities are utterly visible – to the viewer, at least, as the filmmakers use the medium to render the metaphysical physically, as if to suggest that there is no ontological difference between them. I would argue, though, that there is also in this an element of that communal "sharing" of cultural meanings through the manipulation of the medium's specific representational capacity.

"when i swallow his heart and lungs, jesus is pleased"

In the final Igloolik sequence, Rasmussen's colleague Therkel Matthiasen (Jakob Cedergren), in charge of gathering data on material culture, asks Avva's old friend if he, too, is a shaman. The friend responds that, after hearing about Jesus, doubt came into his mind: "I ate the pieces of meat shamans are never supposed to eat. The next time I tried to call them, my helping spirits wouldn't come. Now I'm not a shaman anymore."[34] Spiritual despair and conversion are equally by-products of doubt and broken taboos. As noted, the film thematizes the ever-present threat of famine and even starvation[35] – the real Nanook's rumoured fate – tying it inexorably to the parallel threat of spiritual transformation. Therefore, when Avva's daughter, Apak, describes her thoughts and actions as being "bad," she is not invoking any conventional southern moral schema; rather, she means that they are *literally* bad for the group, for the community; they have caused real suffering and so she is the one who is to blame. Soon after, Apak realizes that an act of self-sacrifice is required, but in the service not of spiritual but *physical* survival. In this vein, the Inuit traditions that are under threat are to the Old Testament what the literal New Testament, translated into Inuktitut, shown in close-up in the hands of the Inuit priest, is to the Gospel narrative: the first is not so much replaced as subsumed by the second. Thus the film's insistence upon the Inuit's measure of responsibility in their own rapid post-contact decline is reiterated; a depressing – and, it seems, reductive – perspective, which is simultaneously offset by the fact of the film itself as twenty-first-century manifestation of the impulse to appropriate outsider technology, dramatized in the opening scene in the trader's cabin.

In the above-mentioned scene featuring the New Testament and the Igloolik Inuit converts singing hymns, Nuqallaq declares: "Turn away from your old way of life. Satan tempts us with old taboos, but Jesus saves us with only ten commandments." His father, Umik, the priest, represents the complete rejection of a communal, external view of sin as the breaking of specific taboos, and the adoption of a Western conception of an interior, morally responsible self – a Christian, which is to say, modern, self-awareness. This shift is analogous to that from Inuit communal bonds to notions of individual Romantic love. Nuqallaq: "Your sins are in your hands and in your minds. Bad acts from bad thoughts." Umik: "Tonight we will cross over, eating organs shamans are forbidden. This way we become Christians. We become ready for Heaven! [...] Joy to all!" In a bitter irony, Umik's words echo the conclusion of Avva's earlier story of his consecration as a shaman: "Joy! Now I will go home!" Mid-way through the film his daughter Apak experiences an aural vision, a flash-forward to the film's climactic scene, in which Avva banishes his helping spirits. At intervals throughout the film, Apak has a recurrent dream of having sex with her dead husband. As noted, these scenes differ stylistically from the main diegesis in their grainy black-and-white imagery, extreme close-up framing and non-diegetic throat-singing aural backdrop. They are also unique in the Isuma canon for their frank representation of otherwise "invisible" subjective interiority: Apak's inner dreamscape, the visual manifestation of guilt-free joy. The scene in question begins with Apak in close-up as she slowly awakens, the sound of Avva's banished spirits' lamentation bridging her dreaming and waking realities. Her dream this time, however, ends with a close-up, still in grainy black and white, of a chuckling, bearded older man. He is in fact the same man seen earlier, laughing softly at Apak in reverse shot, after she awakes from her oneiric tryst. In the penultimate dream scene a quick cut back reveals Apak as she mutters "Asshole" under her breath, self-consciously pulling her clothes over her naked body. The subsequent reverse shot reveals that the man is no longer there, he has in effect disappeared. Was he ever there? Yes and no: the answer is complicated, as the viewer realizes that he is Apak's spirit helper, his sudden vanishing at the end of this scene foreshadowing with the audacity of a straight cut his utter and irreversible disappearance at the film's conclusion. As with Avva's spirit-helpers, he both is and is not there; his concrete visibility, his *presence* in the film, in the form of an actor wearing a special costume, serves to underline the significance of his utter absence, once Apak relinquishes her status as her father's shamanistic heir. In the film's conclusion Apak must kneel to accept the sacrament of prohibited meat while around her the other Inuit sing their versions of Christian hymns. Apak is driven to eat the forbidden organ meat after her confession of having concealed a miscarriage, a broken taboo, which, she claims, is the source of her family's misfortune. Just before she accepts the morsel of food from Umik, a final reaction shot of her spirit helper precedes his final disappearance. Umik makes explicit to his congregation the connection between breaking taboos and taking communion: the organ meats become the body and blood of Christ in an Inuit appropriation of transubstantiation. As the hymn says: "I cross over through my mouth. When I swallow his heart and lungs, Jesus is pleased." By translating scripture and transmediating communion, the Inuit in the film re-frame them in their own terms. At the same time, as shown in the penultimate scene of Apak's first communion, in which she eats the organ meats heretofore forbidden to women, this ironic recontextualization comes at the price of an entire way of life.

conclusion: sacrificial consumption and cultural memory

In the film's final scene, Avva banishes his spirit-helpers, thereby disavowing his identity as a shaman in what is clearly an act of self-sacrifice on behalf of his family group, threatened with starvation in the face of a rapidly spreading Christianity whose zealous followers control the food supply. Informed by a particular historical interpretation,[36] the film's connecting of physical survival with cultural survival is central to its meaning as trans-indigenous art film, the question of *sacrifice* resonating across these two distinct but interconnected registers. As Georges Bataille reminds us, sacrifice means etymologically "nothing other than the production of *sacred* things."[37] This scene, however, represents Avva's sacrifice as a moment of radical *loss* that transcends the individual, embracing the loss of cultural identity as a whole, the basis for Inuit collective memory. How, then, does this or any other scene *produce* the sacred? It is arguable that Avva's gesture *bans* one form or mode of the sacred in order to survive by embracing – or appearing to embrace – another.[38] Bataille's sacrificial production, after all, is implicitly determined by a negative logic of destruction: the sacred is "produced" through the *destruction*, actual or metaphorical, of something *else*, a designated object, animal or person, the proper or surrogate victim, just as the meaning of communion is produced out of the *consumption* of the bread and wine. In the Judeo-Christological framework, as Girard shows, the classic form of victim is the scapegoat as figure of substitution; the substitutive victim whose destruction *produces* something else, the "sacred" as meaning, which justifies or "redeems" the inherent violence of such productive destruction. It is necessary at this point, however, to augment Girard's sacrificial model to achieve a fuller understanding of the experience of the Inuit in this film. In its modern attenuation, after all, such violence, like the victim and the act of destruction itself, may also be metaphorical, adding another layer of displacement onto the initial displacement necessary for the sacrificial act to be something other than a mere act of violence, or straightforward destruction. As the story focuses on historical loss, transformation, and adaptation for the sake of survival, sacrifice in *The Journals* is transformed on the formal level of the film's imagery, where the sacred, or rather the spirit world, is instantiated, given form, made flesh, alongside the quotidian objects and actions of the Inuit in the film's 1922 setting. That is, the violence of Avva's sacrifice – his relinquishing of his spirit-helpers in order to convert to Christianity, in order to avoid starvation – is the violence of hunger, privation, loss; the violence of "living on" – the literal meaning of survival[39] – in what amounts, in the film's diegetic world, to a living death: the dissolution of community.

In many ways the Isuma team embodies what Jacques Rancière means by the "emancipated spectator,"[40] in that through making these films they first achieved artistic emancipation as more-or-less autonomous indigenous cultural producers, a self-transformation predicated upon their initial transformation as spectators of their own (cultural or spiritual) annihilation. Throughout *The Journals*, the dialogue emphasizes the difference between the often difficult "roads" the Inuit must travel in their seasonal migrations and the choice to turn away from their "old ways" and follow the metaphorical "road of Jesus," in a devastating invocation of the Pauline distinction between the letter and the spirit, a distinction which does not hold for the traditional Inuit perspective presented in the film. In this worldview the relation between the natural and the spirit worlds is one of continuity, rather than the metaphysical hierarchy upon which Western post-Christian culture is historically based. This difference in perspective is most powerfully evoked in the form of the appropriated communion ceremony, where the film dramatizes the "transubstantiation" of the old ways, in the form of the ultimate taboo, into a new, effectively "civilizing" ritual, in which collective taboo gives way to moral prohibition, external evil to sin and internalized guilt. In *The Journals* the literal and metaphorical value of communion as sacrament is transformed into the violence of sacrifice, and only the beauty of the images remains as compensation for what has been lost. It is possible that the Inuit, in exchanging their pre-literate orality for a post-literate digitality, might be giving up their future in exchange for a reified past, sacrificed on the altar of digital video.

notes

1 Plate 6.

2 The first film is *Atanarjuat: The Fast Runner*, directed by Kunuk and Cohn (2001), and the third instalment is *Before Tomorrow*, directed by Marie Cousineau and Madeline Ivalu (2008).

3 Voigts-Virchow 140.

4 McLuhan 7.

5 Plate does not address questions of the intersection or clash of indigenous and dominant cultures, whether secular or otherwise. Nevertheless, his argument here tallies closely with that of many scholars of indigenous cinema, concerned about the contradictions faced by such "Fourth World" filmmakers who choose to express or represent themselves via the latest "First World" technologies. See Plate 4–5. Indigenous peoples, existing within (heretofore) First World states, also comprise what is sometimes referred to as the "Fourth World," producing what Barry Barclay terms a "Fourth Cinema":

> While Third Cinema is a postcolonial movement that grew out of cultural and political changes in the 1960s in formerly colonized parts of the world to denounce Hollywood style entertainment in favor of a national, popular, and activist vernacular, indigenous cinema has its roots in specific indigenous aesthetics with their attendant focus on a particular geographical space, discrete cultural practices, social activist texts, notions of temporality that do not delink the past from the present or future, and spiritual traditions. (Raheja 1167)

6 Marsh 211–12.

7 Martos 235.

8 Anderson 6–7.

9 See Kilbourn.

10 Girard 13.

11 In his journals Rasmussen used the term "wizard" to translate the Inuit term (Rasmussen).

12 *Funk and Wagnall's Standard College Dictionary.*

13 Raheja 1174.

14 Mittman and Strand 51.

15 See, for example, Laugrand and Oosten.

16 Chamberlin 83.

17 Norman Cohn, personal interview.

18 Igloolik Isuma Productions.

19 Jasen 9–10.

20 In 1990 Kunuk and Cohn, with Pauloosie Qulitalik and the late Paul Apak, founded Isuma Productions, based in Igloolik, Nunavut, the first all-Inuit independent film and new media production company. "Isuma" is Inuktitut for "think" or "to have a thought."

21 Quoted in Stam and Shohat 393.

22 In addition to Rasmussen, the film also features actors portraying two of the men who accompanied him on the expedition, Peter Freuchen, cartographer, and Therkel Matthiasen, an anthropologist in charge of studying Inuit material culture (Rasmussen 10).

23 Davis 208.

24 I use "Romantic" here to qualify a specifically modern category of love characterized by its focus upon the individual (even in those cases, such as in Wagner, where the transcendence of individual bounds is desired), elaborated in the Romantic period but persisting in its influence through the nineteenth century and into the twentieth. This usage is related to but not coterminous with the musicological appellation "romantic" in the phrase "romantic comic opera" (see *Grove Music Online*).

25 The *Grove Encyclopedia of Music* lists *Martha* as a "romantische-komische Oper" ("Flotow, Friedrich").

26 Ginsburg 81.

27 Milton.

28 See Hearne 314.

29 According to Hearne, "early ethnographic cinema combined documentation with the exotic, seeking to capture a supposed Native 'purity' [within] Euro-American frameworks" (307).

30

> Our film is a vehicle for you to get as close to being inside the events of *The Journals of Knud Rasmussen* as you could possibly be, if you hadn't been there, because you can't have been there, and we can't have been there. So we recreate the events in a way that seems to us as authentic as we can possibly make it. (Cohn, personal interview)

31 Rony 11.

32 Krewani 117.

33 Contrary to Jasen's description, this scene does not involve a "direct address" to the camera (8); rather, Avva's slightly oblique eyeline suggests that he is addressing Rasmussen, his off-screen interlocutor, with whom the viewer unavoidably identifies.

34 Re the crucifix as symbolic of death and rebirth for Inuit, cf. Laugrand and Oosten 55.

35 This is quietly illustrated in a scene late in the film of Avva's sons bringing to him one of their sled dogs, which they have just killed for food.

36 See, for example, Laugrand and Oosten re an alternative interpretation of the relation between traditional Inuit culture and the newly introduced Christianity in terms of cultural integration or assimilation as a means of survival (xvii–xviii).

37 Bataille 119.

38 Ungureanu.

39 As in the French "sur-vivre." See Jacques Derrida's discussion of Maurice Blanchot's *Death Sentence* [*L'Arrêt de mort*] (Sherwood and Hart 225–27).

40 Rancière.

bibliography

Anderson, Benedict. *Imagined Communities: Reflections on the Origin and Spread of Nationalism.* 2nd ed. London and New York: Verso, 1991. Print.

Bataille, Georges. *Visions of Excess: Selected Writings, 1927–1939.* Ed. and trans. Allan Stoekl. Minneapolis: U of Minnesota P, 1989. Print.

Chamberlin, J. Edward. *If This is Your Land, Where are Your Stories?* Toronto: Vintage Canada, 2004. Print.

Cohn, Norman. Personal interview. 20 Oct. 2012.

Davis, Wade. *The Wayfinders: Why Ancient Wisdom Matters in the Modern World.* Toronto: Anansi, 2009. Print.

"Flotow, Friedrich". Grove Music Online. 2007–2014. Web. 20 Aug. 2014. <http://www.Oxfordmusiconline.com>.

Funk and Wagnall's Standard College Dictionary. Toronto: Fitzhenry, 1976. Print.

Ginsburg, Faye. "Screen Memories and Entangled Technologies: Resignifying Indigenous Lives." *Multiculturalism, Postcoloniality, and Transnational Media.* Ed. Ella Shohat and Robert Stam. New Brunswick, NJ and London: Rutgers UP, 2003. 77–98. Print.

Girard, René. *Violence and the Sacred.* Trans. Patrick Gregory. Baltimore: Johns Hopkins UP, 1977. Print.

Hearne, Joanna. "Telling and Retelling in the 'Ink of Light': Documentary Cinema, Oral Narratives and Indigenous Identities." *Screen* 47.3 (2006): 307–26. Print.

Igloolik Isuma Productions. 2006. Web. 15 Feb. 2014. <http://www.isuma.tv/isuma-productions>.

Jasen, Sylvie. "'The Archive and the Reenactment': Performing Knowledge in the Making of *The Journals of Knud Rasmussen.*" *The Velvet Light Trap* 71 (Spring 2013): 3–14. Print.

The Journals of Knud Rasmussen. Dir. Zacharias Kunuk and Norman Cohn. Perf. Natar Ungalaaq and Sylvia Ivalu. Igloolik Isuma Productions, 2006. DVD.

Kilbourn, Russell J.A. "If This is Your Land, Where is Your Camera? *Atanarjuat, The Journals of Knud Rasmussen* and Post-Cinematic Adaptation." *Journal of Adaptation and Theatre Performance* 7.2 (2014): 195–208. Print.

Krewani, Angela. "Through the Camera Lens: Cultural Practice as Media Image." *Zeitschrift für Kanada-Studien* 28.1 (2008): 108–18. Print.

Laugrand, Frédéric B., and Jarich G. Oosten. *Inuit Shamanism and Christianity: Transitions and Transformations in the Twentieth Century.* Montreal and Kingston: McGill-Queen's UP, 2010. Print.

Marsh, Clive. "Did you Say 'Grace'? Eating Community in *Babette's Feast.*" *Explorations in Theology and Film: Movies and Meaning.* Ed. Clive Marsh and Gaye Ortiz. Oxford: Blackwell, 1997. 207–18. Print.

Martos, Joseph. *Doors to the Sacred: A Historical Introduction to Sacraments in the Catholic Church.* Liguori, MO: Liguori/Triumph, 2001. Print.

McLuhan, Marshall. *Understanding Media: The Extensions of Man.* Cambridge, MA: MIT P, 1994. Print.

Milton, John. *Paradise Lost.* 1674. Ed. Scott Elledge. New York and London: Norton, 1993. Print.

Mittman, Elizabeth, and Mary R. Strand. "Representing Self and Other in Early German Romanticism." *Theory as Practice: A Critical Anthology of Early German Romantic Writings.* Ed. and trans. Jochen Schülte-Sasse. Minneapolis: U of Minnesota P, 1997. 47–71. Print.

Nanook of the North. Dir. Robert Flaherty. Perf. Allakariallak and Nyla. Les Frères Revillon, 1922. DVD.

Plate, S. Brent. "Introduction: Filmmaking, Mythmaking, Culture Making." *Representing Religion in World Cinema.* Ed. S. Brent Plate. New York: Palgrave, 2003. 1–18. Print.

Raheja, Michelle H. "Reading Nanook's Smile: Visual Sovereignty, Indigenous Revisions of Ethnography, and *Atanarjuat (The Fast Runner).*" *American Quarterly* 59.4 (2007): 1159–85. Print.

Rancière, Jacques. *The Emancipated Spectator.* Trans. Gregory Elliott. London and New York: Verso, 2011. Print.

Rasmussen, Knud. *Intellectual Culture of the Iglulik Eskimos, Report of the Fifth Thule Expedition 1921–24, vol. 7, no. 1.* 1929. Copenhagen: Glydensdalke Boghandel, Nordisk Forlag, 1930. Rpt. New York: AMS, 1976. Print.

Rony, Fatimah. *The Third Eye: Race, Cinema and the Ethnographic Spectacle.* Durham, NC: Duke UP, 1996. Print.

Sherwood, Yvonne, and Kevin Hart, eds. *Derrida and Religion: Other Testaments.* New York: Routledge, 2005. Print.

Stam Robert, and Ella Shohat. "Film Theory and Spectatorship in the Age of the 'Posts.'" *Reinventing Film Studies*. Ed. Christine Gledhill and Linda Williams. Oxford and New York: Arnold, 2003. 381–401. Print.

Ungureanu, Camil. "Re: Cinema and Sacrifice." Message to the author. 15 Mar. 2013. E-mail.

Voigts-Virchow, Eckart. "Metadaptation: Adaptation and Intermediality – Cock and Bull." *Journal of Adaptation in Film and Performance* 2.2 (2009): 137–52. Print.

robert sinnerbrink

ANATOMY OF *MELANCHOLIA*

Justine: The earth is evil. We don't need to grieve for it ... Nobody will miss it.
Leo: Dad says there's nothing to do then. Nowhere to hide.
Justine: If your dad said that, then he's forgotten about something. He's forgotten about the magic cave.
Melancholia

Lars von Trier is a director renowned for his treatment of sacrifice. Many of his films feature female characters who sacrifice themselves, their social standing, their dignity, or even their lives, for others, whether husbands, children, community, or cinema itself.[1] As a number of critics have observed, his films are also pervaded by theological motifs and a sacrificial logic of exchange.[2] Sacrifice, however, is not only a thematic concern in his work; it is *cinema itself* that von Trier attempts to sacrifice, most explicitly in his recent film, *Melancholia* (2011), the second in what one might call von Trier's "trauma trilogy" (bookended by *Antichrist* (2009) and *Nymphomaniac: Vol. I* and *Vol. II* (2013).[3] *Melancholia* is a remarkable fusion of Dogme-style melodrama, apocalyptic disaster movie, and mock-Wagnerian *Gesamtkunstwerk*. Combining Bergmanesque psychodrama and Tarkovskian melancholia, Schopenhauerian pessimism and German romanticism, von Trier creates an enchanted cinematic world consecrated to the disenchanting idea of "world-sacrifice." The film presents a devastating portrait of depressive melancholia, dramatising the main character Justine's (Kirsten Dunst's) harrowing experience of a "loss of world" that finds its objective correlative in a cinematic fantasy of world-annihilation. In what follows I shall analyse some of the aesthetic and philosophical strands of *Melancholia*, focusing in particular on the film's remarkable Prelude, arguing that it performs a complex ethical critique of rationalist optimism in the guise of a neo-romantic allegory of world-destruction. At the same time, I want to suggest that *Melancholia* seeks to "work through" the loss of worlds – cinematic but also cultural and natural – that characterises our historical mood, one that might be described as a deflationary apocalypticism, or a melancholy modernity. Indeed, a number of critics have noted the aesthetic and theological aspects of *Melancholia* along with its environmental and ethico-political resonances.[4] From this perspective, *Melancholia* belongs to a genealogical lineage that links it with two earlier films important for von Trier: Ingmar

Bergman's *Shame* [*Skammen*] (1968) and Andrei Tarkovsky's *The Sacrifice* [*Offret*] (1986). All three films share a concern with apocalypticism, world-sacrifice, and historical melancholia; but they also explore different responses to the imagined experience of a catastrophic loss of world. By examining these films in relation to *Melancholia* we can trace the logic of this loss, culminating in *Melancholia*'s radical gesture of world-sacrifice; this aestheticisation of world-destruction has the paradoxical ethical meaning, I suggest, of preparing for a post-humanist beginning.

"of an apocalyptic tone recently adopted in cinema ... "

One of the more intriguing phenomena in contemporary cinema has been the resurgence of the apocalyptic disaster movie. This has been a recurring topic in the movies, a subgenre of science fiction typically featuring religious, ideological, and more recently economic and ecological themes. Apocalyptic fiction, in the modern sense, dates back to the nineteenth century. The most famous example is Mary Shelley's novel *The Last Man* (1826), a post-apocalyptic "last man standing" narrative including critical reflections on romanticism and humanism.[5] We could also mention Edgar Allan Poe's early science fiction story "The Conversation of Eiros and Charmion" (1836), in which the two eponymous characters have a posthumous conversation about the response of humankind to the destruction of the world due to a comet strike.[6] As is well known, movies have long been fascinated by apocalyptic tales. The 1950s saw a wave of popular apocalyptic disaster movies, typically featuring alien invasion/War of the Worlds scenarios, or fatal viral-biological epidemics, but also exploring cosmic catastrophes in which a random astronomical event destroys life on Earth. Rudolph Maté's *When Worlds Collide* (1951), for example, features a newly discovered planet, called Bellus, set on a collision course with the Earth. The impending catastrophe provides the backdrop for an anarchic Hobbesian "war of all against all" as desperate individuals vie for a place in the "arks" that will set forth for another planet and thus save the human race from extinction.

From the mid-1980s the apocalyptic/post-apocalyptic movie made something of a comeback, typically centred on the threat and aftermath of a global environmental or nuclear apocalypse. Two representative examples are Geoff Murphy's post-apocalyptic love-triangle scenario *The Quiet Earth* (1985), a contemporary remake, set in New Zealand, of a 1950s movie,[7] and Steve de Jarnatt's *Miracle Mile* (1988), a chronicle of the last night on Earth before nuclear war erupts, a scenario in which a wide range of characters respond in very different ways, evincing shock, panic, despair, suicide, denial, maintaining normality, pursuing pleasure, and committing heroic acts. Don McKellar's cult film *Last Night* (1998), a classic "last night on Earth" scenario, features, for example, a failed suicide pact as the film's central couple decide to embrace and kiss before their (and the world's) definitive destruction. Abel Ferrara's *4:44 Last Day on Earth* (2011) is a contemporary revisiting of this theme, again centred on a central couple, a successful actor (Willem Dafoe) and his artist girlfriend (Shanyn Leigh) in New York City, whose lovemaking after observing the shocked and panic-stricken responses of those around them concludes their intimation of mortality.

In recent years, however, another kind of apocalyptic/post-apocalyptic movie has appeared.[8] These movies tend to thematise more explicitly contemporary anxieties over environmental devastation, geopolitical threats, and economic crises, often by way of religious-theological speculation. This is not surprising, given our contemporary ideological-historical mood, which Slavoj Žižek describes as "living in the end times."[9] A good example of this kind of apocalyptic/post-apocalyptic fantasy is Alex Proyas's *Knowing* (2009), a film that stages the destruction of the Earth and of all life on the planet as a spectacle that certain privileged characters – and viewers – are able to enjoy; an apocalyptic fantasy laced with vague speculation over free will and determinism, religious themes of prophecy and salvation, and the Darwinian indifference of nature to human suffering. Blockbuster post-apocalyptic movies, such as Roland Emmerich's *Independence Day* (1996) and *2012* (2009), take a more practical approach, affirming their faith in the nuclear family, in the American Way, reinvesting belief in the world-saving virtues of what Deleuze called the sensory-motor action schema. Their redemptive version of post-apocalyptic renewal typically features enterprising individuals, "love conquers all" couples, even the American president, cast in mythic roles of all-powerful heroes who avert catastrophe and re-found humanity by purifying acts of violence against alien forces, aided by an unstable blend of fringe science and esoteric religious prophecy.

It will not be surprising to remark that von Trier's *Melancholia* is a determinate negation of all of these apocalyptic and post-apocalyptic fantasies; a resolutely tragic film that refuses any humanistic consolation or metaphysical comfort afforded by post-apocalyptic redemption fantasies, reassuring visions that reconstitute the couple, the family, or civilisation as we know it after the "divine violence" of cosmic catastrophe. What *Melancholia* shares with more arthouse "end of days" movies, however, is the manner in which the apocalypse – in the biblical sense of a revelation of all secrets, and in the generic sense of a fantasy of world-destruction – is reflected or refracted by a familial drama or melodrama. Michael Haneke's remarkable post-apocalyptic film *Time of the Wolf* (2003) is noteworthy here, with its "biopolitical" focus on a mother (Isabelle Huppert) and her two children reduced to "bare life," struggling to survive as refugees in a makeshift lawless "camp" following an unspecified social/ecological disaster.[10] Terrence Malick's cosmic epic *The Tree of Life* (2011) also includes – following the familial melodrama, evolution of life, and memory film sequences – Jack's (Sean Penn's) apocalyptic vision of the destruction of the Earth and eschatological vision of redemption through love. Jeff Nichols' *Take Shelter* (2011) is another interesting case, centring on the possibly schizophrenic visions of a character, the breakdown of his family, work, and personal life as he obsessively constructs a storm shelter, and concluding with what appears to be the film's confirmation of his apocalyptic visions of preternatural storms, waterspouts, and tsunamis.

This fascination with the "end of the world" topos inflected through familial melodrama is significant for a number of reasons. On the one hand, it reflects culturally pervasive anxieties over a variety of social, cultural, economic, political, and environmental concerns (threats to the nuclear family, fragile social and cultural identities, psychological and social dislocation due to globalisation, geopolitical terrorist threats, economic crises, climate change and environmental threats). On the other, such films can also be read allegorically, that is, as reflective of a sense of cultural and political paralysis, scepticism or deadlock (the "end of the world" as an allegory of the unsustainable character of the globalised consumer capitalism, and of our inability to envisage a different world as our own confronts the threat of cascading ecological, economic, and geopolitical crises). Whereas some films opt for a fragile, ambiguous political possibility (Haneke's *Time of the Wolf*), and others for moral-religious forms of transcendence (*The Tree of Life* or *Take Shelter*), von Trier's *Melancholia* refuses any straightforward political, religious, or ideological solution. Instead it reworks the "romanticist" strategy of staging the "end of the world" as a sublime aesthetic spectacle, one that refuses psychological or moral comfort to be drawn from the devastating thought of world-annihilation. As I discuss below, it does so in a highly reflexive manner, staging this aesthetic spectacle of world-sacrifice as a metacinematic reflection on the corruption, but also possible redemption, of art (cinema) today.

romanticism

I have described von Trier's *Melancholia* as a neo-romanticist work, but what does this mean? According to early German romantics such as the Schlegel brothers, the romantic work of art is capable of disclosing "the Absolute" indirectly via aesthetic means. These include the aesthetic use of the fragment, of transcendental irony as a way of combining poetic and philosophical discourse, and the poetic merging of aesthetic figures, rhetorical forms, and conceptual reflection. Romanticism is dedicated to creating poetic yet philosophical works that achieve what idealism sought but failed to secure: an (indirect) revelation of being or reality (or what the German idealists and romantics alike called "the Absolute").[11] Although often overlooked, the link between cinema and romanticism remains profound. As Jacques Rancière remarks, the cinema is an artform whose principle, "the unity of conscious thought and unconscious perception," was worked out one hundred years before its advent, namely in Schelling's *System of Transcendental Idealism* (1794).[12] With its capacity to combine the mechanical recording of events with the conscious intentionality of the filmmaker, "cinema, with its unconscious eye [...] enacts the romantic conception of the work as the identity of an unconscious process and a conscious process."[13] The conscious intentionality of the filmmaker combines with the unconscious capturing of an ambiguous reality, the aesthetic manipulation of the images merging with the tapping of "unconscious" currents of mood and meaning made manifest via aesthetic and technological means.

Let us consider, in this light, *Melancholia*'s remarkable Prelude, set to the Prelude of Wagner's *Tristan and Isolde* (1859). This is, of course, not the first von Trier film to begin with a prelude: *Antichrist* (2009) commences with a striking series of black and white images, also shot using the super-slow-motion Phantom HD Gold camera, set to Handel's aria "Lascia ch'io pianga" from the opera *Rinaldo* (1711).[14] *Dogville* (2003) commenced with an overture set to Pergolesi's *Stabat Mater* and von Trier's early film *Epidemic* (1987) – his viral contagion meets metacinematic scriptwriter drama – featured the Prelude to Wagner's *Tannhäuser*. Even *Breaking the Waves* featured *tableaux vivants* in the "intertitle" sections introducing the various chapters of the movie, set to evocative popular songs of the period (by David Bowie, Procol Harum, and Jethro Tull, for example).

Melancholia's Prelude consists of sixteen colour slow-motion shots, slowing the images down to near stasis, using "painterly" composition set to music, turning cinematic images into moving *tableaux vivants* evoking a variety of aesthetic moods. They also evoke a prophetic apocalyptic vision of the catastrophe to come. The opening image is a close shot of a woman's face (Kirsten Dunst), her head slightly to the left of mid-screen, against an indeterminate grey-orange background, opening her eyes and gazing directly at the camera, her hair dank, her face pale, tired, blank. The image is reduced to near stasis, a portrait of melancholia, of time arrested and congealed, with just the barest flicker of movement visible on her face, eyes, and hair.[15] It is an image of time, a veritable time-image. Some moments later dead birds fall slowly from the sky behind her, a popular "apocalyptic" image that signals, in many mythologies, God or nature's disapproval of the conduct of humankind. Here, however, the falling bodies seem poetic, mysterious, and beautiful, adding a vertical movement punctuating the slow passing of time. The second image depicts a symmetrically arranged front lawn, flanked by identical rows of trees, with a large sundial in the foreground (reminiscent of the outdoor garden in Alain Resnais' *Last Year at Marienbad* (1966)). In the background a tiny figure can be seen swinging a child around in a circle, like a tiny clock movement again evoking the mysterious compression and dilation of time. Also striking in the image are the dual shadows that the trees and other objects cast on the ground, anticipating the revelation of the planet Melancholia, with its soft blue light rivalling the Sun and the Moon. Time itself is revealed in the image, its movement reduced to the tiniest point; a child swinging around, marking time, in a movement pointing to the irreversibility of time and anticipating its ultimate end with the destruction of the Earth.

The third shot is of a painting, Pieter Bruegel's *Hunters in the Snow* (1565), showing a weary band of hunters and their dogs, cresting a hill and about to trudge home to their village, dormant in a small valley under a grey winter sky. Ashes appear in the front of the image, falling gently like snow, or like the dead birds, as the image slowly turns to flame. Bruegel's melancholy *Hunters in the Snow* also features prominently in Tarkovsky's *Solyaris* [*Solaris*] (1972), in the library birthday celebration sequence where Kris Kelvin (Donatas Banionis) battles his own bouts of melancholia after the death – and hallucinatory reappearance – of his wife, Hari (Natalya Bondarchuk).[16] Von Trier's homage is thus twofold: to Bruegel's early modern depiction of the mood of melancholia and the spiritual vacuity of crass materialism (later we see Justine's admired advertising image of sprawling models, which is itself modelled on another Bruegel painting, *The Land of Cockaigne* (1567), an allegory of moral vacuity in a land of plenty); and to Tarkovsky's art cinema of the 1970s, to moving images with aesthetic power and metaphysical ambition, now sacrificed, reduced to ash, like the Bruegel painting – a cinematic world consumed in the mindless embrace of consumerist culture and instrumentalised digital imagery.

The Prelude cuts to a cosmic image, recalling Kubrick's balletic planet and spaceship sequences in *2001: A Space Odyssey* (1968), an enormous blue planet (presumably Melancholia) slowly wending its way around a red or orange star (Antarus? Our own Sun?). The image rhymes with the opening shot of Justine's head and face, similarly framed, thus drawing the visual parallel between the melancholic Justine and the planet Melancholia: a pre-figuration of the psycho-cinematic mood of doom and destruction, a Tarkovsky-like coalescence of psychic, unconscious, and emotional memories in romantic, metaphysical, and cosmic imagery.

The next shot is of Justine's sister, Claire (Charlotte Gainsbourg), clutching her son, barely moving across the golf course, her boots sinking deep into the grassy ground, a nightmarish image of sensory-motor breakdown and helpless desperation. The image also features a suspicious flag, the nineteenth hole, which refers, von Trier remarks, to limbo.[17] A metaphysical-visual joke, ambiguous between sensuous immersion and distanced reflection, this shot suggests we are "in limbo"; an indeterminate space and time between past and future, divine prophecy and cosmic nightmare, hallucinatory vision and anticipatory recollection.

This shot is followed by a startling image of a black horse, Justine's beloved Abraham, falling to the ground beneath a night sky glowing with northern lights, a homage, perhaps, to Tarkovsky, recalling the many horses that appear, and sometimes fall, in his films (like *Andrei Rublev*, *Stalker*, and *Nostalghia*). This is followed by an image of Justine, standing on the golf course, arms outstretched like Christ, as moths dance around her in the foreground (a biblical reference, perhaps, to a passage in Isaiah, referring to moths and mortality in the face of God's infinite power).[18] These images, once again, hover ambiguously between romantic sublimity, historical homage, theological allusion, and cinematic self-reflection. This unsettling ambiguity of the Prelude, as developed further throughout the film, perhaps explains the polarised responses that *Melancholia* has evoked, from enthusiastic praise for its visual brilliance to sharp criticism for its "empty" allusions.[19]

A striking *tableau vivant* follows, one of the signature shots in the film. We see the gloomy castle, in crepuscular twilight, with the bride Justine, young Leo (Cameron Spurr), and Claire (Charlotte Gainsbourg) arrayed symmetrically on the lawn, barely moving, flanked by rows of trees. Twin sources of nocturnal light – Melancholia's *blaue Licht* and the Moon's eerie glow – lend the scene a strongly romantic cast, reminiscent of Caspar David Friedrich or the surrealism of Paul Devaux. The ambiguous status of these images, between still photograph and moving cinematograph, intensified by digital manipulation and intensified by slow-motion stasis, creates an uncanny, fantastical effect; a metaphysically tinged melancholy, an intimation of sublimity, expressed in images approximating moving paintings or cinematic hallucinations, images opening up a dimension of temporality that is difficult to place (a time anticipating the end of time; a time in which movement all but ceases, mood is intensified, thought is revealed).

The film cuts to another image of the planets in their *danse macabre*, the planet Melancholia, dwarfing the Earth, performing its teasing fly-by, followed by a shot of Justine, her hands slowly rising, electricity sparking from her fingertips and from the light poles behind her. The interaction between the planets, their mutual attraction, transfigures both nature and culture, transforming the manicured golf course into an elemental cauldron of energy, and Justine into a lightning rod for the collision to come. The coalescing of Justine's psychic visions of catastrophe and the energy connecting her melancholy mood with the impending world-destruction becomes striking at this point – a crisis that is at once psychological and social, metaphysical and modern, cinematic and cosmic.

The images in this Prelude, as becomes clear, are not arrayed chronologically, tracking the movement of the narrative to come. Rather, they cross back and forth between different temporal sections or movements of the film, from Justine's disastrous wedding reception, reminiscent of the early Dogme film *The Celebration* [*Festen*] (Thomas Vinterberg, 1998) to the final collision, catastrophic yet breathtaking, between the Earth and Melancholia. An image evoking the first part of the film appears, one that captures the oppressive feeling of time slowing and one's physical energy ebbing. We see a nightmarish but beautiful vision of Justine in her wedding dress, striding against black, weed-like strands, wrapped around her limbs and holding her back, but also unfurling from the trees, as though nature were refusing to let her go – images that again remain ambiguous between pure visual ideas, independent expressions of mood, and recollection-images attributable to particular characters (like Justine). Another shot of the planets Earth and Melancholia appears, looming larger and more equal in scale this time, the parallel now made explicit between Justine's psychological state, her physical distress, a generalised *Weltschmerz*, and the cosmic catastrophe to come. A shot from inside one of the melancholy rooms in the castle, a Victorian baronial-style interior framed by archways and intricate window-frames, reveals a burning bush in the garden outside, another image combining a biblical reference with an elemental, Tarkovsky-like evocation of fire. The film then cuts to a decidedly romantic image of the drowning bride clutching her wedding bouquet, half-immersed in a watery pond, slowly sinking amidst the lily pads and wavering weeds, reminiscent of John Everett Millais's well-known Pre-Raphaelite painting *Ophelia* (1852) – another homage image that provides both an aesthetic correlate for the character's mood and for the film's Tarkovsky-like evocation of earlier historical and cultural imagery.

The oneiric vision flashes forward to Justine and Leo in the forest, Justine approaching from a distance, Leo whittling a stick he will offer for Justine's "magic cave" that the surviving trio will build for their final moments together before the Earth is destroyed. What becomes clear at this point, to the viewer who has seen the film before, is that these are proleptic or prophetic images of events still to come (Justine, seated on a stone wall will watch Claire return carrying her son during a hailstorm; Justine's horse Abraham that will fall to the ground rather than cross the bridge to the village; Leo whittling sticks in the forest in preparation for the final collision between Melancholia and the Earth). This vision of world-destruction weighs heavily upon Justine and is perhaps the deeper reason for her profound melancholia; the lost object here being not only her own life (her marriage, career, and family) but sheer attachment to the world itself, not to mention the film's attachment to the universe of cinema, which will itself be sacrificed at the film's end.

Leo looks up from whittling wood and gazes off into the distance, just as the image cuts to a long shot of Melancholia approaching the Earth; the Prelude now swelling to its climax, the image suggests a perverse cosmic embrace as Melancholia pulls the Earth into itself, a *Liebestod* to end all others. As the image fades to black the Prelude ends with a primordial rumbling that persists beyond the blackness, accompanying the painted screen title that announces the film proper: Lars von Trier *Melancholia*. The Prelude is also an ironic elegy; von Trier's hint that the (cinematic) world that we are about to enter is going to be sacrificed, showing us that it, and all the characters in it, are to be utterly destroyed.

melancholia

For all the brilliance of Kirsten Dunst's performance, and the authenticity of the film's presentation of melancholia, it would be a mistake to interpret the film too literally as a psychological study of depression or as a nihilistic negation of the "human project." Rather, melancholia is evoked in the film as a mood, an aesthetic sensibility, a way of experiencing time; a visionary condition and mesmerising aesthetic experience that contemporary cinema has all but forgotten. Indeed, von Trier attempts to reclaim for cinema the romantic association of melancholia with prophetic vision and artistic genius (hence the references to Bruegel, Wagner, but also Tarkovsky). From this point of view, the film is an exercise in the aesthetic evocation of melancholia as an anachronistic yet historically resonant mood; one that expresses some of our contemporary cultural-historical maladies, while at the same time meditating on the corruption and redemption of cinema in the digital age.

The fact that Justine, for example, is both a melancholic and an advertiser should give us pause. Justine has a refined aesthetic sensibility, she "knows things," but is unable to cope with the everyday world of commerce and culture, refusing to give her boorish boss, Jack (Stellan Skarsgård), the tagline he desperately seeks (on her wedding night, a signal that commerce really owns and controls art). Justine eventually gives him her acerbic (and ironically Heideggerian) tagline – "*Nothing* is too good for you, Jack" – one that best describes Jack and what he stands for (the corruption of art through advertising). Jack is the embodiment of pure negativity, cultural capitalism personified, a destructive force bent on the annihilation of anything that stands in the way of business. It is this world that Justine sacrifices, renouncing her promotion (as "artistic director"), insulting her boss, losing her job, thus negating the entire sphere of her social and professional identity bound up with the world of advertising, her self-destruction as architect of the culture industry.

One way of reading this episode is to treat Justine and Claire as two complementary but also conflicting surrogate figures for the director: Justine, melancholic artist/advertiser ("artistic director"); Claire, caring sister and anxious "organiser" trying to keep up appearances and see through the event (the wedding as defining social ritual of future domestic happiness). Indeed, it is not difficult to see the chiasmatic crossing over of character traits in the two parts of the film – Justine's cheer turning into melancholy, Claire's impatience giving way to care; Justine's calm and resolve in the face of catastrophe, Claire's mounting panic and desire to escape – suggesting that these two characters can be seen as two halves of the one person (in a manner recalling Alma (Bibi Andersson) and Elisabeth Vogler (Liv Ullmann) in Bergman's *Persona* (1966)). If Justine and Claire, moreover, are contrasting aspects of Von Trier's directorial persona, we could take the film's presentation of melancholia as an allegory of the "corruption" of cinema as art; a self-critique of von Trier's own ambivalent role as at once melancholic artist, anxious controller, and cynical manipulator of images – a loss resulting, as we shall see, in a melancholic act of (cinematic) world-destruction.

At the same time, however, *Melancholia* manages to reinvent the possibilities of art cinema in a commercial-digital age by channelling modernist cinematic masters while fusing genre cinema with hybrid forms (domestic melodrama meets metaphysical disaster movie). In an important scene, Justine, having retreated from the wedding, reacts violently to the pictures of modernist art in the books proudly on display in the library, abruptly replacing them with pre-modern and romantic images (Bruegel, Millais, and so on); as though her melancholia were itself a symptom of the decadence of modernist optimism, a debilitating malady linked with her rejection of the corruption of modernist art in contemporary advertising design. There is something rotten, for Justine, in modernism's degeneration into consumer culture. Indeed, Justine's gesture of refusal and negation signals that these ideas – the corruption of modernist art by advertising, and the need to retrieve, in a therapeutic gesture, the spirit of romanticism as a countermovement to nihilism – prefigure the destruction of the image-world that is to come (recalling the image of Bruegel's *Hunters in the Snow* consumed by flame and turning to ash).

What is it that defines Justine's – and the film's – melancholia? According to Freud's classic account, melancholia is a pathological condition in one's inability to grieve and "work through" the loss of a loved object through the normal process of mourning that allows the subject to detach from the lost object and invest its desire in new ones.[20] In mourning, the subject's basic capacity for affective engagement with the world remains intact. In melancholia, by contrast, the loss is so catastrophic that the subject negates its own self and withdraws itself from the world; the ultimate object of melancholia is unnameable, something unconscious that cannot be readily identified with an object; a negation of the self so radical that it results in a complete withdrawal from social reality leading to a negation of the world itself. In *Melancholia*, Justine's negation of self and withdrawal from the rituals of everyday life – notably the socially and symbolically defining ritual of marriage – leaves her bereft of the capacity for affective engagement and meaningful agency. She strives to perform the socially sanctioned ritual of marriage, to play the smiling bride, but like the oversize limousine that she has chosen to bring her to the event, she does not fit into the parameters of the social world in which she exists – the rituals strike her as unavoidably trivial, empty, and absurd. In the course of the evening, she withdraws from the wedding reception, withdraws from her husband, rejects the demands of her boss to produce an advertising tagline, loses her promotion and career, provokes her husband to leave her, is abandoned by her family and falls into a deep depression that leaves her bedridden and unable to move.

The melancholia, however, is not confined to Justine's crippling depression. It pervades the entire world of the film, suggesting that melancholia is a mood that negates the movement defining everyday activity, thus revealing an uncanny, "prophetic" dimension of time. Justine's self-negation extends from her family and work to her investment in the world itself; it is almost with relief that she learns about the impending collision of Melancholia with the Earth. Her sister Claire becomes increasingly anxious and frightened about the event to come, while her husband, initially reassuring, citing his faith in science, but then despairing once he realises that the collision is inevitable, commits suicide rather than face his family and the humiliating certainty of their deaths. Justine, by contrast, slowly emerges from her depression, gains a quiet strength, and becomes almost calm, contemplative, seduced by the vast planet, bathing nude in its eerie blue light, beguiled by its implacable presence as it hurtles towards the Earth, pulling our planet into its fatal embrace. Justine's melancholia takes on cosmic dimensions, her negation of self and world enveloping "the world itself." Her melancholia thus achieves its end, just as the planet Melancholia destroys the Earth, along with Justine, Claire, and Leo in their "magic cave," and just as the film *Melancholia* annihilates the image-world it had so carefully composed.

world-sacrifice (creation and destruction)

Justine's experience of depression finds its objective correlative in the cataclysmic encounter with the planet Melancholia, fulfilling her prophetic vision – and von Trier's cinematic fantasy – of sacrificial world-destruction. What is this metaphysical comfort afforded by cinematic tragedy, by the sublime spectacle of world-destruction? At one level, *Melancholia* can be described as a Nietzschean tragedy drawing on Wagnerian romanticism and Schopenhauerian pessimism; on another, it is a meta-cinematic meditation on the "end of cinema" as an artform capable of revealing, composing, and destroying new worlds. Indeed, *Melancholia* is a film fable that finds its completion in a sublime depiction of the destruction of life on Earth – the only life in the universe, according to Justine – rendered as a random, implacable act of cosmic justice: "The earth is evil. No one will grieve for it when it is gone ... " What are we to make of this seemingly nihilistic attempt to negate "the human project" via the imagined destruction of life on Earth?

One way to approach this question is to look at *Melancholia* in light of two films, by directors important for von Trier, which also explore the theme of the "end of the world," albeit more firmly within the conventions of the apocalyptic/post-apocalyptic disaster movie: Bergman's *Shame* [*Skammen*] (1968) and Tarkovsky's *The Sacrifice* [*Offret*] (1986). *Shame* centres on a troubled couple, Eva (Liv Ullman) and Jan (Max von Sydow), former musicians who have moved to a remote island to escape an outbreak of civil war on the mainland. They live a simple but domestically tense life, seeking refuge from political strife in the country, an idyll interrupted by the arrival of army troops and the eruption of a violent military conflict. The film uses the relationship between the couple to explore how these characters react to the sudden disruption of their familiar world, the destruction of their conventional frames of reference. Jan is initially presented as withdrawn, ineffectual, overly sensitive, retreating to a corner of their cottage and crying when criticised by Eva; she, for her part, is initially tense, frustrated, angry with Jan at his incompetence and ineptitude for their new life as farmers (her anger at his refusal to pay the phone bill, fix their car, and so on). After the war begins in earnest and Jan is forced, then willingly undertakes, to execute a "traitor," Eva, while deeply shocked, becomes more emotional and sympathetic (wanting to help a young soldier who has deserted), whereas Jan becomes colder, more ruthless, indifferent to anything other than his own survival (killing the soldier, stealing his gun and boots, and taking his berth on a ferry off the island).

There is an interesting parallel here between the transformation of both Eva and Jan as a couple and that between Justine (Kirsten Dunst) and Claire (Charlotte Gainsbourg), who both undergo a similar transformative exchange of character traits: Justine's depressive withdrawal and inability to enjoy giving way to a calm clarity of vision, a Heideggerian "anticipatory resoluteness" in the face of mortality; Claire's competence and care giving way to an increasing desperation and inability to face the truth of certain death. Both films focalise the destruction of world via the domestic drama of a troubled couple or family. Bergman's film ends, however, with the couple adrift in a crowded boat with other refugees, facing an uncertain future in a post-apocalyptic world (resonating with the Cold War fear of nuclear apocalypse very palpable in 1968). There is no redemptive finale, or possible escape; the couple, like the other refugees, are cast adrift by the forces of history and politics, which seem to hit them like a violent natural disaster they can neither understand nor control. The shame of the film's title emerges more emphatically as the film unfolds; the shame of moral depravity when one is unable to sacrifice oneself for others, or which accompanies the refusal of self-sacrifice in favour of naked self-preservation.

Tarkovsky's last film, *The Sacrifice* [*Offret*] (1986) is also filmed, like Bergman's *Shame*, on the island of Gotland, Sweden. In many ways an extended homage to Bergman (the film bears a Swedish title, is shot in Swedish, and stars veteran Bergman ensemble actor Erland Josephson), it tells the story of Alexander (Josephson), a former actor, critic, journalist, and aesthetics lecturer, celebrating his birthday with his family (wife Adelaide (Susan Fleetwood), daughter Julia (Valerie Mairesse), mute young son Gossen or "Little Man" (Tommy Kjellqvist)) in their idyllic, rather Tarkovskian, country retreat. The film opens with an extraordinary long take, which we might call a philosophical prelude. Alexander, a *Japonisme* enthusiast, and "Little Man" are planting a tree together by the island shoreline as Bach's *St Matthew Passion* plays on the soundtrack. Local postman and friend Otto (Allan Edwall) approaches, wishes him happy birthday, and embarks on a meandering philosophical discussion about Nietzsche's concept of eternal recurrence. As they walk back from the shore towards the forest, Alexander reveals that he "has no relationship with God" and seems unimpressed by Otto's vaguely Nietzschean meditations. Meanwhile, "Little Man" plays a little practical joke on the postman, engrossed in philosophising, by tying his bicycle to a tree branch. Once they return home, Alexander's restrained birthday celebrations begin; he receives a seventeenth-century map of Europe as a present from Otto, and argues with his theatrical wife Adelaide over why he left the theatre, a sore point in their relationship. In this midst of this Bergmanesque domestic drama, including hints of a possible affair between Adelaide and dashing family friend Victor (Sven Wollter), a sudden air raid heralds the start of war, a nuclear Armageddon announced over the radio by the president to the stunned familial gathering.

Like *Shame* and *Melancholia*, *The Sacrifice* focalises the catastrophic threat of world-destruction – here through a nuclear confrontation rather than planetary collision – through the responses of an intimate yet conflicted family group. Like *Shame*, *The Sacrifice* focuses on the responses of the family to the news of war, the imminent threat of death and the destruction of their familiar world. Unlike *Shame*, however, the drama is not psychological, social, and physical, but principally existential, moral, and spiritual: a meditation on the spiritual power of belief and sacrifice rather than its moral or political significance.

Indeed, the central question of *The Sacrifice* turns on Alexander's desperate prayer, his anguished pleading with God to reverse the coming Armageddon and to spare his family. Alexander promises God that he is willing to sacrifice everything most dear to him – his family, and his beloved house – if only God will restore everything to how it was before. Given Alexander's avowed atheism and philosophical scepticism, his profession of faith comes as a surprise and marks a dramatic caesura in the film's narrative arc. After spending a troubled night, and heeding Otto's prophetic plea that Alexander should sleep with Maria (whom he describes as a benevolent witch), Alexander visits her and does sleep with her in a Tarkovsky-like moment of levitating ecstasy. Next morning Alexander awakes, from what may or may not have been a dream, and is stunned to discover that everything has been restored to "how it was," his family preparing for his birthday as though nothing had happened. Thinking that God has indeed granted his wish, Alexander must now fulfil his promise to sacrifice everything in order to ensure that his family, and the world, will survive. Thus he steals away from the house, overhearing his wife and lover Victor discussing future plans, and plots to fulfil his promise to God by burning down his own house to give thanks for the gift of life he has been granted. As Otto remarks earlier in the film, when he gifts Alexander an early modern map of "the known world," thus pre-figuring the sacrifice to come, "[e]very gift involves a sacrifice, otherwise what kind of gift would it be?"

Comparing the two films, we can discern a distinctive shift from shame (in Eva's and Jan's responses to war) to sacrifice as redemptive and as self-destructive (Alexander goes mad and is rounded up by an ambulance that arrives unexpectedly as the family watches their beloved home burning down). *The Sacrifice* ends on a note of miraculous redemption thanks to Alexander's unlikely act of faith: Little Man, watering the tree he helped his father plant, lies down at its base and utters his first words: "In the beginning was the Word. Why is that, Papa?" as the camera pans upwards, following the tree trunk and resting on the branches disappearing in the sunlight glittering off the surface of the sea. Alexander's "impossible" act of faith – an act of spiritual self-sacrifice that cannot but seem "mad" from the perspective of those outside – is at one with the power to reverse the inevitability of history and fate, heralding a new world in which all can be redeemed. His act of self-sacrifice is also an implicit rejection of Otto's pagan Nietzschean belief in life-affirmation via the eternal recurrence of the same. Indeed, Otto's interest in collecting "incidents" that cannot be rationally explained by science foreshadows the "inexplicable" event of a reversal of Armageddon thanks to a sacrificial act of faith. *The Sacrifice* negates the refusal of sacrifice and commitment to self-preservation that defined the world of *Shame*; it posits the metaphysical dignity of self-sacrifice as an "impossible" leap of faith with the power to reverse time and transform the world, even a world on the brink of self-destruction. Like many Tarkovsky films, *The Sacrifice* thereby makes thematic the struggle of an individual to become a person, to achieve moral personhood thanks to a spiritual source within a disenchanted world, no matter how mad this makes him or her appear to others.[21]

Melancholia takes the further step of negating this negation, rejecting Tarkovsky's theological solution to the problem of world-destruction: his affirmation of spiritual belief in a destitute world as capable of transfiguring our experience, transforming the "now" into a moment of divine transcendence – one that can also be experienced through cinema. The theological possibility of faith is refused, as is faith in the power of science and instrumental rationality to know and master nature. Instead, von Trier proffers an aestheticist response that stages the sublime spectacle of world-annihilation as an ironic tragedy without metaphysical comfort or spiritual redemption. Yet this is neither, as some critics claim, a nihilistic gesture of despair nor a cynical manipulation of sublimity. It can be read, rather, as an ethical moment of sacrifice: staging the thought of "world-sacrifice" as an aesthetic spectacle, one that "traverses the fantasy" of world-destruction but without the reassuring narrative perspective of a vantage point from which we might contemplate our own demise.[22]

Melancholia thus takes the "logic" of sacrifice traced in the previous two films to its aesthetic conclusion: from *Shame*'s depiction of the destructiveness of refusing sacrifice in favour of self-preservation to *The Sacrifice*'s valorisation of self-sacrifice as offering a spiritual power capable of overcoming fate and transfiguring the world. *Melancholia* negates this spiritual or theological valorisation of sacrifice, undermining any psychological resolution, metaphysical comfort, or spiritual transcendence. Instead, it presents an aesthetic staging of the sublime spectacle of world-destruction as an ironic gesture of cinematic self-sacrifice. Here we find the hidden ethical gesture in *Melancholia*; the self-destruction of the image, the cinematic spectacle of world-sacrifice that opens up a mood and sensibility capable of contemplating the possibility of extinction without sentimentality or spiritual compensation. This may be precisely the kind of ethical gesture we need today in order to experience and think anew the implications of our own "end times"; a cinematic self-sacrifice that gestures towards whatever post-humanist world may or may not come "after the end."

epilogue

I have argued that *Melancholia*'s staging of the act of world-destruction is also one of (cinematic) world-sacrifice: von Trier's Manichean cinematic destruction of an "evil" world of corrupted or enervated images in order that a new one may emerge; a world of images born of spirit and born again (as Hegel remarks in his *Aesthetics*) from its pulverised ashes. The "end of the world" thus becomes an apocalyptic spectacle staged as an aesthetic phenomenon; a sublime tragedy viewed from an "impossible" perspective – the "magic cave" of cinema itself. One could imagine Justine's ironic tagline for the film: *fiat cinema, pereat mundus*.

At this point, a harsh critic might object: this is precisely what makes *Melancholia* an exercise in empty nihilism; worse still, it shows von Trier is not only a pretentious neo-romantic but possibly a misguided proto-fascist. Walter Benjamin's famous words (from the conclusion of the "Work of Art" essay) could even be cited as evidence:

> "*Fiat ars – pereat mundus*," says Fascism, expecting from war, as Marinetti admits, the artistic gratification of a sense perception altered by technology. This is evidently the consummation of *l'art pour l'art*. Humankind, which once, in Homer, was an object of contemplation for the Olympian gods, has now becomes one for itself. Its self-alienation has reached the point where it can experience its own destruction as a supreme aesthetic pleasure.[23]

Here one could reply that Benjamin was talking of the Futurists and the fascist aestheticising of politics, to which he opposed the communist politicising of art. It is highly dubious, however, to graft this historically specific critique directly onto our contemporary (post-fascist and post-communist) historical-cultural situation. Nonetheless, there are critics who would link von Trier's fascination with romanticism, his scepticism about utopian politics, his admiration for Speer, and his confused relationship with Nazism and Judaism, with a nihilistic aestheticising of violence – like Justine, von Trier too appears to be "longing for shipwrecks and sudden death," to quote, as he does, Danish poet Tom Kristensen.[24]

Such a reading, however, would be mistaken, for a number of reasons. It forgets that this is a film about "the end of film," about the end of modernism in film, about the destruction of the image-world and the fragile possibility of a new one. It forgets, in a word, the "magic cave" that is cinema itself. It projects a literal meaning onto the film and thus remains blind to *Melancholia*'s mode of aesthetic presentation. It demands moral-political certainty in art, and thereby ignores the sceptical questioning of the present and future that defines contemporary aesthetics as much as our melancholy modernity. As Žižek remarks, *Melancholia* is, from a dialectical point of view, a profoundly *optimistic* film: one that "traverses the fantasy" of world-destruction to its end, evoking a shattering spiritual-existential acceptance of our finitude, an experience necessary for the transformation and strengthening of our ethical attitude towards a world under threat of destruction.[25]

Although the film resonates with contemporary "apocalyptic" themes, there is no didactic political message within it. Rather, we find within it an ironic critique of rationalist optimism: the conviction that, given our irrational faith in instrumental reason and fantasies of controlling nature through technology, the only foreseeable end is a scenario of world-destruction. At the same time, it resonates with contemporary ecological anxieties concerning the threats to the biosphere and the environment, even the "unthinkable" thought of species extinction. Indeed, *Melancholia* is a film that makes the destruction of the Earth thinkable, imaginable, as an aesthetic spectacle; it does so as an ethical challenge to a world that refuses to face this threat, reverting instead to banality as usual and melancholy denial. As Bruno Latour remarks:

> In the amazing final scene of a most amazing film the hyper-rational people fall back onto what old primitive rituals are supposed to do – protecting childish minds against the impact of reality. Von Trier might have grasped just what happens after the sublime has disappeared. Did you think Doomsday would bring the dead to life? Not at all. When the trumpets of judgment resonate in your ear, you fall into melancholia! No new ritual will save you. Let's just sit in a magic hut, and keep denying, denying, denying, until the bitter end.[26]

This is a tragic insight, to be sure; an ethical experience of sublimity, of the finitude and fragility of our shared world. It is a provocation to question our naive rationalism, our collective refusal to countenance the potentially catastrophic threats that face our planet, our stubborn propensity to continue "denying, denying, denying," that our ways of life must drastically change if we are to avert disaster. At the same time, *Melancholia* is an aesthetic spectacle of world-sacrifice, a sacrifice of the "corrupted" image-world defining our melancholy modernity. As Justine prepares for the end with her sister

Claire and frightened Leo, we can share their harrowing experience from within von Trier's "magic cave," awe-struck yet mindful of the existential challenge posed by the thought of world-destruction, the ethical difficulty of imagining a liveable future, of keeping imagination alive, beyond the "end of the world."

notes

I would like to thank Alex Ling and Magdalena Zolkos for inviting me to participate in the Sydney Seminar for the Arts and Philosophy, Seminar 20: "Melancholia non Grata: Lars von Trier and the Infinite Sadness" (2012), where I first presented some of the ideas developed in this article. I gave another version of this paper at the Film-Philosophy Conference 2013 (Amsterdam), and am grateful for the excellent questions and insightful comments I received there. I would also like to thank Louise D'Arcens and Magdalena Zolkos for their stimulating discussions of von Trier's work, and Costica Bradatan for his excellent editorial suggestions.

1 Von Trier's video version of *Medea* (1988) shows, in graphic detail, Medea's sacrifice of her own children in order to punish her husband, Jason, for accepting as an award the hand of Glauce, King Creon's daughter, in marriage. In *Breaking the Waves* (1996), Bess McNeill (Emily Watson) sacrifices herself, becoming a sexual martyr, in order to save and heal her crippled husband Jan (Stellan Skarsgaard), a sacrifice "confirmed" by the infamous concluding shot of heavenly pealing bells. In *The Idiots* (1998), Susanne's (Anne Louise Hassing) grief-driven "spassing" is taken to its limits in her unbearable encounter with her family, where she simulates a humiliating condition of drooling imbecility, sacrificing her dignity and social identity. *Dancer in the Dark* (2000) centres on the travails of blind, battling mother Selma (Björk), who sacrifices herself in order to ensure the money stolen from her by deceitful policemen Bill (David Morse) can be used to cure her blind son's affliction, a decision that culminates in her brutal execution by hanging. *Dogville*'s (2003) fugitive heroine and "moral example," Grace (Nicole Kidman), destroys the town of Dogville in a sacrificial act of fiery retribution for the suffering she endures at the hands of its morally hypocritical and socially exploitative "good folk." *Antichrist*'s (2009) disturbing "cognitive therapy" session cum psychosexual struggle between He (Willem Dafoe) and She (Charlotte Gainsbourg) culminates in the husband's sacrificial burning of his wife's corpse on a funeral pyre, an act summoning up the female forest spirits of a misogynistic past. Even von Trier's comedy *The Boss of it All* (2006) is premised on the "sacrifice" of authorial creative control and decision making, which is assumed by the random computer-generated angles and shots of von Trier's "Automavision," a sacrifice of artistic freedom that mirrors the protagonist's "outsourcing" of managerial authority to a fictitious persona (the American "boss of it all").

2 See Bradatan; Buch-Hansen; Mandolfo; Pohl.

3 See von Trier's interview with Nils Thorsen ("Longing for the End of All") in the Press Release for *Melancholia* where he mentions his research into nymphomania and the frequency of cutting and self-harm among women with hypersexuality.

4 See Matts and Tynan's ecological reading of the film, and Latour's comments on its ecological-ethical aspect. See also Žižek, "Optimism of *Melancholia*," who argues that the film is not pessimistic or nihilistic but "profoundly optimistic," even ethical.

5 "Last man" narratives have proven popular in film; Richard Matheson's novel *I am Legend* has inspired adaptations such as *The Last Man on Earth* (1964), *The Night of the Living Dead* (1968), *Omega Man* (1971) and the recent *I am Legend* (2007).

6 At the end of H.G. Wells' *Time Machine* (1895), the expansion of the Sun causes the death of all life on Earth.

7 The film is *The World, The Flesh, and the Devil* (1959).

8 Apocalyptic movies (e.g., *4:44 Last Day on Earth* or *Melancholia*) are centred on characters' responses to the catastrophic destruction of civilisation or even the Earth itself, whether due to nuclear war, biological catastrophe, or planetary collision. Post-apocalyptic movies (e.g., *Time of the Wolf*, *28 Days Later*, or *The Road*), focus on the aftermath of the apocalyptic event and how survivors struggle to keep alive in a devastated and anarchic environment. Some films (*2012*, for

example) attempt to straddle both apocalyptic and post-apocalyptic scenarios.

9 Žižek, *Living in the End Times*.

10 I discuss this aspect of *Time of the Wolf* in Sinnerbrink.

11 See Critchley; Nancy and Lacoue-Labarthe.

12 Rancière, *Film Fables* 166.

13 Rancière, *Aesthetics*. Schelling writes: "The work of art reflects to us the identity of the conscious and unconscious activities" (225). See Garneau and Cisneros.

14 Like many recent movies, the rest of *Melancholia* was shot in high definition digital video using an Arri Alexa camera.

15 See Remes for a fascinating discussion of images of stasis in experimental cinema as revealing an ontology of duration.

16 The painting also appears in Tarkovsky's *Mirror* (1975).

17 The golf course at which the wedding reception is to be held has only eighteen holes (as we are told twice in the film).

18 Darghis remarks that the image could be a reference to Isaiah 51.8: "For the moth shall eat them up like a garment, and the worm shall eat them like wool: but my righteousness shall be for ever, and my salvation from generation to generation."

19 See, for example, the contrasting reviews by French and by Ebert.

20 See Freud.

21 See Kovács.

22 Žižek discusses the fantasy situation of being in a position to contemplate our own death or absence from the Earth. Žižek, *Less than Nothing* 273ff.

23 Benjamin 122.

24 "If you ask me, she is longing for shipwrecks and sudden death, as Tom Kristensen wrote. And she gets it, too. In a way, she succeeds in pulling this planet from behind the sun and she surrenders to it" (*Melancholia* Pressbook 5). For such a critique, see Brody. For a different view, see Williams.

25 Žižek, "The Optimism of *Melancholia*."

26 Latour.

bibliography

Andrei Rublev [*Andrey Rubylov*]. Dir. Andrei Tarkovsky. Mosfilm, 1966. Film.

Antichrist. Dir. Lars von Trier. Zentropa Entertainments, 2009. Film.

Benjamin, Walter. "The Work of Art in the Age of its Technical Reproducibility: Second Version." *Selected Writings 1935–1938*. Ed. Michael W. Jennings, Howard Eiland, and Gary Smith. Harvard: Harvard UP/Belknap, 2002. 251–83. Print.

The Boss of it All [*Direktøren for det hele*]. Dir. Lars von Trier. Zentropa Productions, 2006. Film.

Bradatan, Costica. "'I was a stranger, and ye took me not in': *Deus Ludens* and Theology of Hospitality in Lars von Trier's *Dogville*." *Journal of European Studies* 39.1 (2009): 58–78. Print.

Breaking the Waves. Dir. Lars von Trier. Argus Film Produktie, 1996. Film.

Brody, Richard. "Lars von Trier, *Melancholia*, and the Remarks." *The New Yorker* 3 Oct. 2011: n. pag. Web. 1 Sept. 2012.

Buch-Hansen, Gitte. "Lars von Trier's *Antichrist*, the Bible, and Docetic Masculinity." *Relegere: Studies in Religion and Reception* 1.1 (2011): 115–44. Print.

The Celebration [*Festen*]. Dir. Thomas Vinterberg. Nimbus Film Productions, 1998. Film.

Critchley, Simon. *Very Little ... Almost Nothing: Death, Philosophy, Literature*. 2nd ed. London: Routledge, 2004. Print.

Dancer in the Dark. Dir. Lars von Trier. Zentropa Entertainments, 2000. Film.

Darghis, Manohla. "This is How the End Begins." *The New York Times* 30 Dec. 2011: n. pag. Web. 1 Sept. 2012.

Dogville. Dir. Lars von Trier. Zentropa Entertainments, 2003. Film.

Ebert, Roger. "Melancholia" Review. *Chicago Sun Times* 9 Nov. 2011: n. pag. Web. 1 Sept. 2012.

Epidemic. Dir. Lars von Trier. Elementfilm A/S, 1987. Film.

4:44 Last Day on Earth. Dir. Abel Ferrara. Fabula, 2011. Film.

French, Philip. "Melancholia – Review." *The Guardian* 2 Oct. 2012: n. pag. Web. 31 Oct. 2012.

Freud, Sigmund. "Mourning and Melancholia." 1917. *The Standard Edition of the Complete Psychological Works of Sigmund Freud, Volume XIV (1914–1916): On the History of the Psycho-Analytic Movement, Papers on Metapsychology and Other Works*. London: Random, 2001. 237–58. Print.

Garneau, Michele, and James Cisneros. "Film's Aesthetic Turn: A Contribution by Jacques Rancière." *SubStance* 33.1 (2004): 108–25. Print.

I am Legend. Dir. Francis Lawrence. Warner Bros./ Village Roadshow Pictures, 2007. Film.

The Idiots [Idioterne]. Dir. Lars von Trier. Zentropa Entertainments, 1998. Film.

Independence Day. Dir. Roland Emmerich. Twentieth Century Fox, 1996. Film.

Knowing. Dir. Alex Proyas. Summit Entertainment, 2009. Film.

Kovács, András Bálint. "Andrei Tarkovsky." *The Routledge Companion to Film and Philosophy*. Ed. Carl Plantinga and Paisley Livingston. London and New York: Routledge, 2009. 580–91. Print.

Last Night. Dir. Don McKellar. Rhombus Media, 1998. Film.

Last Year at Marienbad. Dir. Alain Resnais. Cocinor, Terra Films, Comoran Films, 1966. Film.

Latour, Bruno. "Waiting for Gaia: Composing the Common World through Art and Politics." Lecture at the French Institute, London. Nov. 2011: n. pag. Web. 27 Sept. 2012.

Mandolfo, Carleen. "Women, Suffering and Redemption in Three Films of Lars Von Trier." *Literature and Theology* 24.3 (2010): 285–300. Print.

Matts, Tim, and Aidan Tynan. "The Melancholy of Extinction: Lars von Trier's *Melancholia* as Environmental Film." *M/C Journal* 15.3 "Ecology" (2012): n. pag. Web. 24 Sept. 2012.

Medea. Dir. Lars von Trier. Danmarks Radio (DR), 1988. TV movie.

Melancholia. Dir. Lars von Trier. Zentropa Entertainments/Memfis Film, 2011. Film.

Miracle Mile. Steve de Jarnatt. Hemdale Film, 1988. Film.

Mirror [Zerkalo]. Dir. Andrei Tarkovsky. Mosfilm Studios, 1975. Film.

Nancy, Jean-Luc, and Philippe Lacoue-Labarthe. *The Literary Absolute: The Theory of Literature in German Romanticism*. Trans. P. Bernard and C. Lester. Albany: State U of New York P, 1988. Print.

Nostalghia. Dir. Andrei Tarkovsky. Opera Film Produzione, Rai 2, Sovinfilm, 1983. Film.

Persona. Dir. Ingmar Bergman. Svensk Filmindustri (SF), 1966. Film.

Pohl, Jan. "Melancholia." *Journal of Religion and Film* 16.1 Article 10: n. pag. Web. 23 Sept. 2012.

The Quiet Earth. Dir. Geoff Murphy. Cinepro, 1985. Film.

Rancière, Jacques. *Aesthetics and its Discontents*. Trans. Steven Corcoran. Cambridge: Polity, 2009. Print.

Rancière, Jacques. *Film Fables*. Trans. E. Batista. Oxford and New York: Berg, 2006. Print.

Remes, Justin. "Motion(less) Pictures: The Cinema of Stasis." *British Journal of Aesthetics* 52.3 (2012): 250–70.

The Road. Dir. John Hillcoat. Dimension Films, 2009. Film.

The Sacrifice [Offret]. Dir. Andrei Tarkovsky. Film Svenska Filminsitutet (SFS), 1986. Film.

Schelling, F.W.J. *System of Transcendental Idealism*. Trans. M.G. Vater. Charlottesville: U of Virginia P, 1978. Print.

Shame [Skammen]. Dir. Ingmar Bergman. Cinematograph AB, Svensk Filmindustri (SF), 1968. Film.

Sinnerbrink, Robert. "A Post-Humanist Moralist: Michael Haneke's Cinematic Critique." *Angelaki* 16.4 (2011): 115–29. Print.

Solyaris [Solaris]. Dir. Andrei Tarkovsky. Creative Unit of Writers and Cinema Workers, Kinostudia "Mosfilm," Unit Four, 1972. Film.

Stalker. Dir. Andrei Tarkovsky. Kinostudia "Mosfilm," 1979. Film.

Take Shelter. Dir. Jeff Nichols. Hydraulx, REI Capital, Grove Hill Productions, 2011. Film.

Time of the Wolf [*Le Temp du loup*]. Dir. Michael Haneke. Bavaria Film/Canal+, 2003. Film.

The Tree of Life. Dir. Terrence Malick. Fox Searchlight, 2011. Film.

28 Days Later. Dir. Danny Boyle. DNA Films, British Film Council, 2002. Film.

2001: A Space Odyssey. Dir. Stanley Kubrick. Metro-Goldwyn-Mayer (MGM), Stanley Kubrick Productions, 1968. Film.

2012. Dir. Roland Emmerich. Columbia Pictures, Centropolis Entertainment, 2009. Film.

Von Trier, Lars. "Melancholia: Lars von Trier." Press Release, Zentropa Entertainments, 2011: n. pag. Web. 23 Sept. 2012.

When Worlds Collide. Dir. Rudolph Maté. Paramount Pictures, 1951. Film.

Williams, Steve. "Longing for Shipwrecks and Sudden Death – Lars von Trier, German Romanticism, and the Nazis." *Kamera.co.uk Film Salon*: n. pag. Web. 1 Sept. 2012.

The World, The Flesh, and the Devil. Dir. Ranald MacDougall. HarBel Productions, 1959. Film.

Žižek, Slavoj. *Less than Nothing: Hegel and the Shadow of Dialectical Materialism*. London and New York: Routledge, 2012. Print.

Žižek, Slavoj. *Living in the End Times*. London: Verso, 2009. Print.

Žižek, Slavoj. "The Optimism of *Melancholia*." Big Think Series. Web. 30 July 2012. <http://www.youtube.com/watch?v=eUljoYDKETM>.

The world came about through a mistake. For he who created it wanted to create it imperishable and immortal. He fell short of attaining his desire. For the world never was imperishable, nor, for that matter, was he who made the world.

Gospel of Philip

costica bradatan

"WE WILL DIE AND WILL BE FREE"

a gnostic reading of the double life of véronique

where the world turns out to be a farce ...

Towards the end of *The Double Life of Véronique* [*La Double Vie de Véronique*, 1991; hereinafter *The Double Life* ...], as Alexandre Fabbri, *le marionnettiste*, discloses that the film we've been watching is a story of his own making, Véronique receives the revelation of her life. Noticing the puppet in Fabbri's hands, she asks him: "Is that me?" "Of course it's you," answers the puppeteer. She then discovers a second puppet, the perfect copy of the first, lying lifelessly on the master's desk. "Why ... why two?" she asks. The answer comes promptly: "I handle them a lot when I perform. They get damaged easily." That Véronique may have had a double somewhere in the world she already knows; she came across pictures she had unwittingly taken of her copy, the Polish Weronika, during a trip to Eastern Europe. Unsettling as such an ontological duplication may be, what eventually devastates Véronique is the realization that she and her double are nothing but playthings in the hands of some manipulating entity. She discovers now that she is an alien to herself: her whole life has been scripted, her biography is nothing but the enactment of someone else's story. In the language of the *marionnettiste* himself, she has always been "handled" by someone else's invisible hand – pulled, pushed, dragged, used and abused. This is all very "damaging" if you are a puppet, but the puppeteer is not worried: when one puppet is damaged beyond repair, he just replaces her. The master discards the exhausted item, pulls out another from his inventory, and the show goes on. From his own point of view, this must be a great performance; for anyone "handled" and "damaged" in this fashion, however, such an existence cannot be other that an enormous *farce*.

The Double Life ... pushes to its ultimate conclusion an insight that Krzysztof Kieślowski first explored at length in *Blind Chance* [*Przypadek*, 1981]. In both films, human existence is part of an ontological arrangement that deprives it of any sense of autonomy and self-determination. No matter how hard you try, you are never in control of your life. The trajectory of your biography, the contours of your life-story, eventually the meaning of your entire existence are all in the hands of an outside entity – something foreign and hostile, as remote from humanity as possible. In *Blind Chance*, Witek, the main character, finds himself thrown into three different existential scenarios, one more oppressive than the next. Falling from one existence into another, he becomes entangled in an increasingly complex web of competing forces, chance events, and fateful encounters. As you immerse yourself in the story, you cannot help wondering: who is this spider-God who's toying with Witek before devouring him?

In *The Double Life …* Kieślowski changes his approach. Here the victim of the cosmic farce is not thrown into different stories, but multiplied. First, it is Weronika, in Poland. An adorable young lady, she is a gifted singer, and blessed with a curious, beautiful mind. Yet, as it turns out, she was made in haste by some careless creator, has a faulty constitution, a weak heart, and gets damaged all too easily. She has a vague intuition that a playful god has made her in two copies ("I have a strange feeling. I feel like I'm not alone. Like I'm not alone in the world"), but her life is cut short before she can do anything about it. She dies on stage – a most fitting setting for the ending of someone whose life has been a farce. Then, it is Véronique, in France (both characters are played exquisitely by Irene Jacob). We meet her immediately after the funeral of her double in Poland. Somehow she senses the other's death: "I don't know why. It's as if I were grieving." She tells her father about it. "Not long ago," Véronique says, "I had a strange sensation. I felt that I was alone. All of a sudden." He prompts her: "Someone disappeared from your life." "That's right," she answers. In spite of the same faulty constitution, Véronique does her best to stay alive: visits the cardiologist, quits singing, and takes care of herself. She also dedicates herself to understanding what is going on behind the scenes. In the end, she learns of the cosmic farce in which she's been cast from the master puppeteer himself. That's the kind of knowledge that can kill you.

What Kieślowski fleshes out in both films is in fact an older philosophical insight, if not a philosophical sensibility altogether. Its broader thematic context is what has been called *theologia ludens*:[1] the notion that the world has been created through an act of divine play. The group of thinkers and artists that Kieślowski joins, however, chooses to focus on a particular facet of this notion: the world as farce. Within the broader context of *theologia ludens*, they advance the argument that the type of play that divinity engages in, far from favoring the human subject, crushes it. Humans are not partners in the divine play – on the contrary, they are toyed with. They are God's playthings. Schopenhauer's philosophy, for example, could be read in this light. In his system, the omnipotent Will (*der Wille*) is such an oppressive, playing entity, always in full control of the cosmic game, turning us into its puppets, doing and undoing our lives as it sees fit. Within this ontological arrangement, save for a handful of exceptional individuals (e.g., mystics, artists and philosophers of genius such as Schopenhauer himself), the human being is nothing but a powerless marionette, mercilessly "handled" and "damaged" by a ferocious, alien entity.

The notion of world as farce also lies at the heart of Ivan Karamazov's philosophy. In *The Brothers Karamazov* Dostoevsky has him articulate a vision of the universe as divinity's source of entertainment.[2] For Ivan, God is just a cynical experimenter, an irresponsible Demiurge who creates the world out of boredom, just to kill time. We are made with no higher purpose in mind as we are just "unfinished, trial creatures created in mockery."[3] Like an ancient Roman, this God takes delight in raw spectacles of gratuitous cruelty, in the suffering of small children, the demolition of the innocent. Ivan admits that this may be needed for some superior, mysterious harmony, but he finds the price for it way too high. As far as he is concerned, God runs an indecent, bloody cosmic show, and he does not want to have anything to do with it. He "respectfully" returns the "admission ticket."[4]

In twentieth-century European philosophy the perception of human existence as mockery, a farce set up by a jesting Demiurge, becomes even more acute. In a certain sense, to give just one example, E.M. Cioran's whole work is dedicated to exposing the cosmic farce. He talks of human existence as a "fraud" and a "cheat." We really have no business being here – it would have been preferable to have never been born. We are "thrown into this world and don't know why."[5] Indeed, our inability to understand – our fundamental idiocy when it comes to grasping the ultimate things – is meant to be part of the farce. In *A Short History of Decay* Cioran writes that we "are engulfed in a pleonastic universe, in which the questions and answers amount to the same thing."[6] Being human in such a setting – as opposed to being vegetable or stone – doesn't make much of a difference. The ultimate enlightenment – which Cioran calls an "initiation" – is to grasp "the mockery of being alive."[7] Only such learning could give us some consolation.

From Lev Shestov Cioran learned how to look at Dostoevsky as a philosopher. And what he found in the latter's novels would leave a deep imprint on his own thinking. In particular, Ivan Karamazov's notion that we "have been set up only for mockery"[8] must have touched him profoundly: the Russian writer gave expression to an insight that lies at the heart of his entire philosophy.

… and that hits home

The Double Life … is something of a paradox. On the one hand, the film is strikingly plotless. Almost nothing happens in it, as Kieślowski himself is ready to admit. *The Double Life …*, he says, is "a film about emotions and nothing else. There's no action in it."[9] On the other hand, for all its plotlessness, the film's impact on the viewer is powerful, lasting, haunting. There is something "unresolved" about its story that arrests your attention – you want to see it again and again. This is due in part to the exquisite artistry Kieślowski displays throughout, but it can't be only that. Beyond its aesthetics, the film affects us viscerally because it addresses issues pertaining to our ultimate ontological make-up and our situatedness in the world. As often happens in Kieślowski, he misleads us: the film is not just about emotions. Emotions play an important part, but *The Double Life …* is about much more than that.

We are so affected when we watch the film because we sense, whether clearly or in a more obscure manner, that our own existence, too, has something of a marionette show at its core. Indeed, *Véronique, c'est nous.* We, too, have been "thrown into the world," and are expected to perform a nonsense part until we become too "damaged" to go on, and have to be replaced. Just like Weronika/Véronique, we find ourselves entangled in the cosmic play, without ever having been asked whether or not we want to take part in it. A host of invisible yet always efficient strings determine the best part of our lives: the economic system, the political context, the laws and societal norms, the culture in which we grow up, the fashions we follow not only in dress but in everything, the many conventions that shape our thought and actions, most of which we are not even aware of. This is already a vivid picture of servitude – and I haven't even mentioned some of the strongest strings such as our biological make-up and genetic baggage, our fundamental precariousness, our mortality and finitude.

To be human, then, is to be scripted: to perform a well-defined role, to act within prescribed limits, to move on a predetermined trajectory. Our lives come already written. We don't live them, they live us. For better or worse, however, we rarely become fully aware of the vast web of entanglements that constitute our existence. Most of the time, we don't pay attention to the strings that move us and the hands that pull them. We live as if they are not there, as though we are in charge. That's why a film like *The Double Life …* affects us so profoundly: it makes the invisible visible, the unnoticeable obvious. We are so unsettled by Kieślowski's work because it reveals something about us that, for most of the time, remains hidden.

When you finally realize that you live the life of a marionette, your first impulse is to try and find out who pulls the strings. For what makes the marionette show a marionette show is the agency of the *marionnettiste*, the master puppeteer. This almost amounts to a novel argument for God's existence: a farce is an intentional act; if the world is a farce (and the evidence is overwhelming), then it must have an author; therefore, God must exist. The farce would make no sense without the farceur. In *The Brothers Karamazov*, Fyodor Karamazov – who seems to share his son's philosophical views, and who is a clown and a farceur himself – formulates the argument with brevity and precision. If God does not exist, he asks Ivan, then "who is laughing at mankind?"[10]

where the author of the farce is identified ...

Yet what kind of God would be laughing at mankind? What kind of divinity would be turning us into his marionettes? Is it even theologically conceivable to talk of such a God? Has the notion of such a divinity ever entered the minds of theologians and religious thinkers? Yes, it has. This divinity is the Gnostic Demiurge: not the real God – the God of light, "the unknown," "the hidden" or "the alien God," as Marcion called it – but "the God of this world," the one that has created it and has always remained close to it, entangled with it in fact. The world, in all its imperfection, mirrors the nature of the Demiurge: himself imperfect and flawed. From the Gnostic *Gospel of Philip* we learn that "the world came about through a mistake." He who "created it wanted to create it imperishable and immortal," but his plan utterly failed. For "the world never was imperishable, nor, for that matter, was he who made the world."[11]

This catastrophic episode occurs in virtually all Gnostic cosmologies. Kurt Rudolf refers to the event as "the presumption (*hybris*) of the Demiurge."[12] In the literature of Gnosticism no adjective is too harsh to capture this divinity's imperfect nature. Hans Jonas sees him as "a blind and arrogant Creator," who thinks he is "the Most High and lording it over the creation," but who in fact is the "product of fault and ignorance," just like the creation itself.[13] Such an incompetent God creates without a plan or superior purpose, just "out of ignorance and passion."[14] Similarly, Slavoj Žižek talks of a "perverse and confused, idiotic God who screwed up the work of Creation."[15]

Jacques Lacarriere's classic work *Les Gnostiques* (1973) is of particular interest for understanding the Demiurge as a universal exploiter and cosmic trickster. Under the rule of an "incompetent and profoundly malevolent Demiurge," Lacarriere writes, humans are placed at the bottom of creation. "Exploited on a cosmic scale," we are spared no humiliation. We are "the proletariat of the Demiurge-executioner," miserable "slaves exiled into a world that is viscerally subjected to violence." Almost nothing can save us where we are: "we are the dregs and sediment of a lost heaven, strangers on our own planet."[16] The world is an utterly failed project, and so we are. Failure is not something accidental and remediable, but lies at the core of the human condition. Out of the many possible manners in which we could have been created, the way in which we turned out to be is the worst, thinks Lacarriere:

> The sadistic and perverse Demiurge responsible for this world and our existence in it must have racked his brains to find these incredible combinations of molecules, these indissoluble aggregates of matter, which make any escape from the carnal and planetary prison impossible or, at least, very aleatory.[17]

Yet this picture of the human condition in Gnosticism looks familiar: it presupposes the notion of existence as farce, of which I spoke earlier. The whole thing is "a cheat and a sham." The world in which we live, says Lacarriere, is above all "born of a monumental machination."[18] And true knowledge is understanding this machination: exposing the farce of existence should be the task of any honest thinker. For Lacarriere, to start taking the world for what it is, so as to avoid falling prey to "the beguiling trickery of the world,"[19] is the beginning of the *gnosis* – the only wisdom worth its name: the Gnostic thought.

Like Hans Jonas before him, Lacarriere sees in Gnosticism not just a religion, or a religious movement, which was active at a certain moment in history and then faded away, but a *way of thinking* that has given birth to a body of timeless insights into the human condition. Beyond its luxuriant, often disorienting mythic imagery, fables and stories, Gnosticism conceals an articulated philosophical vision on what it is to be human, something that remains valid beyond the historical context in which it emerged. And such a vision, this line goes, proves helpful especially in the twentieth and twenty-first centuries.[20] That's what compelled both Jonas and Lacarriere to relate Gnosticism to developments in contemporary philosophy, especially existentialism. Whereas Jonas tied the Gnostic thought to Heidegger, Lacarriere – even though to a lesser extent – connected Gnosticism especially to the works of E.M. Cioran. For him, *A Short History of Decay*, *The Temptation to Exist*, and *The New Gods* – some of Cioran's best-known works – are "texts which match the loftiest flashes of Gnostic thought."[21]

Given what I said earlier about Cioran, his affinity with the Gnostics should not surprise. Indeed, he is modern Gnostic, as Lacarriere and others have observed. Gnostic ideas and insights permeate his thinking. He sees creation as a lamentable failure: human history and civilization are nothing but "the work of the devil," which is the Demiurge's other name. In *A Short History of Decay*, Cioran deems the God of this world "incompetent." "Of all that was attempted on this side of nothingness," he wonders, "is there anything more pathetic than this world, except for the idea which conceived it?"[22] He explicitly engages with the Gnostics – he praises them, borrows from them, and places himself in their tradition. The French title of one of his books, which in English has been published as *The New Gods*, is telling: *Le Mauvais Démiurge* (1969) – "The Evil Demiurge." Here he endearingly calls the Gnostics "fanatics of the divine nothingness" and praises them for having "grasped so well the essence of the fallen world."[23] In an earlier work, *History and Utopia* [*Histoire et utopie*, 1960], in good Gnostic tradition, Cioran establishes a link between the precariousness of the world and the chronic sickness of its creator: "Without the hypothesis of a feverish deity subject to convulsions, giddy with epilepsy, we could not explain a universe that everywhere shows signs of an original sputum."[24] Ivan Karamazov could not have agreed more.

... and exposed for what it is

Kieślowski's religion is not easy to pin down. Even though he grew up in a Catholic environment, later in life he was not on friendly terms with the Catholic Church – especially after *No End* [*Bez końca*, 1985], which was poorly received, when not openly criticized, in Catholic circles. But he was not anti-Catholic either, and even less so atheist. People who knew him well talk of a certain religious dimension of his personality. Agnieszka Holland, a close friend, recalls:

> Krzysztof is somebody who had an incredibly deep need to believe in something transcendental. He did believe, but at the same time he wasn't really a member of any church, and his relationships toward the religious were less theological than ethical and metaphysical.[25]

For someone who grows up Catholic, but also grows distant from Catholicism, who still believes, but has very personal views on faith and religion, and goes as far as to express them in his work, the Church has a name: *heretic*. And of all the Christian heresies, Gnosticism would suit Kieślowski like a glove. Not that he read Gnostic authors or engaged with Gnostic literature: some people don't need to, they are born that way. Indeed, if we look closely enough, we are bound to discover a distinct and quite well articulated Gnostic sensibility in Kieślowski. This has already been noticed by other scholars such as Slavoj Žižek (*The Fright of Real Tears*; *The Double Life of Véronique*), who, however, didn't go into too much detail.

In his book of interviews with Danusia Stok, Kieślowski comes across as someone for whom this world is a dark, uncomfortable, dysfunctional place; there is something intrinsically alien and alienating about it that troubles him. And if something matches the world's imperfection, it is the wretchedness of those who inhabit it. Kieślowski complains of "all this mess which surrounds us," of all "this dirt, powerlessness, human impotence, this inability to finish anything, to do anything well."[26] Moreover, in good Cioranian tradition, he sees our inability to understand the full extent of our predicament as part of the predicament itself. Because of the "the limitation of our knowledge and the imperfection of our intelligence," says Kieślowski, "there's no way we can gauge the reality or the gravity of sin, the extent of guilt."[27] For all our best efforts, whatever we achieve remains shallow and marred in contradictions. "We're tiny and imperfect," he notices bitterly.[28] Human history is nothing but the endless recycling of the same errors and stupidities, the reenactment of the same disasters. We are bound to repeat history because we are not equipped to understand it. We never learn from our mistakes, never improve. For all the technological and scientific progress, we remain incapable of gaining control over that which controls us. Unwittingly employing an image dear to many Gnostics – the world as a prison of the human soul – Kieślowski observes that we are "just as much prisoners of our own passions, our own physiology, and certainly our own biology, as we were thousands of years ago."[29] We are doomed, and there is nothing we can do about it. Locked in this cellar of a world, we don't know true light nor genuine hope. "The most optimistic thing I can say is 'I'm still alive.'"[30]

Unsurprisingly, this sensibility shows up in Kieślowski's cinematic work. "All my films," he says, "are about individuals who can't quite find their bearings, who don't quite know how to live, who don't really know what's right or wrong and are desperately looking."[31] *Blind Chance* is a good example of Gnostic film. Here an incompetent, still-in-training Demiurge makes and remakes Witek, the main character, without any clear plan and purpose. As the cosmic puppeteer creates successive versions of the character, he throws them into the world to see if they stick. If they don't, he just drops them, and keeps trying. The three Witeks in the film are indeed, as Ivan Karamazov would put it, just "unfinished, trial creatures created in mockery." Yet, perhaps more than in *Blind Chance*, it is in *The Double Life ...* that Kieślowski reveals himself as a Gnostic artist. I use the phrase "Gnostic artist" in a deliberate, considered manner. As Jonas and Lacarriere made the case, Gnosticism is not just part of our past: one can still be a Gnostic in the twentieth (or twenty-first) century. As I hinted earlier, Hans Jonas speaks of Gnosticism as a certain mode of being in history, and an attitude to the world around, which are not at all the monopoly of the Gnostic religion strictly speaking. In the same sense, a major Catholic theologian such as Jean Guitton could say that "the Gnostic spirit is always present and continues to inspire" today's world.[32]

A Gnostic "feel" is discernible even in the opening scene of *The Double Life ...*. As the film begins to roll, we suddenly find ourselves in a world turned upside down, an image common in Gnosticism.[33] It is as though we've been "thrown" into an alien apace, some labyrinth from which we now have to find our way out. We soon realize that this is how the universe appears to little Weronika, who is making a huge discovery: her existence in the world. She is all eyes, doesn't move, doesn't utter a word – she is overwhelmed and confused by the immensity of it all. Her mother guides her gaze: "look at all the haze there below. It's not haze. It's really millions of little stars." The world reveals itself to Weronika (and, obliquely, to us) as a Gnostic universe: heavy, disorienting, as remote from the source of meaning as possible. In this place you feel indeed "tiny and imperfect." Such a universe, says Hans Jonas, "is like a vast prison whose innermost dungeon is the earth, the scene of man's life."[34]

Just as with *Blind Chance*, a persistent sense of cosmic claustrophobia permeates *The Double Life ....* The world is too narrow a place, too suffocating, we need to get out – that's the feeling that gradually develops in the viewer. Much of what is going on in the film is about overcoming the physicality of the universe in an attempt to find something larger, higher, more fulfilling, and non-material in nature[35]. That's why, in this sense, *The Double Life ...* is an exercise in dismantling the material world. Through alienating camera angles, distorted lenses, lighting effects, filters and other devices, Kieślowski questions its substantiality, undermines its solidity, and knocks down its walls. As Weronika travels to Krakow to see her aunt, she looks casually through a transparent ball. This "magic ball" distorts everything; not only does it turn the world upside down, but somehow it also liquefies it; the universe starts dematerializing under its spell. What we see through the train window, in the same scene, is an equally distorted, "deconstructed" version of the outside world, which is melting down before our eyes. It is as though Kieślowski's cinematic program is to "dissolve" all the matter of the world in the process of showing it on screen so that his characters can break free.

Seeking to escape from the realm of matter is a typically Gnostic approach. In many Gnostic narratives of creation, due to some unfortunate accident, the soul finds itself entangled in the physical world. The attraction is almost erotic in nature – it is as though the soul falls madly in love with matter. The Harranites of Mesopotamia, for example, believed that

> The Soul once turned toward matter, she became enamored of it, and burning with the desire to experience the pleasures of the body, she no longer wanted to disengage herself from it. Thus the world was born. From that moment the Soul forgot herself. She forgot her original habitation, her true center, her eternal being.[36]

This powerful image encapsulates much of what's at stake in Gnosticism. Reduced to its bare essentials, the Gnostic doctrine is a wake-up call: we are here only by accident, somehow we've lost our way, and have forgotten where we were going – otherwise, we have nothing in common with this place. Therefore, there cannot be anything worthier than escaping from it – that should be our first task. Gnostic soteriology is all about breaking free from the entanglements of the physical world. As Jonas puts it, Gnosticism is a narrative about the human soul "trapped and lost in the labyrinth of the world, seeking to escape and frightened by the gatekeepers of the cosmic prison".[37] Jonas uses a metaphorical style as he borrows from the Gnostics' imagery, yet what the Gnostic recipe for salvation boils down to is simply a diminishing of the importance of matter in our lives. "To discard or lighten all the matter of this world, that is the strange end the Gnostics pursued," says Jacques Lacarriere.[38] Through specific ascetic practices, meditation, abstention from certain foods and from procreation, but above all through *gnosis*, the Gnostics sought to extract themselves from the many entanglements that keep us tied to matter. They refused to play the cosmic game. Referring to the Marcionites, Tertullian said that they "impudently turn up their noses at creation and reject the work of the Creator."[39] Just like the Gnostics of old, Kieślowski is actively looking for a way out of the labyrinth of the material world[40] – and what better escape than knocking down its walls?

Yet perhaps the most conspicuously Gnostic feature in *The Double Life ...* is the figure of the puppeteer. His very name, Alexandre Fabbri, suggests a demiurgic role: the Italian "Fabbri" must originate in the Latin "faber": craftsman, maker, creator. Fabbri is a maker of stories, puppets, worlds.[41] Indeed, he is the maker of Weronika/Véronique and of their whole universe. Just as *The Double Life ...* is about to end, he starts sketching it. The film we've just seen is the story he is about to tell:

> November 23, 1966, was the most important day of their lives. That day, at 3.00 in the morning, they were both born, each in a different city on a different continent. They

> both had dark hair and brownish-green eyes. At two years old, when both knew how to walk, one of them burned her hand on a stove. A few days later, the other one reached out to touch a stove but pulled back just in time. Yet she couldn't have known she was about to burn herself... I think I will call it *The Double Life of*...

This is when, as I noticed earlier, Véronique learns that she is nothing but Fabbri's fabrication. He has manipulated her throughout, preyed on her weakness, teased her, aroused her, and toyed with her as he saw fit. To catch her in his game, he would call her in the middle of the night, send her mysterious objects, and prompt her to look for him in unexpected places. And yet, throughout his toying, he reveals himself as a Demiurge in the good Gnostic tradition: arrogant, weak, insecure, incompetent. He does not seem to have any clear purpose, does not know what he is doing with his creation, nor where he's headed, if he's headed anywhere.

Indeed, Fabbri is frustrated because he is stuck with minor stories and children's literature: "I want to write a book, a real book." He doesn't know how to come up with more complex narratives. Yet what he lacks in imagination he makes up in arrogance. Unable to figure out female psychology, he uses Véronique as a guinea pig: "I wanted to be sure. I wanted to see if it was possible ... Whether it was psychologically possible ... " for a woman to answer the calls of a complete stranger. So much for demiurgic omniscience! When she asks him "Why me? Why did you choose me?," his answer borders on the pathetic: "Because ... I don't know." When cornered by Véronique, the Demiurge apologizes like a schoolboy: "I'm sorry. Please forgive me."

The creatures of this poor Demiurge are badly made, flawed, vulnerable. Weronika dies young due to a congenital disease, Véronique gives up singing because of the same condition, but that may not save her from living a precarious life. They both feel certain things, but remain unable to understand, let alone articulate, what they feel. Their knowledge of themselves is feeble, obscured. "What do I really want, Papa?," Weronika asks her father. Véronique is in love, but does not know with whom. She feels compelled by some invisible force ("I always sense what I should do"), but can't name it ("It's hard to explain"). Neither Weronika nor Véronique are on a firm footing in this world – they can't find their way, they are left in the dark when it comes to grasping what really matters. They do their best, strive and fight, yet the results are mediocre. They are, you've guessed, "unfinished, trial creatures created in mockery," like all of us.

As though this were not bad enough, the master puppeteer, towards the end of the film, admits that he can't do any better than he does. His mastery over the situation is limited, and so are his creative abilities. When Véronique asks him why he needs two identical marionettes for the same show, his answer is a monument of defeatism: "I handle them a lot when I perform. They get damaged easily." The Demiurge can't envision a better, more enduring version of us.

As Fabbri has this exchange with Véronique, one of the puppets hanging in his hand, we can briefly see the second one, which is lying on his work desk. It's inert, inanimate, somehow eerie in its immobility. You can't really say whether the creature is dead or unborn – a corpse or an aborted fetus. Just some lump of matter, with human appearance, but without human life. This image uncannily brings to mind a myth about the creation of man we owe to Saturninus, a Gnostic who lived in Hadrian's time. Seven angel-Demiurges, the story goes, had seen "a brilliant image (εἰκών) descend from the supreme power, and had striven to detain it." They couldn't get a good enough look at it, but were so smitten with what they glimpsed that they encouraged each other: "Let us make man after the image and after the likeness." And so they did, and the result was a disaster. It was humanoid, but since these Demiurges were "too feeble to give him power to stand erect," the creature "lay on the ground wriggling like a worm."[42] Except for the wriggling, the humanoid in Saturninus' myth looks strikingly similar to Fabbri's puppet.[43]

where the puppeteer sacrifices the puppet …

The puppet lying lifelessly on Fabbri's work desk is of course Weronika. Singing, which she had taken up almost by accident, has proven fatal to her heart. Obscurely, as always in *The Double Life …*, she felt that music was a dangerous pursuit. Soon after her successful audition, her aunt enquired: "How did it go?" "Well," she answered. "Even too well, I'm afraid." She had the premonition of something bad that would come with her performance – she hesitated and delayed, but didn't give up, and readied herself for the big night. In the first, Polish part of the film, there is a clear build-up towards the event of Weronika's performance, which represents this part's climactic point. Weronika is a promising singer, has a captivating, unforgettable voice ("unusual," says the musical director), and expectations are high. As it turns out, however, her first performance is also her last.

But Weronika's performance is much more complex than anyone might have expected. On stage she performs her part in the concert, but more importantly she performs her own death – her sacrifice. At the end of the scene, lying dead on that platform, in front of the expectant crowd, she strikingly looks like a sacrificial victim on the altar. *This* is the climax we've been prepared for, not the singing. Weronika is young, beautiful, gifted, innocent – the perfect offering. Strangely, when she silently falls down, we *know* that she has died, and, after perhaps a moment of confusion, we accept her death. The film's conspicuously "transcendental style" – to use Paul Schrader's phrase – has surreptitiously prepared us for such an outcome, so that we are not totally surprised when an eminently transcendent event such as death irrupts into the story. The camera's dissolving gaze, the alienating angles, the filters and the lighting – the "unreality" of it all – have punctured Weronika's universe deep enough to make us realize that she is being toyed with by some outside entity. We haven't made the acquaintance of the master puppeteer yet, but we sense his presence and see his work. *Of course* Weronika dies in the end – that's how it should be. What else can one expect from a *marionnettiste*-God? A final bird's-eye shot, strongly suggesting a distant, indifferent observer, seals the scene.

• • •

Just a few years after the release of *The Double Life …* on another work desk – an operating table, this time – lying lifelessly there was another discarded puppet: Krzysztof Kieślowski himself. He died in Warsaw on 13 March 1996, during open-heart surgery, which followed a heart attack. He was only fifty-four years old. Relatively young, tremendously gifted, with much still to say – Kieślowski, too, was the perfect sacrificial offering. His performance, like Weronika's, was a complex, multilayered one: it started in art and ended in death. Just as Weronika wouldn't stop singing in spite of her premonitions, so Kieślowski worked himself to death. The documentary that Krzysztof Wierzbicki dedicated to him (*I'm so-so*, 1995) features a number of people, of different professions (a priest, a doctor, a clairvoyant, a graphologist, etc.), who speak of Kieślowski as they see him from their specific perspectives. Here's what the doctor has to say: "His job is very harmful to his health and it demands that he often works under great pressure. Having led a life like this for many years, he now has problems with his circulatory system. It's inevitable." The discarding of exhausted, useless puppets is always inevitable. We should also remember that they "get damaged easily," as the *marionnettiste* himself puts it.

… which turns out not to be such a bad thing …

"God is a man-eater. For this reason men are [sacrificed] to him."[44] The "God" to whom the *Gospel of Philip* refers here is not the Demiurge but the "true," "hidden," "secret," "alien God" of the Gnostics. And with this God of light the world – an embodiment of darkness – has nothing in common. For the Gnostics everything in the world is failed and corrupt: "life, thought, human and planetary destiny," says Lacarriere, are a "failed work, limited and vitiated in its most fundamental structures." Absolutely everything, "from the distant stars to the nuclei of our body-cells, carries the materially demonstrable trace of an original imperfection."[45] And yet, for all the imperfection that structures human existence, within the Gnostic scenario there is hidden in every human being a divine "spark" that comes from – and aspires to return to – the originary light. To be human is to be here and, at the same time, to miss being elsewhere. "I am *in* the world but not *of* the world" is the ultimate credo of the Gnostic. For anyone entertaining such views, death cannot be but a form of liberation. To be sacrificed to the "man-eater" is a blessing for the people so persuaded. You are not destroyed – on the contrary, you are freed from the world of destruction. Sacrifice helps you get rid of the lump of matter – your body – that keeps you tied to a place with which you – the divine spark in you – have nothing in common. To the "pneumatics," as those who possess the *gnosis* are called in Gnosticism, this world can do no harm, no matter how hard it tries. They are already out of the Demiurge's reach.

And yet things are not that simple, as the Gnostics themselves admitted. The God of light is unlike anything we know. We cannot even imagine it. It's so inaccessible to the ordinary human faculties that Marcion called it "the unknown God." Basilides went one step further and talked of it as the "non-existent God." It's totally understandable, then, that for those of us who don't possess the *gnosis* – in Gnosticism they are called "fleshly" or "hylic" – sacrifice is a different business altogether. We, too, can say that "God is a man-eater," but what we mean is not the Gnostics' God. It's the *marionnettiste*-God, the spider-God, it is Cioran's *mauvais démiurge*, the manipulator that sets up the cosmic farce. And how are we going to deal with this cannibal? How on earth can such a sacrifice – Kieślowski's, yours and mine – be meaningful?

In fact, it can. Granted, when you are an "unfinished, trial creature created in mockery" there is not much you can do, but the little you can may be enough to redeem you from total meaninglessness. Human existence may be a farce, but there are ways to resist it, and to poke fun at the cosmic farceur. Dostoevsky's underground man, one of Ivan's earlier incarnations, sticks his tongue out at it all, and finds satisfaction. That gives him a reason to live. When Antonius Block, Ingmar Bergman's hero in *The Seventh Seal*, is about to be crushed, he does the most unexpected thing: he challenges Death – the farceur's messenger – to a game of chess. Of course Block cannot win, but he does not play to win. He plays for the sake of the game, to savor the way Death has to submit to the rules of the game, unable to do anything to change them. Block plays to shame the farceur, to trick the trickster, and that gives him a reason to be. For there is a certain dignity, a freedom and a meaning, that the crushed can get from the crushing itself. Simone Weil once said that, whatever does the crushing, it does not feel anything. Instead, "it is the person crushed who feels what is happening." If one does not "place oneself on the side of the oppressed, to feel with them, one cannot understand."[46]

It's precisely this understanding that makes all the difference. There is something distinctly insensitive, unintelligent, and unrefined about the "man-eater." Any beasts, if they are beastly enough, can be man-eaters, but they don't know, let alone understand, what they are doing. So the man-eater devours the man, but it can never know what it is that it devours. *Being eaten up* – that's a different story altogether. The anxiety that her imminent annihilation brings about in the victim places her in a unique existential situation: it makes her acutely aware of her own existence, but it also opens her up towards a larger ontological horizon, and prepares her for self-transcendence. From where she is now, everything – the world around, the victimizer, she herself, the nothingness behind it all – looks very different. And a reversal of values and priorities takes place: that which seems powerful is proven powerless, and the powerless gains tremendous power. The victim turns out victorious and the victimizer impotent. The anxiety triggered by her impending death raises the victim above the ontological arrangement in virtue of which she's is made "for mockery." As she is being crushed, she gains something that the cosmic regime that does the crushing can never have: a sense of boundless freedom.

When the world reveals itself to be a farce, for the farce's victim such a revelation can turn out to be an exhilarating experience: she can turn the tables on the farceur by being the first who does the laughing. Such a response will surely throw him off balance: it is the last thing the man-eater expects. When the mocking cosmic machine is about to devour you, you can spoil its designs by starting to mock yourself. The self-awareness thus caused is so intense, the anxiety so shattering, the experience so liberating that, in a certain sense, you can pull yourself out of the situation. You transcended yourself: in a way, you are no longer there, even though your body stays behind. You are crushed, but that no longer affects you. There is nothing the mocking machine can do to you because it always comes for victims, and you are no longer one.

Sacrifice thus becomes an experience of boundlessness. In dying, you have nothing to lose but the chains. As some marionettes – on their way to destruction, the man-eater already in sight – once quipped: "We will die and will be free."

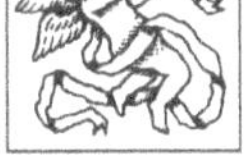

... and the story ends

notes

1 The notion has been famously explored by Hugo Rahner. More recently Giuseppe Mazzotta employed it in his reading of Dante (227). See also my essays "'I was a Stranger, and ye took me not in'" and "To Die Laughing."

2 I discuss at length Ivan's notion of world as farce in my essay "To Die Laughing." See also my essay "'God is Dreaming You.'"

3 Dostoevsky 261.

4 Ibid. 245.

5 Cioran, *Entretiens* 82–94.

6 Cioran, *Short History of Decay* 49.

7 Ibid. 74.

8 Dostoevsky 261.

9 In Stok 189.

10 Dostoevsky 134.

11 In Robinson 145.

12 Rudolph 75.

13 Jonas xxxi.

14 Ibid. 327.

15 Žižek, "*The Double Life of Véronique*."

16 Lacarriere 29.

17 Ibid. 30.

18 Ibid. 20.

19 Ibid. 38.

20 As Hans Jonas put it:

> something in Gnosticism knocks at the door of our Being and of our twentieth-century Being in particular. Here is humanity in a crisis and in some of the radical possibilities of choices that man can make concerning his view of his position in the world, of his relation to himself, to the absolute and to his mortal Being. (Jonas xxv)

21 Ibid. 127. Lacarriere adds the telling detail that "*A Short History of Decay* has, since its publication, been a constant bedside book for me."

22 Cioran, *Short History of Decay* 142.

23 Cioran, *New Gods* 8.

24 Cioran, *History and Utopia* 73.

25 In Kickasola 34. See also his interview with Paul Coates (*Lucid Dreams*).

26 In Stok 69.

27 Ibid. 122.

28 Ibid. 150.

29 Ibid. There are also some subtle Marcionite echoes in the way he conceives the "two Gods" of the Old Testament and the New Testament, respectively:

> when I think of God, it's more often the God of the Old Testament rather than the New. The God of the Old Testament is a demanding, cruel God; a God who does not forgive, who ruthlessly demands obedience to the principles which He has laid down. The God of the New Testament is a merciful [...] who just forgives everything. The God of the Old Testament leaves us a lot of freedom and responsibility, observes how we use it and then rewards or punishes, and there's no appeal of forgiveness. It's something which is lasting, absolute, evident. (Ibid. 149)

30 Ibid. 205.

31 Ibid. 79.

32 In Filoramo xvi.

33 In Gnosticism, says a modern scholar, this "cosmos of ours is a pale, eroded, if not deformed (and upside down) image of the true world" (Filoramo 57).

34 Jonas 43.

35 Joseph Kickasola employs the term "threshold" when talking of Kieślowski's approach: "Kieślowski charts the liminal spaces, demarcating the apparent thresholds of metaphysical and physical, transcendent and immanent, eternal and temporal" (x).

36 In Jonas 63.

37 Ibid. xxxi.

38 Lacarriere 19.

39 In Filoramo 164.

40 Central to Kickasola's interpretation is that the film is about a "spiritual search" and an instinctive quest for a higher reality. "The film is about longing – deep, internal longing – and the attempt to follow one's intuition, which is part of the reason it is so difficult to write about" (244–46).

41 This is how Kieślowski describes his first contact with the puppeteer-actor who played Fabbri: "He animated those dolls and immediately, within the space of a second, a whole new world appeared" (Stok 180–81).

42 Smith and Wave 587.

43 It was "hominoid in appearance," says Lacarriere commenting on Saturninus, but "incapable of standing upright on his atrophied legs" (31–32).

44 Robinson 138.

45 Lacarriere 10.

46 In McLellan 93.

bibliography

Bradatan, Costica. "'God is Dreaming You': Narrative as *Imitatio Dei* in Miguel de Unamuno." *Janus Head – A Journal of Interdisciplinary Studies in Continental Philosophy, Literature, Phenomenological Psychology and the Arts* 7.2 (2004): 453–67. Print.

Bradatan, Costica. "'I was a Stranger, and ye took me not in.' *Deus Ludens* and Theology of Hospitality in Lars von Trier's *Dogville*." *Journal of European Studies* 39.1 (2009): 58–78. Print.

Bradatan, Costica. "To Die Laughing." *East-European Politics and Societies* 25.4 (2011): 737–58. Print.

Cioran, E.M. *Entretiens*. Paris: Gallimard, 1995. Print.

Cioran, E.M. *History and Utopia*. Trans. R. Howard. London: Quartet, 1996. Print.

Cioran, E.M. *The New Gods*. Trans. R. Howard. London: Quadrangle, 1974. Print.

Cioran, E.M. *A Short History of Decay*. Trans. R. Howard. Oxford: Blackwell, 1976. Print.

Coates, Paul, ed. *Lucid Dreams: The Films of Krzysztof Kieślowski*. Trowbridge: Flicks, 1999. Print.

Dostoevsky, F.M. *The Brothers Karamazov*. Trans. and annotated Richard Pevear and Larissa Volokhonsky. New York: Farrar, 2002. Print.

Filoramo, Giovanni. *A History of Gnosticism*. Oxford: Blackwell, 1990. Print.

Jonas, Hans. *The Gnostic Religion: The Message of the Alien God & the Beginnings of Christianity*. Boston: Beacon, 2001. Print.

Kickasola, Joseph. *The Films of Krzysztof Kieślowski: The Liminal Image*. New York: Continuum, 2004. Print.

Lacarriere, Jacques. *The Gnostics*. Foreword Lawrence Durrell. New York: Dutton, 1977. Print.

Mazzotta, Giuseppe. *Dante's Vision and the Circle of Knowledge*. Princeton: Princeton UP, 1993. Print.

McLellan, David. *Utopian Pessimist: The Life and Thought of Simone Weil*. New York: Poseidon, 1990. Print.

Rahner, Hugo. *Man at Play*. Trans. Brian Battershaw and Edward Quinn. New York: Herder, 1972. Print.

Robinson, James M., ed. *The Nag Hammadi Library in English*. San Francisco: Harper, 1977. Print.

Rudolph, Kurt. *Gnosis: The Nature and History of Gnosticism*. San Francisco: Harper, 1983. Print.

Schrader, Paul. *Transcendental Style in Film: Ozu, Bresson, Dreyer*. Berkeley: U of California P, 1972. Print.

Smith, William, and Henry Wave. *A Dictionary of Christian Biography, Literature, Sects and Doctrines*. London: Little, 1877. Print.

Stok, Danusia, ed. *Kieślowski on Kieślowski*. London: Faber, 1993. Print.

Žižek, Slavoj. "*The Double Life of Véronique*: The Forced Choice of Freedom." Essay published in the booklet accompanying the DVD release of *The Double Life of Véronique* in the Criterion Collection (2006). Print.

Žižek, Slavoj. *The Fright of Real Tears: Krzysztof Kieślowski between Theory and Post-Theory*. London: BFI, 2001. Print.

ashley woodward

A SACRIFICIAL ECONOMY OF THE IMAGE

lyotard on cinema

Jean-François Lyotard's writings on cinema have achieved some sporadic attention in anglophone cinema studies, but this has so far been accompanied by two significant lacks: they have exhibited a striking ignorance of some directly relevant material, and have missed the potentially far-reaching significance of Lyotard's work for the study of cinema. On the first point, this attention has been focused on Lyotard's two essays which have appeared in English translation: "Acinema" and "The Unconscious as Mise-en-Scène," as well as involving some attempts to draw implications for cinema from his wider writings.[1] In fact, Lyotard published two further essays on film – "Deux métamorphoses du séduisant au cinéma" [Two Metamorphoses of the Seductive in Cinema] and "Idée d'un film souverain "[The Idea of a Sovereign Film] – of which existing discussions in English make no mention. Significantly, issues treated by Lyotard in these essays have direct bearing on arguments made in English discussions. For example, Simone Knox has recently called for a renewed attention to Lyotard's "neglected" essay "Acinema" and its potential fecundity for cinema studies, while mounting an argument that Lyotard's own work is limited by an excessive focus on avant-garde and experimental cinema, and suggesting that it might be possible to combine his analysis with mainstream, narrative ("Hollywood") film.[2] However, Lyotard has already done much of this work himself (in the essay "Idée d'un film souverain"). Oversight of this work is therefore a significant lack in need of remedy if scholarship in this area is not to cover ground unnecessarily and to move forward effectively.[3] I have no wish to labour here the shortcomings of existing scholarship, but rather to widen the pathway it has opened. My first aim in this essay is to provide an overview of all four of Lyotard's essays on cinema in order to bring the full range of his work in this area to the attention of anglophone film theorists. Much of the work here is thus exegetical, since this is what is called for by the current state of scholarship. However, this exegesis is necessarily interpretive, as Lyotard's essays on cinema are framed within quite different theoretical terms, and what I aim to provide here is ultimately a reading which synthesises them in order to outline a "Lyotardian philosophy of cinema."

I will argue that the key theme which can be used to give coherence to Lyotard's writings on cinema is that of sacrifice. This theme appears not in terms of any representational content but in terms of the economy of the images from which a film is composed. Sacrifice is here understood in a sense derived from Bataille, and is related to his notions of general (as opposed to restricted) economy, and of sovereignty. Bataille critiques capitalist "restricted" economy for its utilitarian principle of maximising usefulness and attempting to eliminate waste and "useless" expenditure: in a restricted economy, everything is channelled into maximising "the good." The basis of Bataille's critique is the view that there is a natural *excess* of energy in the world, which must spend itself in ways which cannot be channelled into the restricted economy of usefulness. This excess is driven to express itself through "useless" expenditures. Bataille finds examples of this both in the natural world (the constant expenditure of energy, without replenishment, of the sun) and the cultural world (sacrifice, the gift as *potlatch*, death, war, non-reproductive sexuality). For Bataille, sacrifice makes potentially useful objects sacred by withdrawing them from profane circulation; such sacrificial objects are subtracted from restricted economy and take part in the kind of consumption which has a place only in general economy.[4]

This notion of sacrifice can also be applied in the arts. In a short text on the photography of Corinne Filippi, Lyotard writes:

> Bataille used to say that true poetry consists in a *sacrifice* where the words are the victims. It removes them from the use we make of them (or believe we are making) when we speak to each other. It spends them without calculating gain (our "interaction" [...]), it offers them, surrenders them to the power of language.
>
> Corinne Filippi's photography is a sacrifice of photons: they are surrendered by her to their energetic spirit, whose purpose is by no means to enlighten the human horizon.[5]

While Lyotard does not speak explicitly of sacrifice in relation to cinema, in the essay "Idée d'un film souverain" Bataille's connected notion of "sovereignty" is central. Sovereignty, for Bataille, refers not to an authority figure in a hierarchy but to a mode of consumption which implies the ability to consume without taking part in work and production: the sovereign is thus insubordinate in relation to a given system based on a restricted economy, and is able to consume in a "sacrificial" manner.[6] Bataille's terms opposed to restricted economy have their own specificity. Nevertheless, they are sufficiently similar, when developed analogically in relation to the arts, that we may draw out Lyotard's philosophy of film under the title "a sacrificial economy of the image." The sacrificial image involves a sterile consumption; Lyotard gives the example of a child playing with matches:

> A match once struck is consumed. If you use the match to light the gas that heats the water for the coffee which keeps you alert on your way to work, the consumption is not sterile, for it is a movement belonging to the circuit of capital: merchandise-match merchandise-labour power money-wages merchandise-match. But when a child strikes the match-head *to see* what happens – just for the fun of it – he enjoys the movement itself, the changing colors, the light flashing at the height of the blaze, the death of the tiny piece of wood, the hissing of the tiny flame. He enjoys these sterile differences leading nowhere, these uncompensated losses; what the physicist calls the dissipation of energy.[7]

My second aim is to indicate the so-far largely untapped potential I believe Lyotard's work may have to contribute to film theory. This potential, I will argue, takes its bearings from Lyotard's critical opposition to Lacan, whose influence in film theory is of course very well known. The "first wave" of Lacanianism began in the 1970s with the work of film theorists such as Christian Metz, Jean-Louis Baudry, and Jean-Louis Comolli, and achieved a crystallising moment in Laura Mulvey's widely influential article "Visual Pleasure and Narrative Cinema." This work focused on Lacan's idea of the mirror stage and the register of the Imaginary. It mobilised a psychoanalytic approach to cinema by understanding it as a space which invites us to phantasise and which has the ideological effect of producing an unfree subjectivity in the spectator, an effect which should be destroyed by the demystifying function of critical theory.

More recently, after the wave of "post-Theory" which began to dominate cinema studies in the 1990s,[8] some notable scholars – such as Joan Copjec, Slavoj Žižek, and Todd McGowan – have called for a return to theory in film in the form of a return to Lacan.[9] However, this Lacan is not the same Lacan, but the later one who concentrates on the register of the Real. The emphasis of this Lacanian film theory is no longer on breaking the spell of the Imaginary phantasy set up in film through proper theoretical conceptualisation, but rather on recognising that film itself presents the Real – that is, breaks and ruptures in the Imaginary and Symbolic worlds they present. Key to this second wave of Lacanianism in film is a shift in understanding of "the gaze," from the spectator's scopic drive for mastery, as it was for Mulvey and the earlier Lacanians, to Lacan's own proper understanding of the gaze as the objective "blind spot" which destroys mastery, along with the fullness of meaning and interpretation. As I will argue, we may gain purchase on the significance of Lyotard's writings on film, on their potential to impact and transform the field, by viewing them as critically intersecting both waves of Lacanian theory.[10]

The fact that Lyotard's contributions to cinema theory are dispersed throughout his diverse and changing oeuvre necessitates an independent analysis of each essay. In what follows I will therefore briefly examine these essays one by one in chronological order of their composition, drawing out their common themes through the frame of sacrifice, and indicating their implications for film theory.

libidinal movement, sterile consumption

Lyotard's first essay on film, "Acinema" (1973), is the most well known and commented on in English. In short, Lyotard proposes here a "libidinal economy" of cinema, and develops a privileged notion of cinema which he calls "acinema." In the later essay "Idée d'un film souverain," Lyotard briefly revisits "Acinema" and suggests that the main aim there is to oppose avant-garde cinema to commercial cinema.[11] These forms of cinema are opposed according to the way they treat *movement*, and the relative economies in which movement is inscribed. Commercial cinema is characterised as obeying an economy of "the repetition of the same," whereby the movements portrayed in the images from which the film is constructed contribute to establishing the identity of the film as a whole. In libidinal terms, this economy is associated with the "organised body" of "normal" adult sexuality, where desires circulating in the body are all subordinated to the aim of reproduction. Movements in commercial cinema are analogously subordinated to the aim of the overall *narrative* of the film; the story that it tells.

Further drawing out this analogy in Nietzschean terms, Lyotard portrays the commercial film director as a *nihilist*, because of the way movements which do not serve the purpose of the narrative are excluded from the construction of the film. By "exclusions" he means the usual processes of mise-en-scène, editing, etc. Directing is a nihilist art for Lyotard because it eliminates the contingent immanence of movements themselves (i.e., the moving images and sounds), devaluing them in relation to a higher purpose which is supposed to give them meaning: the narrative of the film as a whole functions analogously here to God, the "true world," and all other modifications of the transcendent ideal which Nietzsche sees as devaluing immanent life. In Lyotard's terms, the movements themselves portrayed through cinematic images are capable of transmitting "intensities" to the audience in and of themselves, but these intensities are eliminated or dampened by the director's work, which subordinates the sensuous immediacy of the cinematic material to a narrative meaning.

On the other hand, Lyotard distinguishes experimental cinema by the allowance of movements which are useless to the narrative whole of the film. The economy here is what Lyotard calls "the repetition of the other," and he associates it with Nietzsche's eternal return.[12] In libidinal terms, this economy accords with the production of desires according to partial drives, which escape the reproductive aim and are therefore characterised (in the strictly Freudian sense – see his *Three Essays on Sexuality*) – as perversion. Experimental cinema allows movements which escape narrative structure and are able to transmit intensities to the bodies of the audience on the basis of their sensorial qualities. Lyotard sees this as so far from what typically passes as cinema that he calls it "acinema."

As Lyotard sees it, commercial cinema structures its images according to a rhythm which is accepted as establishing an effect of "reality." When we see images unfold on the screen at a certain pace, we believe we are seeing reality (or its faithful reproduction). Lyotard then argues that "acinema" is evident at two extremes where this rhythm is violated – when the movements slow to a virtual halt, or become very fast. He develops these notions through an analogy with other visual arts, particularly painting, associating cinematic immobilisation with the *tableau vivant*, and acceleration with lyric abstraction (such as Jackson Pollock's action painting).

While Lyotard does not make explicit in this essay any influence from Bataille, Lisa Trahair and Graham Jones have noted that the two economies of (a)cinema appear to accord with Bataille's distinction between a restricted and a general economy.[13] This is evident in the way that commercial cinema obeys a rule of productive, utilitarian usefulness in the economy of the images themselves:

> No movement, arising from any field, is given to the eye-ear of the spectator for what it is: a simple *sterile difference* in an audio-visual field. Instead, every movement put forward *sends back* to something else, is inscribed as a plus or minus on the ledger book which is the film, *is valuable* because it *returns* to something else, because it is thus potential return and profit.[14]

That is, every image in commercial cinema is judged according to its relation to other images and its utilitarian value in relation to the overall narrative *meaning* of the film as a whole. By contrast, acinema obeys a general economy where at least some images are allowed the status of a sacrifice: they portray a movement which is simply allowed to exist in and of itself, to transmit its sensorial intensities to the viewer and to be enjoyed as a useless, sterile expenditure, like the child striking the match simply to see it burn.

somatography, diagraphy, perspectivism

Lyotard's next essay dealing significantly with cinema is "The Unconscious as Mise-en-Scène" (1977). Here he develops an analogy between two types of mise-en-scène: the *psychoanalytic* variety, in which desire is "put in scene" by the unconscious and manifests in symptoms, dreams, and so on, and the *artistic* variety, in which the script or other form of instruction is "put in scene" by the director and manifests as a film (or an opera, or a theatrical production, etc.). Lyotard's aim here is to demonstrate a displacement of the problematic of the unconscious and mise-en-scène "from Freud to Nietzsche and beyond."[15] He continues to make much of Freud, however, in an argument familiar from his earlier works, that Freud's own aesthetics remain bound to a *Quattrocento* model of representation and ignore the artistic avant-garde contemporaneous to his own work. Nevertheless, there are resources within his works – in particular, the ideas of desire as energy and the "irrational" operations of the unconscious – which provide resources for an understanding of avant-garde art.[16] A key point for our concerns that Lyotard develops here is that, contra Lacan, desire should not be understood as a legible text, to be interpreted and read, but as a *force* which manifests through contemporaneous figures. This approach contrasts significantly with the "Imaginary Lacan," for whom desire can and should be fully symbolised in order to overcome the lure of the image.

Lyotard defines mise-en-scène as follows: "'Mettre-en-scène' (to stage) is to transmit signifiers from a 'primary' space to another space, which is the auditorium of a theatre, cinema, or any related art."[17] He describes the primary space as consisting of "groups of signifiers forming so many messages,"[18] and the mise-en-scène as "giving life" to these messages by transcribing them onto the bodies of the performers, who turn written signifiers into sensory equivalents such as speech, song, and bodily movements (i.e., acting out the script, playing the music, etc.), which can then be transmitted to the bodies of spectators in the performance itself. Lyotard thus characterises mise-en-scène as a *somatography*: a transcribing of linguistic signifiers on and for bodies, and as a *diagraphy*: a change in the *space* of transcription, from linguistic signifiers (primary space) to sensations affecting the bodies of the audience (the other space).[19]

In the psychoanalytic analogue to the artistic mise-en-scène, the primary space is desire, the director or "*metteur-en-scène*" is the unconscious, while the other space is the symptom, phantasy, or dream in which desire is staged in disguised form. Psychoanalysis, Lyotard tells us, is a theory of *the interpretation* of desire, and in its "classical" Freudian model the unconscious is understood as a kind of translator which acts to simultaneously stage and hide desire by translating one intelligible language – desire – into another – symptoms, dreams, etc. The classic statement of this model is *The Interpretation of Dreams*, in which desire is understood as dreamthoughts (*Traumgedanke*), or the latent content, and the dream itself as dreamcontent (*Trauminhalt*) or manifest content. The unconscious is understood as mise-en-scène in so far as it submits the dreamthoughts to certain operations, which Freud calls the dreamwork (*die Traumarbeit*), which act to stage and hide it. According to Lyotard, Freud here follows the model of "classical" mise-en-scène, which was dominant, for example, in nineteenth-century Viennese opera, or in the Hollywood films of the 1930s.

On these "classical" models of mise-en-scène and the unconscious, the primary space is understood as a legible text, which has been *translated* by the work of the unconscious or the director into the performance of the other space. However, Lyotard argues that this model is displaced in Freud's later writings by an increasingly sophisticated understanding of desire, and of the operations of the unconscious. The possibility of seeing desire as a legible "truth" is clearer in relation to Freud's earlier understanding of desire as "wish" – desire is an absent object, what the person wants (such as the mother's love etc.). Yet in the later works Freud elaborates desire as a force (libido) with dynamic and economic properties, which never manifests in a "pure" form but always through the *drives* (roughly, the instincts as they are shaped by environmental influences). Lyotard quotes a passage from "Instincts and their Viccisitudes"[20] in which Freud describes the drives as being like successive eruptions of lava, where each of these eruptions may undergo radical transformations (e.g., from love to hate concerning the same object), yet continue to exist in the same "space," such that desire takes on the quality of *ambivalence*.[21] This quality is also expressed in Freud's 1915 paper on the unconscious. Here, the primary processes, which are "the metamorphoses of the drives," are described as being "irrational" with respect to logical, spatial, and temporal properties.[22] If we follow this displacement of mise-en-scène in the later Freudian texts, we find ourselves with a Nietzschean perspectivism, where there is no single, legible "truth" of desire, but multiple and inconsistent desires. The implication for the arts is that "works must not be taken as symptoms symbolically expressing a concealed discourse, but as attempts to state perspectives of reality."[23] Relating these themes back to economy and sacrifice (though they are not mentioned explicitly here), we can see the classical model of mise-en-scène as analogous to the restricted economy of narrative cinema, while the perspectivism that Lyotard champions allows and necessarily involves the sacrificial images of a general economy. Lyotard argues that this perspectivist problematic is in fact operative in "Underground" cinema, and gives as an example Michael Snow's classic experimental film *La Région centrale* (1971), in which a specially designed camera multiplies perspectives – producing a plethora of unusual, sacrificial images – thanks to a fully spherical range of motion.

A key point of difference with Lacanian film theory which emerges in this essay concerns ideology. The early Lacanians drew on not only Lacan but significantly on Louis Althusser's appropriation of Lacan for a theory of ideology. In this theory, capitalist society reproduces its relations of production by "interpolating" subjects, that is, by forming in its citizens a subjectivity which makes them accept existing conditions. Althusser bases his theory of how such subjectivity is formed on Lacan's theory of identification in the mirror phase.[24] For Althusser, as for Marx, ideology is "false consciousness," a mystification covering the truth, and can be dispelled by the deployment of "scientific" theory. While a notion of ideology is still operative in Lyotard's thought in the orbit of *Discourse, Figure*, this quickly disappears: the Nietzschean perspectivism he adopts seems to render inoperative theories of ideology in so far as they maintain a Platonic structure of reality vs. appearance. Early Lacanian film theory seems wedded to this Platonic perspective especially in so far as it sees sensuous enjoyment as a sensible (Imaginary) lure, to be overcome by intelligible (Symbolic) analysis. From a Lyotardian perspective, such an analysis would appear as yet another in a long line of theoretical indictments of art.[25] For Lyotard, "the function of the image is no longer to deceive by means of false recognition [...] and film is not made to disguise truth on a fantasmatic stage." Cinema is an "inexhaustible means for experimenting with new effects, never seen, never heard before." It creates its own reference and its own addressee, "a disconcerted body, invited to stretch its sensory capacities beyond measure."[26]

seductive pragmatics, hyperrealist cinema

So far, we have seen Lyotard critique traditional conceptions of cinema, and argue for an experimental film which is endless in its possibilities and which operates on bodies, through sensations, rather than in terms of narrative and intelligible meaning. This focus, and the displacement of the category of ideology, might seem to render Lyotard's theories of film completely apolitical. However, the 1979 essay "Deux métamorphoses du séduisant au cinéma" extends these ruminations in a more explicitly political register. We see here Lyotard's well-known "turn" from psychoanalytic, libidinal philosophy to philosophy of language fully in effect. Many of his concerns, however, remain recognisably those of his earlier works: cinema is analysed according to a contrast between the film as a whole with its narrative and effect of representing a reality, and certain images and sequences which operate independently of this narrative, which defy intelligible meaning, and which work by transmitting sensations directly to bodies. Yet the problematic proposed here is a little different: it is the political effect of film construed as *seduction*. Lyotard examines two examples of "political film" (i.e., films with a more-or-less explicit political content): Francis Ford Coppola's *Apocalypse Now*, and the works of Hans-Jürgen Syberberg. His treatment of Syberberg is perfunctory, however, and I will focus my analysis on what he has to say about *Apocalypse Now*. The question he poses is this: is it possible for film to function in a way which does not "seduce" its audience?

He elaborates the idea of seduction in the framework of linguistic pragmatics by drawing on Gorgias and Plato. Gorgias was fascinated by the power of language to deceive and seduce, and he explained seduction as consisting in the *metastasis* (displacement) of the opinions of the listener.[27] Plato suggests in the *Menexenus* that seduction consists in the metastasis of names on the pragmatic places of addressee and referent. The example he gives is the way that the citizens of Athens can be seduced into *being* virtuous citizens by hearing tales *of* virtuous citizens (the addressees shift to the place of the referent).[28] Cashing this out, Lyotard suggests that seduction is *a case* of the pragmatic efficacity of discourse (i.e., it is one way in which discourse *works to effect* its listener). The specific way in which seduction works is this: *a non-prescriptive utterance acts like a prescriptive*: it imposes an *obligation* on the addressee. Seduction would then involve a metastasis of opinions in Gorgias's sense because the addressee comes to hold an opinion – that they ought to believe or to do something – which they did not previously hold. Moreover, there is a metastasis of the names attached to the addressee and referent in Plato's sense if the prescription is carried out.

What this means for "theatrical arts" such as cinema is that the director does not speak directly to the audience, telling them what they ought to believe or do. Rather, the actors speak to each other, and the "prescriptive" effects on the audience arise indirectly. Here, Lyotard tells us, the conditions are favourable to seduction (the transmission of a non-explicit prescriptive discourse) because the positions of director and audience are hidden behind the positions between the staged characters.[29] In a way which is now familiar from his previous two essays on cinema, Lyotard links the function of "classical" cinema with realism, which he now defines as follows: "The term realism, in cinema, must designate a perfect occultation of the places of the narrator and the narratee, that is to say the perfect mimesis."[30] This occultation is linked to the exclusions involved in cinema which he had previously detailed, but now he focuses on the exclusion of one particular element: the explicit intervention of a director. Yet he also notes that the spatial and temporal frame of realist cinema must be "in conformity with what is culturally and socially acceptable according to the norms of perception."[31] According to Lyotard, then, realism facilitates seduction, and realist cinema is an art form conducive to seductive effects. This seduction is also associated with the narrative effect of film, since it is the narrative which establishes the reference of the film as a representation of reality, and which unfolds through the images of the film according to the "norms of perception." It is the narrative, moreover, which establishes the discourse – the meaning of the film – which may then implicitly convey prescriptive effects.

Lyotard presents *Apocalypse Now* as precisely such a realist film. It unfolds various narratives, and beneath them is a political message about the futility of the Vietnam War which is conveyed seductively, as a non-explicit prescription. Yet there is one sequence of images in this film which, Lyotard hypothesises, escapes the seductive effect and conveys an effect of a very different type: the sequence of the attack by the American soldiers on the Vietnamese village. He analyses this as a shift from the realism of the film as a whole to a *hyperrealism* characteristic of this sequence. The term "hyperrealism," he reminds us, is taken from the field of painting, where it arose as a response to the invention of photography, and where it is associated with the machinic reproduction of images, and with what Walter Benjamin called "loss of aura."[32] Recalling one of the poles of the acinema, Lyotard suggests that it is also associated with an "immobilisation." He defines hyperrealism with reference to Bataille's writings on Manet, and the loss of "eloquence": "Eloquence is the possibility of inscribing the painted scene in the narration, whether its character is mythological, religious, historical, intimist, or even simply intimate."[33] With hyperrealism, painting no longer refers to a meaning; the painting itself becomes the event, the thing of significance. Hyperrealism *destroys narrative*; not by moving away from the depiction of reality but by focusing on it too intently, immobilising it, or by multiplying images of it at speed. Thus, under the heading of hyperrealism, Lyotard presents here an alternative account of what remain recognisably the themes of the acinema, and a modality of the sacrificial economy of the image: in hyperrealism, the images are sacrificed; they are useless from the perspective of narrative. Since it destroys narrative, Lyotard contends, the hyperrealist effect disrupts the "prescriptive murmur," which can only issue from an intelligible story. There is no longer a director sending an implicit prescription to the audience; both addressor and addressee form part of the "machine" (mechanical reproduction), like

Warhol wanted.[34] Lyotard testifies that "[t]he sequence of the attack on the village in *Apocalypse Now* placed me in something close to this condition."[35]

While the idea of hyperrealism is introduced through an association with immobilisation, Lyotard's description of the attack sequence allows us readily to identify it (although he himself does not explicitly do so) with the other pole of the acinema, extreme excitation:

> [...] the scene is saturated by sonorous and visual elements all in ultra-rapid displacement, where the eye and the ear are exceeded by the given and where the addressee is made to suffer from an excess of reality. There is a panic on the scene. All the little stories concerning the principal and secondary characters sketched previously are wiped out or blurred, rendered ungraspable in an instant. The scene empties itself of meaning. The eloquence, and the implicit prescriptions which are associated with it, sink in the overflow of information.[36]

Lyotard suggests, then, a positive answer to his initial question: there *are* pragmatic effects possible in cinema which are other to seduction, and which consist in the somatic effect of images and sounds on the body which defy narrative meaning, and which are associated with the two poles of the acinema and with what he here calls hyperrealism.

Yet what are the political implications of this analysis? In significant respects Lyotard's theorisation of seduction significantly parallels the Lacanian film theorists' notion of ideology: seduction is a problematic political manipulation of a film's spectators. Lyotard insists that this seductive effect is what needs to be opened to critique, and it is precisely the artistic effects he privileges which offer such an opening by destroying narrative closure, the reality effect, and the seductive, prescriptive murmur. Whether or not one *agrees* with the messages portrayed by films such as *Apocalypse Now* is entirely irrelevant to Lyotard's politics of aesthetics. What he opposes is the seductive effect in general, which deceives its audience and blinds them to all but a single perspective. Lyotard's politics differ from a critique of ideology, however, in rejecting the idea that there is a single reality which lies behind sensuous appearances, which can and should be intelligibly explicated. Nevertheless, he advocates a critical attitude with political significance: the exposure of the audience to multiple perspectives of reality, which allows them to reflect on and make their own judgements concerning these realities, as well as simply to enjoy the sensuous creations of cinematic art. In this way, the sacrificial image may be seen as politically efficacious in so far as it acts as ideology critique.

stases, sovereignty, space-time

Lyotard's final essay on cinema, "Idée d'un film souverain" (1994), frames the problematic of cinema in terms of Bataille's notion of sovereignty. Many now-familiar themes are repeated, yet perhaps surprisingly, given Lyotard's previous critical discussions of realism in film and his privileging of experimental film, the main focus of this essay is neo-realist cinema.[37] Lyotard distinguishes neo-realism from the kind of cinematic realism which remains largely negative in his appraisal, yet this essay nevertheless bears witness to an important shift of emphasis: the acinema is no longer relegated primarily to the realm of avant-garde film but is clearly established as a possibility *within* films which for the most part remain narrative-realist. Neo-realism, for Lyotard, is taken as an example of the possibility of combining both narrative and the "sacrificial image" not only in the same film but also within the same images and sequences.

Lyotard introduces neo-realism and its distinction from the realism of "classical" cinema by invoking Gilles Deleuze's now well-known distinction between the movement-image and the time-image:[38] *grosso modo* cinema prior to the Second World War was characterised by the movement-image, the unfolding of the film in conformity with the "sensori-motor schema" of the body, and the conformity of the image with the narrative of the film, while post-war cinema, beginning with neo-realism (first in Italy, then elsewhere), began to break with this, and to present time in a new way, allowing "blocks of temporality" which assert themselves with indifference to the narrative.[39]

Lyotard identifies these blocks of temporality as *sovereign* in Bataille's sense. The images in classical cinema would all be "servile" (the term to which Bataille opposes "sovereign") in so far as they obey the authority of the narrative form, while the neo-realist blocks of temporality are independent of such an authority, indifferent to it. These sovereign moments can allow a kind of "communication" which has nothing to do with the exchange of signs (either linguistic or socio-economic). Rather, what sovereign film communicates are "intense instants, temporal spasms."[40] While such instants are analysed here in somewhat different terms, clearly Lyotard has in mind what he had earlier identified as libidinal intensities, as the somatographic inscription of sensations on bodies, and as the hyperrealist production of non-seductive pragmatic effects. Moreover, it is with these blocks of temporality that Lyotard finds the presence within neo-realism of the two poles of the acinema, immobilisation and extreme movement. Both, he suggests, are common in neo-realist films. In the "Acinema" essay Lyotard had already suggested a certain unity of these two apparently opposite extremes, but here it is further explained, first in terms of perception:

> in truth, the two cases are sensorially little different: an object fixed at length by the gaze conceals itself to the point of not being seen, because it loses its bearings in the context; inversely, a very rapid movement, like a whirlpool hollowed out in a sheet of water, can be perceived like an immobile form.[41]

Second, this unity is elaborated through the temporal paradox which Lyotard here develops in order to characterise these exceptional filmic moments. Borrowing the term from Paul Schrader, he calls these moments "stases."[42] Stases suspend chronological time and express the *transcendental condition* of time, which is time's paradoxical *form*. Lyotard elaborates this with reference to Kant and Deleuze; briefly, the argument is this: time is the condition for the passage of things, and so time itself must not pass – it must remain the stable frame in or through which all else passes. It is paradoxical, because in the space of time the past and the future are held together in a present instant, and as such time is both passing and not passing in this instant. Thus, both immobilisation and extreme movement can express, and can both be combined in, the transcendental condition of time, since this condition paradoxically involves both.

Lyotard notes the similarity of this achronological time and the timelessness of the unconscious according to Freud, yet insists that the "stases" evident in neo-realist films are not to be understood as pure blocks of the unconscious. Neo-realist films, unlike those of the surrealists, do not attempt to depict dreams, but *reality*, and unlike the unconscious, the images in neo-realist films do not divorce themselves from the reality principle. Rather, *sovereign* images do not rebel against the authority of the filmic form but are *indifferent* to it. This allows Lyotard to develop the idea of acinematic stases as *immanent* to cinematic realism, rather than *transcendent* to or outside of it. In the simplest terms, Lyotard means that the images he has in mind remain recognisable; they maintain their role in the unfolding of the narrative. And yet at the same time they are indifferent to this narrative, and present something which cannot be reduced to it. Lyotard writes that with these stases, "[w]hat is altered, rendered other, is the space-time in which this situation, that object or this person which yet belong to the narrative are presented."[43] From within the realist framework, something which remains a part of reality presents "something else": "the presence of an unfamiliar reality in the customary reality."[44] Lyotard argues that in neo-realism *reality itself* enjoys an autonomy in relation to the story being told, and sometimes – through the images which form stases – reality is simply presented *as such*. In other words, in some sequences of images, reality ceases to be the background for the narrative being told, and rises to the foreground: we are invited to see it directly, abstracted from its context in the cinematic narrative. This is a real which seems to "emerge" from reality itself, as "[...] outcrops of the visual or the vocal in the surface of the visible and the audible."[45] Lyotard calls what is revealed in such depictions the "ontological real," as distinguished from the reality-effect of the narrative.

With this notion of the ontological real, Lyotard appears to be in significant proximity to "the Real Lacan": both Lacan's Real and Lyotard's ontological real indicate a rupture in meaning.[46] However, the deeper question which underlies such an apparent proximity apropos of film theory is *how* the expression of the Real in film is to be understood. Some, including McGowan, have noted that Žižek's influential work in fact mostly tends to use filmic contents as *examples* for Lacan's ideas.[47] The analysis thus generally remains at the representational level, where film is an indifferent medium for conveying concepts. McGowan himself suggests that there are a number of different ways in which film can generate the Real, structuring his major study *The Real Gaze* according to such a division. Frequently, however, in the new Lacanian analysis the Real remains something represented in the film – as, for example, when it appears as a psychological fact confronting a character in the narrative, or when it is directly represented through a symbol (such as the eponymous creatures in Hitchcock's *The Birds*). What would distinguish a Lyotardian approach would be the attention to film as an art, which means, for him, focusing on the way it works to order and disorder our sensations. From this perspective, a Lyotardian approach to the Real sees it in the filmic images themselves and how they work in terms of their sensuous qualities, not in terms of the concepts they represent.

To summarise: while Lyotard's various essays on cinema take place within heterogeneous theoretical frameworks, certain common themes are evident. Lyotard opposes realist film, which subordinates all images to the narrative in which they unfold, to what I am calling here a "sacrificial economy" of the image. In this economy images take on a value independent of any narrative, and function solely in terms of their sensorial qualities and somatic effects. These images are sacrificial because they function with indifference to the narrative, realist economy. Sacrificial images are produced at the two poles of the acinema, when narrative pace is immobilised, or accelerated. In terms more familiar from some of Lyotard's other writings, the narrative of the whole may be understood as the *structure* of the film, while sacrificial images appear as *events*.

As I have suggested above, I believe that Lyotard's work may have potentially broad and far-reaching implications for film theory. These implications can be discerned from the perspective of Lyotard's critical intersection with Lacan, who remains the Master Theorist in this field. A first promise of Lyotard's approach to cinema is that it offers a conceptual framework for critically engaging with avant-garde, experimental films without representational or narrative content. (By drawing attention to Lyotard's last essay on film, I have shown here how his own work also, however, extends to a consideration of the latter – belying some existing criticisms – and thus engages a broad range of film.) In the semi-autobiographical text *Peregrinations*, Lyotard explains that the resistance he felt towards Lacan was prompted by a defence of the arts.[48] According to Lyotard, Lacan places all sensory qualities in the realm of the Imaginary, where they can act only as a lure for desire. To break the hold of phantasy, and similarly of ideology, we must necessarily accede to the Symbolic register, the realm of cognition and language. The implication of this is that, for Lacan, the sensorial effects of art can never be more than seductive, and escaping seduction requires cognitive intervention. Developing this, Laura Mulvey proposes that political resistance to cinematic ideology must take place through a theoretical analysis which destroys pleasure and beauty.[49] In stark contrast, Lyotard suggests a politics of cinema which invites us to enjoy it *even more gratuitously*. For him, it is the sensorial qualities of images that may liberate us from the seductive effects of the narrative.

Lyotard had attended Lacan's seminars in the mid-1960s, a period during which Lacan's thought was closer to the thoroughly "structuralist" ideas taken up by the early Lacanian cinema theorists that they would later become. To this extent, Lyotard's work appears at its most oppositional in relation to "the Imaginary Lacan." However, as I have also suggested, Lyotard suggests a critical perspective on *how* film can generate the Real, the rupture in meaning which is the focus of current Lacanian film theory, in a way which focuses attention on how film can best be understood as an *art*. I have not attempted anything like a full investigation or resolution of any of these issues here. The aim of the foregoing discussion has simply been to draw attention to the full range of Lyotard's writings on cinema, to indicate its unity around the economy of sacrifice, and to indicate some key points on which I believe his work, if further critically developed, has the potential to impact significantly on current debates. I hope this paper will provide a useful prolegomena to such further work.

notes

1 See Turim; Rose; James; Krauss; Bignall; Trahair, "Figural Vision," *Comedy of Philosophy*, and "Jean-François Lyotard"; Knox; and Jones.

2 Knox. Maureen Turim has similarly argued that there is the danger in the Lyotardian perspective of ignoring the representational content of art (146–47).

3 This is not the case in francophone scholarship, which has seen a relatively recent thorough study, Jean-Michel Durafour's *Jean-François Lyotard: questions au cinema* (2009).

4 See, for example, the essays collected in Part III of *The Bataille Reader*.

5 Lyotard, "Syncopes, Landscapes" 621, 623.

6 See the essays collected in Part V of *The Bataille Reader*.

7 Lyotard, "Acinema" 53–54.

8 See Bordwell and Carroll.

9 See Copjec; Žižek, *Fright of Real Tears*; and McGowan. See also Žižek's essay "The Undergrowth of Enjoyment," a pioneering introduction to "The Real Lacan" in the domain of cultural theory.

10 Two useful historical overviews of Lacanian film theory, on which I have drawn here, are McGowan and Kunkle; and McGowan, "Introduction: From the Imaginary Look to the Real Gaze" in *The Real Gaze*.

11 Lyotard, "Idée d'un film souverain" 214.

12 Idem, "Acinema" 55.

13 Trahair, "Jean-François Lyotard"; Jones.

14 Lyotard, "Acinema" 170.

15 Lyotard, "The Unconscious as Mise-en-Scène" 97.

16 See in particular the essay "Freud selon Cézanne" for a concise statement of this argument, which is developed in more detail and through various nuanced modifications in the major works of this period, *Discourse, Figure* and *Libidinal Economy*, as well as the essays collected in *Dérive à partir de Marx et Freud* and *Des dispositifs pulsionnel*.

17 Lyotard, "The Unconscious as Mise-en-Scène" 87.

18 Ibid.

19 Ibid. 88.

20 Called here – more accurately – "Drives and their Vicissitudes." The unfortunate elision of the distinction between instincts and drives in James Strachey's Standard Edition English translation of Freud is well known.

21 Lyotard, "The Unconscious as Mise-en-Scène" 94.

22 Ibid.

23 Ibid. 98.

24 See Althusser, "Ideology and Ideological State Apparatuses" and "Freud and Lacan."

25 Second-wave Lacanian film theory, influenced by Žižek's defence of the category of ideology, continues to use this term, but in his significantly modified understanding of it. (See his "Introduction: The Spectre of Ideology.") The complex question of the relation between Lyotard's displacement of ideology and Žižek's renewed understanding of it is

one I can here only pose for further discussion. Briefly, however, we may note that Žižek's understanding of ideology posits a cynical relation to social reality in which we are aware of ideology yet conform to it anyway, because we suppose this cynical awareness is sufficient to place us beyond its grasp. Yet the key point, for Žižek, is that this cynicism still functions ideologically in so far as it removes any motivation for changing social conditions. This view of ideology is not so clearly opposed to Lyotard's Nietzschean perspectivism in so far as it circumvents the Platonic structure of "traditional" ideology which distinguishes illusory appearances from a supposed underlying truth. Some further reflections on Lyotard and ideology are made in the following section above, and at the end of the paper.

26 Lyotard, "The Unconscious as Mise-en-Scène" 98.

27 Lyotard, "Deux métamorphoses du séduisant au cinéma" 93. All translations from this text are mine.

28 Ibid. 93–94.

29 Ibid. 95–96.

30 Ibid. 96.

31 Ibid.

32 See Benjamin.

33 Lyotard, "Deux métamorphoses du séduisant au cinéma" 98.

34 Ibid.

35 Ibid.

36 Ibid.

37 This essay may also be regarded as Lyotard's most extensive discussion of film. With reference to "Acinema" and "The Unconscious as Mise-en-Scène," Lisa Trahair suggests that Lyotard gives so few filmic examples that his theories verge on not really being about film at all (Trahair, "Jean-François Lyotard"). However, he makes up for this lack somewhat in this essay, citing (in addition to various directors and experimental films) many neo-realist films, including Rossellini's *Paisà*, De Sica's *The Bicycle Thief*, Antonioni's *Story of a Love Affair*, Fellini's *La Dolce Vita*, Welles's *Citizen Kane* and *The Magnificent Ambersons*, and Laughton's *The Night of the Hunter*.

38 See Deleuze, *Cinema I* and *Cinema 2*.

39 Lyotard, "Idée d'un film souverain" 213.

40 Ibid. 212. All translations from this text are mine.

41 Ibid. 214.

42 See Schrader.

43 Lyotard, "Idée d'un film souverain" 215.

44 Ibid.

45 Ibid. 220.

46 More broadly, Lacan's and Lyotard's later works would appear to be in closer proximity than they were in the late 1960s and early 1970s. Anne Tomiche provides an instructive discussion of the changing relationship of their thought in "Rephrasing the Freudian Unconscious."

47 McGowan, *Real Gaze* 213–14 n. 19. For a critical discussion of the insufficiency of Žižek's work in accounting for art, see Dean.

48 Lyotard, *Peregrinations* 10–11.

49 Mulvey 8.

bibliography

Althusser, Louis. "Freud and Lacan." Trans. Ben Brewster. *Lenin and Philosophy, and Other Essays*. London: New Left, 1971. 181–202. Print.

Althusser, Louis. "Ideology and Ideological State Apparatuses." Trans. Ben Brewster. *Lenin and Philosophy, and Other Essays*. London: New Left, 1971. 121–73. Print.

Bataille, Georges. *The Bataille Reader*. Ed. Fred Botting and Scott Wilson. Oxford and Malden, MA: Blackwell, 1997. Print.

Benjamin, Walter. "The Work of Art in the Age of Mechanical Reproduction." *Illuminations: Essays and Reflections*. Ed. Hannah Arendt. Trans. Harry Zohn. London: Pimlico, 1999. 211–44. Print.

Bignell, Jonathan. *Postmodern Media Culture*. Edinburgh: Edinburgh UP, 2000. Print.

Bordwell, David, and Noël Carroll, eds. *Post-Theory: Reconstructing Film Studies*. Madison: U of Wisconsin P, 1996. Print.

Copjec, Joan. *Read my Desire: Lacan after the Historicists*. Cambridge, MA: MIT P, 1996. Print.

Dean, Tim. "Art as Symptom: Žižek and the Ethics of Psychoanalytic Criticism." *Diacritics* 32.2 (2002): 20–41. Print.

Deleuze, Gilles. *Cinema 1: The Movement-Image*. Trans. Hugh Tomlinson and Barbara Habberjam. Minneapolis: U of Minnesota P, 1986. Print.

Deleuze, Gilles. *Cinema 2: The Time-Image*. Trans. Hugh Tomlinson and Robert Galeta. Minneapolis: U of Minnesota P, 1989. Print.

Durafour, Jean-Michel. *Jean-François Lyotard: questions au cinéma*. Paris: PUF, 2009. Print.

Freud, Sigmund. "Instincts and their Vicissitudes." *On the History of the Psycho-Analytic Movement, Papers on Metapsychology and Other Works*. Trans. James Strachey. The Standard Edition of the Complete Psychological Works of Sigmund Freud vol. XIV. London: Hogarth, 1953. 111–40. Print.

Freud, Sigmund. *The Interpretation of Dreams*. Trans. James Strachey. The Standard Edition of the Complete Psychological Works of Sigmund Freud vols. IV and V. London: Hogarth, 1953. Print.

Freud, Sigmund. "Three Essays on Sexuality." *A Case of Hysteria, Three Essays on Sexuality, and Other Works*. Trans. James Strachey. The Standard Edition of the Complete Psychological Works of Sigmund Freud vol. VII. London: Hogarth, 1953. 123–243. Print.

Freud, Sigmund. "The Unconscious." *On the History of the Psycho-Analytic Movement, Papers on Metapsychology and Other Works*. Trans. James Strachey. The Standard Edition of the Complete Psychological Works of Sigmund Freud vol. XIV. London: Hogarth, 1953. 166–215. Print.

James, David E. *Allegories of Cinema: American Film in the Sixties*. Princeton: Princeton UP, 1989. Print.

Jones, Graham. *Lyotard Reframed*. London and New York: Tauris, 2014. Print.

Knox, Simone. "Eye Candy for the Blind: Re-introducing Lyotard's Acinema into Discourses on Excess, Motion, and Spectacle in Contemporary Hollywood." *New Review of Film and Television Studies* 11.3 (2013): 1–16. Print.

Krauss, Rosalind E. *The Optical Unconscious*. Cambridge, MA: MIT P, 1994. Print.

Lyotard, Jean-François. "Acinema." Trans. Paisley N. Livingston. *The Lyotard Reader*. Ed. Andrew Benjamin. Oxford and Malden, MA: Blackwell, 1989. 169–80. Print.

Lyotard, Jean-François. *Dérive à partir de Marx et Freud*. Paris: Union Générale, 1973. Print.

Lyotard, Jean-François. "Deux métamorphoses du séduisant au cinéma." *La Séduction*. Ed. Maurice Olender and Jacques Sojcher. Paris: Aubier Montaigne, 1980. 93–100. Print.

Lyotard, Jean-François. *Discourse, Figure*. Trans. Antony Hudek and Mary Lydon. Minneapolis: U of Minnesota P, 2010. Print.

Lyotard, Jean-François. *Des dispositifs pulsionnel*. Paris: Union Générale, 1973. Print.

Lyotard, Jean-François. "Freud selon Cézanne." *Des dispositifs pulsionnel*. Paris: Union Générale d'Editions, 1973. 71–94. Print.

Lyotard, Jean-François. "Idée d'un film souverain." *Misère de la philosophie*. Paris: Galilée, 2000. 209–21. Print.

Lyotard, Jean-François. *Libidinal Economy*. Trans. Iain Hamilton Grant. London: Athlone, 1993. Print.

Lyotard, Jean-François. *Peregrinations: Law, Form, Event*. New York: Columbia UP, 1988. Print.

Lyotard, Jean-François. "Syncopes, Landscapes." *Miscellaneous Texts II: Contemporary Artists*. Ed. Herman Parret. Leuven: Leuven UP, 2012. 622–35. Print.

Lyotard, Jean-François. "The Unconscious as Mise-en-Scène." Trans. Joseph Maier. *Performance in Postmodern Culture*. Ed. Michel Benamou and Charles Caramello. Madison: Coda, 1977. 87–98. Print.

McGowan, Todd. *The Real Gaze: Film Theory after Lacan*. New York: State U of New York P, 2008. Print.

McGowan, Todd, and Sheila Kunkle, eds. *Lacan and Contemporary Film*. New York: Other, 2004. Print.

Mulvey, Laura. "Visual Pleasure and Narrative Cinema." *Screen* 16.3 (1975): 6–18. Print.

Plato. "Menexenus." *Plato: Gorgias, Menexenus, Protagoras*. Ed. Malcolm Schofield. Trans. Tom Griffith. Cambridge: Cambridge UP, 2009. Print.

Rose, Jacqueline. *Sexuality in the Field of Vision*. London: Verso, 1986. Print.

Schrader, Paul. *Transcendental Style in Film: Ozu, Bresson, Dreyer*. Berkeley: U of California P, 1972. Print.

Tomiche, Anne. "Rephrasing the Freudian Unconscious: Lyotard's Affect-Phrase." *Diacritics* 24.1 (1994): 43–62. Print.

Trahair, Lisa. *The Comedy of Philosophy: Sense and Nonsense in Early Cinematic Slapstick*. Albany: State U of New York P, 2008. Print.

Trahair, Lisa. "Figural Vision: Freud, Lyotard, and Early Cinematic Comedy." *Screen* 46.2 (2005): 175–94. Print.

Trahair, Lisa. "Jean-François Lyotard." *Film, Theory and Philosophy: The Key Thinkers*. Ed. Felicity Colman. Chesham: Acumen, 2009. 222–32. Print.

Turim, Maureen. "The Place of Visual Illusions." *The Cinematic Apparatus*. Ed. Teresa De Lauretis and Stephen Heath. London: Macmillan, 1979. 143–60. Print.

Žižek, Slavoj. *The Fright of Real Tears: Krystof Kieślowski between Theory and Post Theory*. London: BFI, 2001. Print.

Žižek, Slavoj. "Introduction: The Spectre of Ideology." *Mapping Ideology*. Ed. Slavoj Žižek. London and New York: Verso, 1994. 1–33. Print.

Žižek, Slavoj. "The Undergrowth of Enjoyment: How Popular Culture Can Serve as an Introduction to Lacan." *New Formations* 9 (1989): 7–29. Print.

Index

Page numbers followed by 'n' refer to notes